The Global Public Sphere

Public Communication in the Age of Reflective Interdependence

Ingrid Volkmer

polity

First published in 2014 by Polity Press

Polity Press
65 Bridge Street
Cambridge CB2 1UR, UK

Polity Press
350 Main Street
Malden, MA 02148, USA

ISBN-13: 978-0-7456-3957-4 (hardback)
ISBN-13: 978-0-7456-3958-1 (paperback)

A catalogue record for this book is available from the British Library.

Typeset in 10 on 12 pt Palatino
by Toppan Best-set Premedia Limited
Printed and bound in Great Britain by Clays Ltd, St Ives PLC

For further information on Polity, visit our website: www.politybooks.com

Contents

Acknowledgements

This book could not have been written without the continuous encouragement of many colleagues. I am deeply grateful for their support and feedback in different stages of this journey!

I also owe special thanks to David Held who has invited me to the London School of Economics in the second half of 2010. In retrospect, these months at the LSE, liberated from University commitments, have been especially crucial for the broadening of the conceptual scope of this book. I am also grateful for having been appointed as a member of the Institute of World Society Studies, University of Bielefeld, Germany where – during numerous research stays – debates with colleagues and students have alerted me to the fine-lined complexities of globalized inequalities.

I should like to express my gratitude to the executives from *Al Jazeera*, the BBC and *Deutsche Welle* who have made themselves available for lengthy interviews despite their busy schedules.

Last – but not least – special thanks go to Susan Beer and Andrew McRae who have been amazing in preparing the final manuscript and to Andrea Drugan, Joe Devanny and Neil de Cort, Polity Press, for their guidance – and great patience.

Illustrations

Figures

Graphics

Tables

Introduction

It is often argued that we live in a time of unprecedented connectivity. Statistics show that not only has one-third of the world's population access to the web but – and this is a change from about a decade ago – the majority of users are now located in Asia, followed by Europe, Latin America, North America and Africa. In addition, visual geographical mapping tools show that no longer are these networked structures reaching mainly urban centres of all world regions but stretch across rural areas and even remote territories – from sub-Saharan Africa to the South Pacific Islands and Central Asia. It is an unprecedented landscape of digital connections and a new architecture of globalized communication, which we are only beginning to understand. Almost two decades ago, Manuel Castells published the trilogy of the *Network Society* (1996), which suggested a novel approach to an inclusive model of networked social, political and economic relations across societies. Today's advanced globalized communication sphere is no longer characterized by these macro-structures of networks, connecting nodes across all continents, which was a fascinating imagination about ten years ago, but nodes are situated within a universe of subjective, personal networked structures linking individuals across world regions. These are dense and authentic networks which are continuously monitored, navigated and configured on commuter trains, on streets and even in university lecture halls. These subjective networks are no longer simply 'social', connecting mainly communities of friends, but have become platforms for subjectively 'lived' public spaces.

This new communicative sphere is no longer mainly 'digital', or even – to use a term which now sounds outdated – a sphere of 'cyber' communication, existing as a distinct sphere from 'mass media'. These distinctions no longer work. Converging media spaces are embedded in content threads, which often resurface on social media platforms available almost anywhere in the world. Media organizations are searching for new ways to 'connect' directly to their users – wherever they live. Content is shifted across platforms and – through cookie codes and pixel tags – increasingly framed along users' interests and according to geographical locations. Newspaper sites are becoming multi-media platforms; for example the *Guardian* in London has launched such a platform, *Guardian Witness*, encouraging readers across the world to upload information as well as images and to collaborate closely with *Guardian* journalists to identify and unfold stories. The once clear contours of the term media are fading and new concepts are being suggested to identify nuances of these emerging, densely entangled dimensions. Concepts such as 'media manifold' (Couldry, 2012), 'polymedia' (Madianou and Miller, 2012) and 'spreadable media' (Jenkins et al., 2013) begin to 'map' the multiple communicative layers of today's media forms within a world where the user, the 'audience' has become the communicative actor: reproducing, delivering, accelerating and magnifying 'content' within the chosen logics of subjective networks across a globalized scope. For the purpose of our discussion I suggest the term micro-networks as a metaphor for the merging of content on individualized platforms within the sphere of a subjectively created communicative universe, incorporating multiple communicative terrains. In this sphere 'bits' and 'pieces' of available media forms are 'assembled' and 'arranged' – from traditional media (e.g. television and newspaper) to communicative sites of local community engagement; from social media (*iTunes* channels and 'apps', *Skype* and *YouTube*), in addition to streaming content of national outlets (from the BBC to Nigerian television) – from mobile communication to networks of direct-to-home satellite platforms.

However, the term micro-networks also allows us to identify the 'connectedness' of the communicative actor across an assembled communicative sphere and helps to address the new trans-border-ness of these communicative flows. Whereas decades ago, trans-border communication was understood as being either 'international' (i.e. is, connecting nations), 'trans-national', (reaching sections of several nations simultaneously) or 'spatial' (a secluded sphere of digital flow), today's globalized communications across advanced micro-networks of subjective platforms are no longer 'trans-border' but rather discursively interrelated. In this sense, the communicative sphere within a globalized scope is no longer an extension but is situated in interrelated subjective micro-networks. In other words, the global and the national and even the local are no longer distinct spheres but merge in particular in contexts of communicative spheres across diverse sites of subjective micro-networks. When students are asked in classes to identify their news sources, they might pick similar media forms; however, each of them names a completely different hierarchy of sources, which relates no longer to the news agenda of a national sphere but is deeply embedded in their own public 'horizons'; these are seamlessly situated within a globalized sphere of interdependence: densely and often linked 'live' to peers and communities anywhere in the world but also to authentic and trusted sources, which may or may not be located on servers in other world regions. These spheres are no longer situated within international or transnational communication but within new sets of communicative interdependence that not only transform the dimension of communication and challenge our understanding of 'media' and civic identity, but also deeply transform the understanding and practice of engagement in 'the public sphere'.

It could be argued that spheres of interdependence within a globalized scope are not new. For example, debates in media and communication which occured at the time when satellite communication emerged as a new form of transnationalization in the early 1990s, identified spheres of reciprocity of globalized communication processes and shifted the paradigmatic foci to a new sense of interdependence across globalized thematic ecologies. CNN (Cable News Network)'s 'breaking news' influenced the daily news agenda of national broadcasters in various world regions. It was also the time when the interdependence of media 'flows' across continents was critically assessed, in addition to an emerging powerful strata of political economy and globalized imbalances, for example along the 'digital divide', to the concreteness of identity politics and – specifically – political activism. However, there are differences between these layers of interdependence. Today, interdependence is intensified, 'dense' and, most importantly, is no longer governed by the national or even transnational media agenda but layers of interdependence are carefully selected from a subjective universe of options, governed by deliberatively chosen 'loyalties' and 'alliances'. In this sense, the sphere of globalized interdependence is no longer 'out there' but very concrete 'right here' in the way content trajectories are chosen, intersect and relate within the site of a subjective networked 'universe', sychronized across devices and always available.

Micro-networks might incorporate Greenpeace news, NGO (Non-Governmental Organization) reports on climate change as well as monitoring sites of transnational pollution, in addition to resources of local community groups. What we see on television is 'filtered' and 're-ordered' through the lens of networks of trust, for example 'live' social networks which enable 'communicative action'. The reference frame for public engagement is no longer within one country, but subjectively assembled across a globalized scope of those who are 'concerned'. When looking for conceptual frames that could help to further assess this emerging sphere of subjective networked locations within a globalized scope, Manuel Castells' term of 'mass self-communication' (Castells, 1996, 2009) comes to mind. It is a term which signifies a 'post-convergence' age as it no longer highlights the merging spheres of content of 'mass' and 'digital' media – which was a key issue a few years ago – but rather the outcome of such a convergence: the sphere of 'individualization' of communicative practices vis à vis networked platforms. Saskia Sassen is another author who is relevant here, however, addressing a different angle of this emerging sphere. She has recently pointed out that we are facing the deconstruction of the traditional 'unitary' bodies of societal knowledge, specifically through the phenomenon of de- and re-contextualization of 'bits' and 'pieces' across digital networks (Sassen, 2012: 74).

Leaving these recent attempts to map in more general terms transformative parameters of the networked communication space to one side, globalization debates are also relevant here for identifying signposts of the emerging communicative landscape within a globalized scope. Globalization debates have over the last decades – especially since the early 1990s – addressed the methodology of interdependence and critically assessed the fine-lined 'logics' of these entanglements across national and local institutional, economical, political and cultural structures and within specific dimensions of globalization ranging from neoliberalism, to global governance as cosmopolitan multilateralism (Held, 2005) to global civil society (see Kaldor, 2003). Recently, interdependence has also addressed a completely new perspective through lenses that have been invisible for too long. This is due to the new densely globalized formations of communication that are no longer merely the domain of the Western narrative of globalized interdependence but include the diverse perspectives of the approaches of Asia, South America and Africa. Authors from South America and Africa in particular suggest to shift the one-dimensional globalization narrative towards new paradigms of 'inclusiveness', i.e. of regional specific world perceptions and a conception of cosmopolitanism that specifically takes into account the new realities of digital networked communication practices in so-called 'developing' regions (see Reguilo, 2009; Ndlela, 2009; Oreget, 2010).

Leaving these larger globalized narratives to one side, it seems that methodologies for the assessment of concrete forms of communicative interdependence begin to emerge in specific areas of media and communication research. For example, approaches of 'conflict' communication – specifically of national political conflicts and crises – are increasingly moving away from transnational angles and, instead, address a broader globalized thematic terrain (Cottle, 2009; Pantti et al., 2012). Another example is journalism studies, a field which began in the 1990s to draw attention to globalized news 'flows', and which focuses traditionally on a professional practice negotiating between national organizational structures and transnational audiences and now begins to define conceptual frameworks of globalized journalism (Hanitzsch and Mellado, 2011; Weaver and Willnat, 2012). Social media research is a third example of a more profound shift towards identifying interrelated transnational communicative forms, for example in contexts of 'viral' publics as a new sphere of public accelerators of political crisis across specific interrelated spheres.

Considering these developments, it is surprising that conceptual frameworks of transnational public spheres are somewhat on the periphery. Despite these transformations of communicative structures within larger frameworks of interdependence, public sphere conceptions even in a transnational context are mainly articulated vis-à-vis modern nation-states and – in this framework – often understand the public sphere as the sphere between civil society and the state. Jürgen Habermas' groundbreaking work on the transformation of the public sphere still serves today – I suppose to his own surprise – fifty years after it was first published in Germany as a core framework for the debate of public discourse in the twenty-first century. Habermas' work provided us with a philosophical understanding of public discourse within the larger paradigm of critical theory but his understanding of public culture needs to be recontextualized. It spoke specifically to the changing societal conditions of a divided Germany in the time of the Cold War – a time when Germany was slowly recovering from an age of fascism. However, the reality of public life is different today. Today's geopolitical order has shifted and the nation-state as such is being incorporated into larger regional and globalized governance structures (from the EU to the

WTO). Specifically the intensified forms of networked communication become the sites of communicative public 'action' among citizens who might never meet in person as they are situated in different world regions as well as different society types.

The reliance on the Habermasian paradigm embedded in the public cultures of Western world regions and the European nation-state – has left us with two gaps which become crucial today. Firstly, a lack not only of alternative historiographies of diverse world regions but especially knowledge of specific understanding of public culture and its transformations of diverse society types. Whereas the so called 'ideal' of the public sphere is often perceived through the historiography of European public life – understood through the public/private dichotomoy established in the nineteenth century – and assessed in the Habermasian methodology of the merging of private and public interests, there is not much knowledge of alternative methodologies, which would show how to assess the fine lines of a quite a different dialectic within trans-border public spheres. This is the more surprising, as trans-border 'flow' is not a phenomenon of the twentieth or the digital networks of the twenty-first century but has existed for centuries, especially – often overlooked – since the time of the invention of the printing press in China and Europe. However, the gap in historiographies of regional traditions of public life and deliberation makes it now quite difficult to conceptualize public communication in non-Western world regions which, for this reason, are too often only studied in the context of the digital sphere, which we are often unable to contextualize across broader layers of local public cultures.

Secondly, the boundedness of national procedural 'mechanisms' of public deliberation has become porous for decades – or some might argue – for centuries. Specifically today, the holes in the boundedness of publics within state spheres are rapidly widening. Not only are public communicative forms 'disembedded' from national territories but core assets of public 'civil' culture, public institutions, are situated within polity regimes of transnational accountability, ranging from legitimacy of the political 'civil' action of governments, to elections and previously non-transparent spheres of intergovernmental relations to forms of deliberation. In addition, today's transnational terrain of 'civil' action and reasoning is situated within – and magnified through – a transnationally available spectrum of public agencies. Not only is it possible to engage with digital activism from almost anywhere with an Internet access but this spectrum has become more 'horizontally' subtle: I can live in Australia, vote in Germany, read news resources from the USA, watch streaming television from Kenya and engage in 'live' debates about saving the Amazon rain forest with NGOs in Latin America. These are the new geographies of public 'horizons' which are – and this is important to realize – no longer central to the democratic nation-state, they are no longer central to other societies as well! It is a shift towards a subjective axis determining and selecting engagement in a globalized interdependent public debate of chosen networked formations which has implications on deliberation and legitimacy – again – in a geographically 'horizontal' spectrum: it is the new calibration of 'polis' and 'demos': my vote contributes to the election outcome in Germany while engage in climate change communities in Australia who are no longer informed by local knowledge or the climate change agenda of national media but rather by discursively shifting public horizons.

In recent times a number of publications have specifically focused on transnational public communication. Public spheres are in these contexts often understood as quite distinct spaces existing in parallel with national public spheres. As this distinction between the national and the transnational represents the core structure of the specific transnationalization of the European publics, it is not surprising that these conceptions relate quite often specifically to Europe as their case study. Only a few authors identify the implications of a transnational public sphere (in a broader institutional context) for global governance (Crack, 2008) or argue for a more profound integration of the global dimension into the understanding of national publics (Spichal, 2012: 149). In this sense it is not about digital life versus 'real' public practices but about a dialectical nexus as an incorporated form of a new sphere of publics in a transnational context. However, despite these new complexities, the public sphere remains a 'blind spot' in globalization and network conceptions.

The global public sphere is often considered to be a 'myth' and, as some have argued, a terrain which becomes 'increasingly difficult' (Gripsrud and Moe, 2010: 10) to conceptualize at all. One reason might be, that paradigms of national embeddedness and the boundedness of public spheres are less related in more general terms to the Kantian notion of 'cosmopolitan' reasoning than to the 'modern' understanding of a public between civil society and 'the state' as a nationally significant terrain of debating and – through this process – the enforcing and re-enforcing of a common 'normative' will, i.e. the negotiation of national 'identity' and of citizenship within newly formed nation-states of the nineteenth century. It is important to realize here that it was the time – to use Hegel's term – of a 'Zeitgeist' of national 'awakening', i.e. the emergence of (national) civil society constituting a civil (translated into civic) counter-power, influencing the government of a state in the distinct public culture of different European nations. Not only the core communicative domains but also their relation to the 'logic' of nationally anchored democratic institutions, processes of elections, the formation of normative consent, legitimacy and deliberation around well established governance structures and polities is deeply anchored in Hegel's understanding of public life.

This is a complex territory where conventional terminologies and conceptual frameworks require a refinement and a fresh and – possibly – 'bold' conceptual lens. The specific construction of the public sphere in the traditions of the European nation-states is a static model which does not follow sufficient space for the assessment of new communicative lines of deliberation. Public engagement within civic spheres has loosened the ties to the nation and has become a communicative practice, negotiating civic identity between values of the 'human condition' of a global civil society and the established sphere of loyalties, 'belonging' and identity.

Taking these debates into the realm of what could be described as communicative globalization reveals that communicative spheres no longer constitute what was once imagined as core territories of globalizing processes, the 'intensifying', the 'stretching' and 'velocity' but rather subjectively chosen, links across globalized scopes. Anthony Giddens remarked that 'time–space distanciation' is a process which 'links distant localities' in such a way that 'local happenings are shaped by events occurring many miles away and vice versa' (Giddens, 1990: 64). Today, interconnectedness exists not only between 'localities' but rather 'observers' and 'actors' who engage in direct 'live' interaction with the outcome of refining contexts and 'meanings' of 'events', 're-ordering' relevance through these subjective points of interconnectedness. It is through this lens that we see public communication changing.

Public communication is no longer 'local', 'national' or transnational but rather constitutes 'reflexive' communication, which unfolds across a sphere of globalized 'reflective' interdependence. Reflective interdependence relates here to horizontal spheres where the core domains of 'communicative action', 'justification', 'verification', 'engagement' are no longer – together – necessarily embedded in the bounded discourse of a community or nation but scattered across different discursive sites within globalized communicative horizons. These spheres of reflective interdependence are positioned in the trajectories of such a 'scattered' territory of public communication, not only overcoming national borders but breaking up paradigmatic boundaries of the global 'North' and 'South', the 'centre' and 'periphery', of individual 'utterance' and public agency. Reflective interdependence situated *across* societies transforms not only conceptions of civic and public engagement but also paradigms of globalization, 'civil' society, international relations and world citizenship.

This book unfolds a conceptual architecture of public communication within a global public sphere which – admittedly – is a huge task. Given the relevance of this new field, it is important to integrate the specific angles in which enlarged transnational political and public terrains have been addressed – not only in media and communication – but also in sociology and political science.

The first chapter sets the stage for this discussion. We begin by positioning 'public space' not only across 'networks' or 'digital' flows but between 'networks of centrality' and the 'centrality of networks'. Based on this approach, the chapter identifies the openings of the boundedness of the state frame as a container of public culture since modernity. It is argued that this opening not only of the boundedness of the nation-state but of the 'state–society' nexus, i.e. the often assumed state 'frame' of civil society is relevant for identifying specific links *between* civic discourses of various types of society which is the core domain for a debate of globalized public communication.

The second chapter takes this discussion further and develops a model of densities of public space which I describe as 'public assemblage'. A term that relates to the 'assembling' mechanism of subjective 'micro-networks' (as discussed earlier) but also to the scope of 'linking' civil society through the widening holes of the 'state–society' nexus. We will assess the few available historiographies of trans-border public communication in different world regions from the time of the printing press to today's digital networks in order to identify the increasing degrees of 'density' of transnational public communication flows, enabled through scalar processes of communication.

The third chapter maps the public space of reflective 'inbetweenness' of deliberative discourse: between the networks of centrality and centrality of networks and the reflective 'verticalization' of this globally interdependent sphere of public engagement.

As media forms change, the notion of micro-networks is further developed into what I call a 'matrix of influence', where diverse communicative platforms take on specific roles, justification, verification and engagement within the subjective location of public space between networks of centrality and the centrality of networks. This model moves away from defining media through organizational forms towards the way media forms are embedded in diverse models of public space. Interview results with executives from the BBC World, *Al Jazeera International* and *Deutsche Welle* provide case studies for a definition of media forms within what I describe as the 'matrix of influence'.

The fifth chapter concludes by proposing a shift to what I call conceptions of public horizons. We will return to the notions of publicness of the Kantian and Hegelian age. The chapter will use Hegel's model to further identify public discursive consciousness not between the state and 'the people' but as an outcome of reflective interdependence.

This book could not have been written without the insight of three key scholars of our time whom I would like to mention after concluding the journey of writing this book. Since my training in social sciences throughout my student years in Germany, my work has been greatly influenced by Jürgen Habermas. Since those early days, critical theory has always been an inspiration for a vision for a better world and, looking back, might have encouraged me to choose an academic pathway. I would also like to mention Roland Robertson here as one of the key theorists of globalization. His work has helped me to understand the relativity of globalization as the 'unity' of diversity. Manuel Castells' visionary work on the network society has inspired me to understand the importance of communication as one of the drivers of the transformation of societal structures.

The Canadian media theorist Marshall McLuhan once coined the term 'global village'. It was a visionary idea at a time of a divided Cold War world and of the first satellites, enabling the occasional 'live' coverage of one event across continents. But it was also the time where the image of the earth appeared behind Neil Armstrong's first steps on the moon, which inspired the term 'global village'. McLuhan's term 'global village' meant an imagination of the world not as a rational, linear, visual space but rather a colourful 'resonance' space of a 'neo acoustic age'. In today's advanced network society, this is no longer a simultaneous 'acoustic space' but rather diverse 'resonance' spaces – spaces of simultaneous reasoning across lively communicative domains. It might be time to begin to chart these new 'resonance spaces' within a global public sphere and to make a contribution to a better world.

1

Public Territories and the Imagining of Political Community

Despite the increasing transnationalization of communication, we are only at the beginning of understanding the implications of this new sphere on public communication and civic deliberation. It is a public architecture that evolves as a networked space within and beyond the nation-state. However, when attempting to assess this sphere of public space, we are facing an ambiguity: on one hand conceptions of the 'public sphere' are framed through an overarching still dominant modern paradigm which centres public communication in nation-states; on the other, political, civic, and, on the other public communicative practices are embedded in public spheres which are meandering across globalized networks – linking citizens of different societies and, through such an emerging sphere of deliberation, influencing the agenda of politics and, sometimes, governments. It seems that the overarching paradigm of modern public spheres tends to blind us to identifying and conceptually mapping how these new structures of public communication take shape. In this chapter, we will begin to situate public space between specific forms of networks: 'networks of centrality', the observing sphere and the 'centrality of networks', the engagement sphere. In order to map this 'terrain' over the next chapters, we must first carefully assess the ways in which existing debates have defined the 'openings' of the nation-state, or in other words, the processes of 'decoupling' civil society from the national boundedness. This discussion will allow us to address more specifically the ways in which the public space evolves through such a 'de-bracketing' of the state–society nexus, across different spheres of public 'action' within a globalized scope.

In his book *The Public and its Problems*, John Dewey remarked that 'in no two ages or places is there the same public' (Dewey, 1927: 33).

Dewey's observation, made in the early decades of the twentieth century relates to the transformation of the public sphere at a time when the traditional centrality of vibrant community public life in the USA was still functional but – and this is Dewey's point – already slowly dissolving. The traditional public life of local communities was merging with larger, more centralized forms which now began to 'mediate' public debate and shape public opinion, which was no longer an outcome of traditional 'local' community reasoning. Such a shift away from the centrality of public discourse of a vibrant local community 'place' of the local townhall to the 'mediating' centrality of national media spheres of newspapers and radio, left local publics – so Dewey concludes – 'eclipsed' and 'diffused' (Dewey, 1927: 137). The deliberative role of a vibrant community public, and this is Dewey's pessimistic assessment, is 'passing away' as 'mediated' spheres of publics emerge where the 'power' and 'lust of possession' is 'in the hands of the officers and agencies' which – and what an irony! – 'the dying public instituted' (Dewey, 1927: 81).

About forty years after Dewey, Jürgen Habermas has identified a second major shift of public spheres. This shift relates to another Western world region: modern European nation-states. In this lens, the shift of public discourse in European nation-states towards 'manufactured publicity' (Habermas, 1964; 1991: 211) and away from reasoned publicness made room for strategically produced 'publicness', a distinct form of public reasoning, which is, however, often translated as 'public opinion' or 'publicity' of private interests. Such a second further shift of mediated public spheres has significantly weakened the public as a 'critically debating entity' (Habermas, 1964, 1991: 162). Furthermore, these 'private' representations of publicity, as Habermas argues, not only 'centralize' – this was Dewey's point – but 'streamline' public debate. A process, Noam Chomsky has called the 'manufacturing' (Chomsky, 1992) of public consent. In consequence, the remaining fractures of public debate disappear 'behind the veil of internal decisions concerning the selection and presentation of the material' (Habermas, 1964, 1991: 169) and further disempower public life.[1] From a quite different perspective, Nancy Fraser (1992) argues for another shift of public spheres not only of 'private' and 'public discourse' but towards 'segmented' or fragmented public debate. Fraser proposes a dichotomy of 'weak' and 'strong' public discourse. Strong publics are those 'whose discourse encompasses both opinion formation and decision making', which means achieving 'legally' binding decisions and in weak publics deliberative practice 'consists exclusively in opinion formation' (Fraser, 1992: 134).

These and many other carefully drawn distinctions between the dialectical space of public spheres (Curran, 1991; Bohman, 2001; Dahlgren, 2009; Coleman and Ross, 2010) rotate around the dialectic of 'private' and 'public', 'weak' and 'strong', 'fractured' and 'mainstream', 'online' and 'offline' publics and have made important contributions to the conceptual refinement of the shifting parameter of the public sphere. However, these conceptions of public spheres and deliberative communication seem to be no longer sufficient for assessing today's emerging non-national, non-territorial 'fluid' publics as an increasingly powerful multi-directional sphere *between* place and space in the logic of intersections. Public communication in these spheres of connected, intersecting layers of, for example, thematic 'threads' is dis-embedded from the traditional dialectic of public formations and, instead, rotates around what Luhmann might have described as 'autopoetic', a self-directed discourse 'absorbing' public engagement across national borders ventilated across a 'viral' public 'system' (Luhmann, 1984). The sphere of climate change debates is an example for such a 'self-directed' transnational debate which offers, due to its transnational angle, multiple 'intersections' as communicative forms across to national climate change spheres from India to Kenya, the USA, China and Australia.

This public space requires a re-thinking of public deliberation beyond the modern model and also beyond the boundedness of national territories, which no longer exists as a secluded sphere. Today, most nation-states are multi-cultural societies where the Realpolitik of public discourse is already situated within worldwide networks of satellite and Internet communication. It seems that even in modern multi-cultural nation-states, the traditional model of public spheres has become an empty category and does not reflect the complex realities of public discourse practices. What is surprising is the dominance of the paradigm of territorial boundedness of publics in the debate of public communication. It is a debate that not only seems to ignore the deep transformation of nation-states to 'network states' (Castells, 2010) but also the varying scopes of transnational public engagement. Such a methodological nationalism of public-sphere conceptions constitutes a – what might be argued – 'normative' methodological exclusion of world regions, where citizens have over the last decade become actors and participants in such a transnational public; however, they are rarely conceptually integrated into the lens of media research methodologies.

Large terrains of world regions, for example in Asia, in Africa and South America are undergoing unprecedented regional specific transformations in contexts of 'compressed' or what Beck might understand as 'reflexive' modernities (Beck, 1992). Dimensions of 'reflexivity', however, are rarely incorporated into the transnationalization of networked communication and, in particular, conceptual debates about transnational public deliberation. I should add that despite a few exceptions, specifically so-called 'non Western' regions are rarely sites of empirical research. Little is known about the shaping of particular urban networked public cultures in the various and adverse societies of African countries through increasing complexities of satellite television, smart-phone mobile communication and the Internet, which have multiplied over the last years. A new communicative landscape emerges that seems to deeply transform the civic identity and 'public orientation' of the emerging middle class in so-called 'developing' regions. In (Western) debates, which mainly highlight implications of neoliberal globalization processes on 'developing' regions, it is overlooked that the enlarged communicative landscape transforms civic discourse, which is increasingly geared towards new forms of deliberation within networked structures of public engagement. These new vibrant publics, for example of African regions and South East Asia are also not addressed in public-sphere debates. For example, Indonesia is one of the most connected countries worldwide, with about half of its population being youth; yet, not much is known about the way in which social media and other forms of network communication create discourse spheres of civic communication within a transnational network space.

Mainly in times of crises, however, these world regions are becoming visible. A visibility that draws attention not only to the use of social media but also to the spheres of connectedness of regions that in the past have been on the periphery of media research. The Arab Spring has shown how little has been known about the role of networked media in a world region long excluded from the communication research mainly conducted in a centralized Western national paradigm. Since the time of the Arab Spring, various studies, increasingly also from the region, attempt to address the role of social media in non-modern societies; what is needed, however, is an inclusive framework for an understanding of the role of networked communication for public spheres and 'connected' civic identities across the complexities of this transnational landscape. These important phenomena require a somewhat inclusive approach to public-sphere conceptions and a conception of the 'reflective' situated-ness of public space.

Public space between 'networks of centrality' and 'centrality of networks'

In order to begin to 'map' this space, it might be helpful to situate such a 'reflective' space in the dialectic of 'network centrality' on the one hand and the 'centrality of networks' on the other.

The term 'network centrality' refers here in a broad way to the networked structure of 'centralized' discourse – in other words to the 'monitoring' of public discourse. The second sphere, 'centrality of networks' relates to the sphere of discursive engagement, the sphere of actors, for example, uploading links, engaging in viral publics, posting comments and blogs but also interacting with 'equals' with shared interest in such a spatial landscape. The sphere of 'centrality of networks' of public discourse relates, in other words, to the broader terms to public engagement through chosen platforms as continuous discursive and interactive 'reference points' but also through engagement in social media and blog sites. These two spheres, network centrality as the monitoring sphere and centrality of networks, the engagement sphere, allow us to unfold the dialectical architecture of advanced globalized public communication, which is no longer exclusively related to modern Western nation-states but to other states (authoritarian, 'failed' states') and has 'reflexive' implications across societies. This inclusive dialectical architecture in the advanced phase of globalized networked communication positions civic identity as 'reflexive' imagination in the subjectively chosen horizons of 'world consciousness' (Robertson, 2011).

This dialectic of such a public space between 'networks of centrality' and 'centrality of networks' emerges today across all world regions, however, in varying fabrics and patterns. Contours of this emerging public space between, for example, national media as a 'networks of centrality' and social media as 'centrality of networks' can be observed in contexts of political conflicts in various world regions. For example, national media in Syria deliver limited – and often argued – censored information; yet, citizens have access to social media forms that not only provide information but discursive sites for engagement in alternative conflict scenarios within regional but also larger transnational spheres. This parallelism of public spaces can also be observed in contexts of European policy debates where, national media might serve as 'networks of centrality' and constitute spaces for active engagement in transnational, cross-European debates. The geopolitics of such a networked public space has increasing impacts on the 'public' agenda not only of Western nation-states but also of diverse state formations. However, such a public space also shapes new formations of public deliberation: forms of deliberation that, for example, emerged in the context of the *Wikileaks* disclosure practices, such as of diplomatic cables and war logs. *Wikileaks* could be considered as a 'network of centrality', a monitoring sphere in some world regions where *Wikileaks* is fully accessible and publicly discussed. The platform might be considered to be a 'centralized network' for discursive engagement in other world regions for political actors who upload information and have access to otherwise banned web content. For example, the so-called 'war logs' disclosure, as well as the disclosure of diplomatic cables, have influenced through the role of 'network centrality' the national public agenda from Spain, Lebanon to Costa Rica, Russia to Cuba. Despite the controversial debates of the *Wikileaks* model of transparency as a deliberative strategy of radical disclosure in transnational publics (see Sifry, 2011; Fenster, 2012), this transparency model has been even adopted by mainstream news organizations; yet, there are different degrees of disclosure across world regions. In some Western regions the focus on public 'impact' in contexts of transnational public engagement was enabled through collaborative links, intersections, with national networks of centrality: mainstream media organizations, such as the *Guardian* in the UK and *Der Spiegel* in Germany. These sites have even enhanced the role of, in this case, *Wikileaks*, as a globalized site for radical transparency. Networks of centrality as the 'monitoring' sphere might also be constituted by the minute-by-minute accounts of subjective perceptions of political crises on micro-blogging sites – from local violence during the crisis in Somalia, to the coordination of demonstrations in Istanbul.

The dialectic of 'networks of centrality' as the 'monitoring' sphere, and the 'centrality of networks' as the 'engagement' sphere, helps to set very broad parameter of the discursive unfolding of public space beyond national boundaries. Furthermore, public discourse across such a diversity of communicative 'networks' can no longer be merely related to 'web-based' spheres or technological 'connectivity', since communicative networks constitute multidirectional, multilayered communicative forms. In this sense the term 'network' as used here reflects a diversity of discursive sites, the Internet as well as satellite channels, traditional media forms and 'apps' on tablets and mobile phones, in addition to new forms of 'networked' television, streamed as IPTV (Internet Protocol Television), social media sites, *Skype* and *Facetime* accessible in local public spheres in an increasingly transnational scope. This is the new dimension of networked complexities of cross-platform communicative practices, which through this multi-layered spatial dimension begins to de-territorialize public communication from the territoriality of national information and communication spheres. The centrality of the local townhall from Dewey's time and the national centrality of the Habermasian age, as well as the assumed 'linearity' of international, cross-border communicative forms are shifting towards a 'reflective' public space emerging in the dialectic of networked discourse.

Conceptions of communicative space in globalization debates

In order to explore this space further, we must realize that such an approach is situated beyond national, transnational and international paradigms and needs to be embedded in the larger paradigmatic scope of globalization theories. This is necessary as the public space in the described networked contexts is not 'just' an approach of transnational communication but rather an approach of 'communicative globalization'. Communicative globalization is used here as a working term for transnational spatial relations, within 'advanced' layers in today's network age through a three-way process: not only nations, 'localities' but also subjective civic spaces are deeply entangled into globalized formations. Despite the key role of communication for political, social and cultural globalization processes, the relevance of transnational publics is rarely discussed in paradigmatic debates of globalization. For this reason it is crucial for our discussion here to assess conceptual 'fragments' offered by globalization theories in order to identify the scope of public space within globalized communication.

Firstly, globalization understood as a process of 'intensification' is relevant here. The first author who comes to mind is Anthony Giddens, whose work is important. In this context, Giddens' understanding of 'relativistic' globalization as a 'stretching' process seems to relate to public communication within the complexity of globalization. Giddens already as early as 1991, at a time when national mass media still prevailed and direct-to-home-satellite delivery and the Internet were just emerging, arguing that globalization constitutes 'the modes of connection', connecting 'different social contexts' but also 'regions' which 'become networked across the earth's surface as a whole' (Giddens, 1991: 64). In consequence, Giddens understands globalization as the 'intensification of worldwide relations which link distant localities in such a way that local happenings are shaped by events occurring many miles away and vice versa' (Giddens, 1991: 64). His notion of 'time–space distanciation' has helped to understand the 'breaking news' genre, for example, used by transnational satellite providers such as CNN about twenty years ago which – through Western, in particular US satellite news dominance – linked localities through 'live' information from almost any point worldwide. However, it seems that public communication in today's advanced stage of globalization diverts in two ways from Giddens' visionary approach: firstly, globalized public communication is not so much characterized by 'intensification' through the somewhat linear axis of trans-local relations but rather by intensification through parallelism of multiple transnationally fluctuating 'densities', continuously shifting terrains of highly fractured forms of public engagement. Secondly, public communication is no longer embedded in taxonomies of 'stretching' as outlined in Giddens' globalization model. Giddens assumes that modern nation-states dominate such a 'stretching process'. A process which not only relates to the neoliberal stretching of corporate structures of (mainly Western) multinational media corporations but also to public diplomacy strategies and security surveillance. Today, the linearity of such a stretching process is transformed into a new dialectical taxonomy of 'contraction' between networks of 'monitoring' and networks of 'engagement'. It is this dialectical taxonomy which constitutes the resonance sphere of a subjective public 'situated-ness' across local, national and transnational discourses. These diverse layers of 'densities' and globalized contractions are phenomena which have implications on modern Western nation-states and increasingly – and it is time that we begin to understand this new reality – on other society types, from authoritarian states to 'failed' states.

Secondly, the resonance 'contractions' emerging between 'networks of centrality' and 'centrality of networks' as a sphere of globalization could be related to what Beck, Giddens and Lash (1994) understand as 'reflexivity' as an epistemic sphere of globalization. They argue that 'reflexivity' is a process of reflexive appropriation of a globalized modernity. However, in contexts of network 'resonance' such reflexive appropriation of the increasing globalized density of subjective spheres is specifically interwoven with public and political communication *not* as a consequence of modernity but as a consequence of *advanced* networked communication. The dimension of 'reflexivity' relates in the context of our discussion to an inclusive (e.g. across diverse society types) resonance of transnational public communication, or, in other words: the macro-structural 'coming-together' of deterritorialized spaces, the transformation of the 'local' site of globalization through the 'reciprocity' of such a networked public *within* the state territory.

Thirdly, the transformation of communicative space has been assessed in the paradigm of the 'spatial turn' through the ontological dichotomy of 'place' and 'space'. Lash and Urry already in the early 1990s addressed such a transformation through a critique of neoliberal globalized economies producing dis-embedded 'place' which, as they argue, colonizes, empties out and displaces traditional social structures (Lash and Urry, 1994). Taking this furher, Castells argues that societies are embedded in spaces of multiple networks of 'space of flows' (Castells, 1996). These flows are 'synchronized' through continuous streams of networked temporality as 'timeless time' with implications on macro- and micro-structures of societies, from political and economic spheres to civic identity formations. Castells relates his term of network society not exclusively to modern society but argues that the structure of a network society incorporates all societies, connected or not, as networked formations are macro-structures that have implications on all world regions. Much has also been written about 'virtual' communities and the formation of identity politics in increasing spheres of 'disembodied' cyberculture (see Turkle, 1995; Slevin 2000; Barkard-jieva, 2005) and networked spaces such as the realm of activism and even 'technopolitics' as a 'new political order' colonizing global civil society (Hassan, 2004: 115).

In more recent approaches 'online' and/or 'digital' public spaces are often understood as side-by-side models, where transnational spatial communications is constructed separately to national publics. However, over the last years intersections between networked interdependence and territoriality have become more distinct. For example, Bohman argues that 'the space opened up by computer-mediated communication supports a new sort of "distributive" rather than unified public sphere with new forms of interaction'. He claims that, the Internet 'decentres' the public sphere and constitutes 'a public of publics rather than a distinctively unified and encompassing public sphere in which all communicators participate' (Bohman, 2010, 2004: 255). In consequence, Bohman concludes that a transnational public sphere combines at least two 'culturally rooted public spheres' which begin to 'overlap and intersect'. He predicts that 'under proper conditions and with the support of the proper institutions, existing vibrant global publics will expand as they become open to and connected with other public spheres' (Bohman, 2010, 2004: 254). These debates have provided important insights; however, for the purpose of our discussion it is crucial to assess public space through the reflexive dichotomy of

'dis-embedding'/'re-embedding' within the dimension of transnational networked 'resonance'.

Fourthly, in addition to such a process of 'de-centring' of links
between 'networks' and 'territoriality', other conceptions address the
transnational/national dichotomy in spaces of 'mobility' across public/
private formations within the traditional public-sphere model (Sheller
and Urry, 2003: 108). It is argued that these 'hybrid' publics stretch
across de-territorialized private/public terrains of modern public-
sphere conception. These 'new hybrids' of 'private-in-public' and
'public-in-private' spheres do not 'automatically imply a decline in
politics or a collapse of democracy, but may instead point to a proliferation of multiple "mobile" sites for potential democratization' (Sheller
and Urry, 2003: 108). The authors note that 'any hope for public citizenship and democracy . . . will depend on the capacity to navigate these
new material, mobile worlds that are neither public nor private' (Sheller
and Urry, 2003: 113).

A fifth stream of debates of globalization centres around the epistemic relationship of – in broad terms – 'networks' and 'territoriality'
through what we might call 'fragmented' publics, for example in contexts of environmental communication (Cox, 2006; Beck, 2007) or even
as thematic spaces as 'issue publics' (Dahlgren, 2009). Other approaches
describe 'tribal' 'mobile selves' as a place-based public in digital formations, 'dispersed nationally and globally, connected to other members
of their own tribes by telecommunications and media' (Varnelis and
Friedberg, 2008: 31). Besides these forms of 'tribal' public spaces, the
role of the Internet as a site for online deliberation in the sense of political mobilization (Lim and Kann, 2008) or *vis-à-vis* traditional media
(Papacharissi, 2007) is often considered as a driver of transnational
public formations. Recent debates focus on 'tactical media' or 'locative'
media, as locally embedded mobile applications, commonly known as
'apps', which identify quite new forms of relationships between networks and in this case local territoriality in such a way that locative
media can be understood as 'flexible', subjectively 'embodied' and
'portable' forms that are 'transforming our use of space and place, but
they are also recontextualizing, repoliticizing, and rehistoricizing our
awareness and engagement with the inhabited neighbourhoods of the
world' (Guertin, 2012: 19). Guertin suggests that advanced mobile technologies (including locative media) create an 'embodiment', and not
merely – in obvious reference to McLuhan (1962) – an 'extension of eye
or ear' (Guertin, 2012: 21).

The public space between networked centralities and territoriality
also signifies (this is a sixth type) what Gilman-Opalsky understands

as a 'transgressive public' which 'refuses to identify its scale and function as either exclusively national or exclusively transnational' (Gilman-Opalsky, 2006: 2). He identifies the space of deliberation of 'transgressive' publics in a particular relationship between national and transnational publics, for example through addressing issues in transnational publics which 'exceed national boundaries' or which 'accumulate solidarity' and 'add weight to national or subnational initiatives' (Gilman-Opalsky, 2006: 120). Processes of 'overlaps' of transnational/national public terrains are also understood as 'porous' publics which emerge through a 'transnational dialectic' (Olesen, 2007: 295). Oleson argues that it is 'theoretically sterile to debate whether the public sphere today is mainly national or transnationalized. The dichotomy is artificial' (Olesen, 2007: 297). He suggests that national publics are 'porous', as public issues 'migrate' and are 'lifted out' of national public discourse.

Moving away from the territorial 'principle': 'decoupling' processes of public 'embeddedness'

These fine-grained conceptualizations of the fracturing of communicative spheres might serve as rough parameters for mapping the public space of 'network centralities'. We should now take this discussion further into the larger realm of globalization debates in order to identify various – to use a Habermasian term – spheres of 'de-coupling' processes, which help to identify the specific areas of porosity of nationally bounded public spheres in globalized structures.

Firstly, these are 'de-coupling' processes of the public sphere from the territorial conceptions of the 'first' modernity where the nation-state and its public institutions constituted not only the territorial centrality of communication sovereignty and the core territories of the epistemic boundedness of democratic discourse. The term 'foreign' journalism might serve as a good example here as it indicates such a centrality of 'domestic territory' where the coverage of events beyond the clearly defined territorial boundness of the nation (and national legitimacy) is referred to as 'foreign' and a separate journalistic field of reporting. The emerging public spaces between globalized networked interdependence and territoriality also reveal de-coupling processes of the 'public sphere' from the 'second' modernity (Beck, 1992). Through the lens of the 'second' modernity, a global public emerges as a sphere of global public awareness or 'risk cosmopolitanism' which, as Beck argues, integrates transnational conflicts and commonalities into everyday practices (Beck, 2006: 34). Despite such a 'radicalized' 'reflexive' sphere (see Beck and Grande, 2010), character-izing the second 'risk' modernity, the underlying paradigmatic frame-work is no longer normatively directed towards the ideal of a 'nation-state', but shifting towards the conceptual parameter of the 'cosmopolitan turn' (Beck and Grande, 2010). The link between cos-mopolitanism in nation-state contexts and public cultures is taken further by Beck who understands the public context of international politics as 'post-state' cooperation (Beck, 2006: 37). Furthermore, trans-international politics constitute 'a level of organized, more or less infor-mal domestic, foreign, interstate and sub-state politics which mirrors all other phenomena: global economic power relations, rises and strate-gies, the situations of nation-states and reactions of individual coun-tries and groups of countries, interventions aimed at a global public, terror, threats, and so on' (Beck, 2006: 37).

Secondly, the social, political and economical 'mechanism' of such a second or so-called 'global' modernity is not only characterized by the 'stretching', for example, of social relations, but by the 'breaking away' of contexts of reflexive 'disembedding' (Beck, Giddens and Lash, 1994). Other recent debates critique the assumed universal approach of 'reflexive' modernity in non-European, for example, South Asian con-texts. Calhoun suggests that 'what is relevant is not the stretching or compression of some normal period of time, but the way in which felt pressures translate into different experiences, strategies, institutions and outcomes' (Calhoun, 2010: 600).

Decoupling processes of public spheres: from 'lifting out' to 'drawing in'

The crucial transformation in the sphere of public communication, an area rarely mentioned in Beck, Giddens and Lash's conceptions, is not so much any more the decoupling process of 'lifting out' or 'breaking away' or in more recent terms, the cosmopolitanization as a 'reflexive outlook' (Beck, 2006) but rather the opposite: the process of discourses being 'drawn into', 'absorbed', and amalgamated into micro-fractured communicative publics, in a way a process of reflexive 'inward' cos-mopolitanization, loosely 'clustering' across diverse sets of territorial spaces. Public communication in an advanced phase of globalization could be described as a sphere of 'spatial reach', as the crucial distinc-tion between previous and today's advanced spheres of communica-tive globalization. A specific sphere of 'spatial reach' which signifies not only a paradigm shift of conceptualizing new globalized – to relate to Held's work – 'social relations and organizations towards the inter-regional and intercontinental scale' (Held and McGrew, 2000, 2006: 3) but also specifically shifts away from national public discourse, from the spatial reach enabled by the 'horizontally' universe of networked communication towards a spatial reach embedded within a much smaller, denser cosmos of public trajectories. of 'linking'; for example, of 'trans-border', 'transnational' or 'globalized' public spaces. These public complexities reveal not so much the 'extension', the reaching-out of transnational spaces, across 'networks' (Castells, 1996) or the 'extensity', and 'velocity' of transnational connectedness (Held and McGrew, 2000, 2006: 68) across social and political spaces (which were key factors of previous phases of transnational public formations) but the 'vertical' densities of public discourse. It is this dimension of subjective, 'vertical', 'reciprocal' density as the reflexive forms of public trajectories which emerges through the dialectical taxonomies of subjectively chosen centralities of networked space.

This emerging public sphere between 'network centrality' and the 'centrality of networks' as a subjective, civic 'situated-ness' has 'vertical' implications for normative consent and legitimacy and for what Hegel once described as the 'universal will' (Hegel, 1952). The public networked sphere is not so much a necessary outcome or extension of 'global modernity' but rather of the 'spatial' merging, the entangling of national *and* transnational public space, not only in modern societies, but – very importantly – in other forms of societal structures rarely addressed in conceptions of globalization debates.

Whereas development communication traditionally addresses communication of developing regions through social and economic processes (see Mody, 2004), it is necessary today where globalized platforms can be accessed almost anywhere in the world to identify specifically the territorial implications of such a vertical 'connectivity' for different state types, such as for 'failed' or 'weak' states in so-called 'low-income' or 'developing'[2] regions where the spheres of civic and public communication are widely under-investigated. The term 'weak' or 'failed' states describes the governance structure, for example, of Afghanistan, Somalia, Chad, Sudan, Yemen and also Iraq, where specific public communicative spheres exist around non-state actors, such as transnational NGOs and local elites (also journalists) who are 'connected' to locally specific forms of network centralities, enabling a specific 'reflective' deliberative public practice. 'Connectivity' in developing regions is still today mainly articulated in contexts of economic development (see, for example, Wilkins, 2004) and through a critical assessment of US dominance in rebuilding failed state governance, such as in Iraq and Afghanistan (Chomsky, 2006). Only recently have spheres of 'connectivity' in civic communication in developing regions been further explored, for example public connectivity among expatriates living abroad and public spheres of their country of origin. Other studies address the role of youth in processes of post-conflict resolution (see, for example, Schwartz, 2010) and, what Farivar has recently described as the Internet of 'elsewhere,' gaining insight into the implications of transnational digital communication in countries beyond the radar screen of communication theory and research (Farivar, 2011).[3] Recent, approaches identify new forms of public communication involving non Western regions and address the role of the particular public communicative sphere of the 'politics of space' of, for example, forced migrants (Witteborn, 2011). Overall, it is this dense overlap, the merging of particular subjective public networks across modern, 'weak' and 'failed' territorial 'places', which seems to characterize the complexity of the politics of today's globalized public. It is *this* emerging centrality of transnational public communications that recalibrates formations of territorial publics and spheres of accountability and governance on a national and transnational level.

Despite the increasing challenge of the normative 'territorial principle' of public-sphere conceptions, it is surprising that forms of 'national non-territoriality' are mainly related to modern nation-states, rather than relation to other state formations. Even the discussion of the so-called 'weakening' of the nation-state circulates around various transformations of otherwise assumed 'intact' European state constructions. Both the broadening scope of imposing 'exogenously' made legitimate decisions on nation-states and the increasing existence of non-territorial governance structures and policy frameworks are increasingly becoming polity parameters in the transnationalization of modern nation-states. Both of these implications are assessed when identifying the 'weakening' factors of the configuration of the nation-state through non-territorial 'systems' of policy networks, of trans-regional intergovernmental organizations, such as the European Union (see Hanley, 2007), the global financial sector, IMF, GO8, WTO and World Bank. However, these processes of transnationalization of the nation-state through high density ex- or post-territorial inter-governmental network spheres increasingly influence the decisions on day-to-day policy practices and constitute an important layer of the transnationalization process of the nation-state. However, the implications of these transnationalization processes of the nation-state also relate to important though under-researched conceptions of public accountability.

As discussed earlier, the public space – as a 'resonance' or 'contraction' – between 'network centrality' and the 'centraliy of networks' is comprised of not only national and 'local' territory but further, 'lifeworld' spatialities. More recent approaches of globalization seem to acknowledge the role of the 'lifeworld' as a political space. For example, Geoffrey Plyers' conception of alter-globalization is quite useful here as it positions political movements in new local subjective 'spaces of experience,' and, at the same time, as deeply embedded within a 'globalized' form of activism (Plyers, 2010: 41). Plyers outlines, through this density, new forms of deliberative spaces in subjective forms of 'reflexive' activism, which, for example, surface in the context of WTO and G08 meetings.

Scalar processes of de-bracketing of the state–civil society nexus: reconceptualizing the public sphere in a transnational context

Having outlined the diverse transnational scopes of transformative de-coupling processes, it is now important to assess further the pathway in which the 'opening' of the national public within larger spheres of transnationalization, the concrete disjuncture of public spheres from the national centrality is addressed here in the lens of public-sphere debates. However, reviewing public-sphere debates in media and communication studies and related conceptions of public deliberation in sociology and political science reveals that this particular disjuncture, the 'decoupling', or what I describe as 'debracketing', of the state–society nexus has been mainly perceived through conceptual frameworks of 'extension' of the modern public sphere beyond national borders guided by the Habermasian narrative. These 'linear' conceptions, viewed from today's perspective, are challenged by at least three levels of complexity.

A first set of conceptual complexities relates to the paradigmatic normativity of public deliberation in the Habermasian model. It is the modern conception of normative nation-state publics and the methodological positioning of public spheres within the terrain not only of traditional European national normative legitimacy but also of the modern European model of deliberative democracy, which defines 'normativity' within deliberative traditions of national communities. National communities are linked – in variations from Weber to Heidegger – by a belief in the collective perception of national 'fate' and historical 'destiny'. In the early days of European nation-building this common fate constituted a political territorial community of 'the people', i.e. the nation as a collective entity marking the deliberative boundaries of the nation-state. Given the pluralism of modern European societies today, such a normative public persists as only one model among various forms of public life, not only transnational but also sub-national public interdependencies. Using Rawls' term 'neutrality' means that the aim of normative consent is to reach an 'overlapping consensus' where individuals 'are able to set aside their personal or non-public conception of the good from the public conception of justice' (d'Entreves, 2002, 2006: 4). Nation-states represent in this sense not only homogenous models of 'demos' and 'ethnos' but rather are internally stratified and differentiated and incorporate quite diverse and distinct multicultural 'demoi' (see also Daniel Chernilo, 2007: Ernst, 2005), which are *not* included. Benhabib argues that a public 'dialogue model' is 'not neutral' in the sense of a 'moral and political epistemology', as the separation between 'the public' and 'the private' leads to 'the silencing of the concerns of certain excluded groups' (Benhabib, 1992: 82). In this sense, the assumption of even a homogenous public *within* the nation-state remains a myth as bounded, linear deliberative space within democratic societies (which is often resurfacing in mediated discourse, such as in national television) as it is already deeply incorporated into multiple networks of public 'trajectories'. Furthermore, it is formations of intergovernmental and public interdependence rather than the European nation-states, are tied into postnational structures, for example through an emerging space of global law beyond the state of autonomous 'private' regimes (Fischer-Lescano and Teubner, 2007: 44). Although 'hybridity' or 'melange cultures' have been addressed in early forms of globalization, the pace of public communication is increasing as societal 'connections' are not only built around political actors but increasingly around direct individual action as an indicator of transnational society building (see Mau, 2007). These are the building blocks of public formations, whereas in the Habermasian form of deliberative publics, global publics and civil society as Scheuerman notes 'do little more than influence or countersteer the commanding heights of global authority' (Scheuerman, 2008: 134).

A second set of complexities relates to the public sphere as a rational discursive framework, i.e. 'utterances' made under certain speech conditions. Habermas himself has noted the conditions under which the 'inclusion of the other' is possible. However, given the variety of communicative spheres, 'public utterances' take on quite diverse formations. Public spheres are often narrowly conceptualized as reasoned discursive terrains; however, they are not always 'reasoned' but incorporate quite diverse forms of public discourses. These forms of mediated discourse also relate to, for example, emotional accounts on television talkshows and other formats of popular culture where the a 'reflexive discourse of the self in the contemporary cultural scene' constitutes a subjective sphere of public life (Lunt and Pantti, 2007: 173: also Kraidy, 2010). Couldry et al. (2007) argued for a broader inclusiveness of public discourse involving the larger scope of mediated communication, such as visual images or subjective narratives.

A third set of conceptual complexities is challenged by the assumed boundedness of public debate – not only within nation-states – often without realizing that transnational forms of public communication have also culturally specific deliberative implications in other world regions in particular in the context of a globalized public and global civil society. For example, the role of satellites and deliberation in Arab states where transregional political communication delivered via *Al Jazeera* contributes to such a formation of intrasocietal deliberation (Sakr, 2007b). This form of dialectical engagement relates to highly specific public 'loyalties' in a supranational context (Slade and Volkmer, 2012). As the examples show these processes are not only emerging in Western contexts, but also in developing countries where, through networked digital trajectories, the engagement with expatriate communities creates important dense spheres of public life. Tittey uses the term 'offshore citizenry' which reflects, for example, the extent to which 'Africans in the diaspora are emotionally invested in home politics' (Tittey, 2009: 146) engaging in political conflicts. This process which, often overlooked, affects national public debates in the residence country of expatriates as well as in their country of origin. These are related to new forms of interdependence, the transnational public engagement by the expatriate, diasporic community with public spheres in countries of origin further sustaining new formations of public culture – as is the case in some African countries – have already been established through the transformations in media structures, and in consequence, information dissemination following democratization processes. In other contexts, these processes of interdependent public cultures allow the bypassing of state control and enables counter discourses, challenging the hegemonic viewpoint of the state (Tittey, 2009: 148). Other studies situate migrants and their 'transnational practices' within a post-territorial sphere and focus on migrant communities centred around 'mobility' and 'locality' (Dahinden, 2010).

These are just some examples of the conceptual complexities arising with new forms of public communication. A critical reflection of the

Habermasian model has quite early on not only addressed the role of pluralist, that is, differentiated societies within a conception of the public sphere but also the need to incorporate, for example, transnational social movements (Calhoun, 1992) in addition to a transnationalization of media in networks of neoliberal market regimes and mediations that establish a new relationship between the 'institutionalized practices of mass communication' and 'democratic politics' (Garnham, 1992: 364).

However, I would like to emphasize that Habermas has identified emerging sections of transnational public terrains, such as new forms of discourse ethics of 'inclusion' and transnational public formations, which constitute an 'intermediary' structure between the political system on the one hand and the private sectors of the lifeworld on the other. It represents a highly complex network that branches out into multitude of overlapping international, national, regional, local, and subcultural arenas (Habermas, 1999: 373). Habermas also notes a diversity of various levels of public spheres, of what he calls 'episodic publics,' publics of 'particular events' and 'abstract' publics 'of isolated readers, listeners and viewers scattered across target geographical areas or even around the globe, and brought together only through the mass media' (Habermas, 1999: 374). Although Habermas' attempts to relate to formations of transnational publics, the notion of 'actors' is mainly articulated through 'modern' social theory, resulting in a perception of 'global' publics as a somewhat peripheral orbit, revolving around the central space of modern public spheres. Not only are political conflicts no longer 'linear' national 'media events' (Dayan and Katz, 1994) but they constitute discursive sites in multiple layers of public spaces within network centralities. Actors in such a model are quite different from Habermas' understanding of 'institutional' national actors, which are 'identifiable', such as actors with a 'functional background', actors in roles of (identifiable) 'self-legitimation' and 'actors as journalists' (Habermas, 1999: 375, 376). Habermas' conception of mediated communication is mainly framed around 'mass media' and, given the time when his work was conducted, does not include the role not only of mediated but specifically *discursive* transnational publics within and across diverse networks of actor discourses in 'real time'.

Over the last years various debates have attempted to situate the Habermasian public sphere *vis-à-vis* a variety of conceptual frameworks of globalization and new public formations. These understand the transnationalization of deliberation through very specific 'extensions' of national 'embeddedness'.

There are three main approaches which specifically extend national publics into a transnational sphere which will allow to further identify departure points in mapping the sphere of public space within network centralities.

Modern publics and transnational extension

The first model is the transnational extension of traditional 'modern' publics. It is not surprising that debates about transnational public spheres are built upon the 'extension' of the modern public sphere, which is situated in what might be called 'spatial congruence' of sovereignty and territory. The main underlying issue of these approaches is the conceptualization of the public, of deliberation and legitimacy through an assumed territorial boundedness of 'voting publics' within the territorial overlap of *polis* and *demos* which is the core component of 'modern' national normative legitimacy: a normative legitimacy that goes back to the political contract which, for the first time, inaugurated a polity affirming the reciprocal acknowledgement of sovereignty. These treaties of the 'Peace of Westphalia' signed in 1648 in Münster and Osnabrück[4] ended the Thirty Years War in 1638 in the centre of modern Europe. The so-called 'Treaty of Westphalia' is only one of these policy frameworks, although a quite important one, as it has outlined the conceptual understanding of 'sovereignty', for a new political order in Europe after the Thirty Years War. The Treaty of Westphalia has laid out the policy framework for the exclusive right to sovereignty over territory which has also implications for legitimizing the embeddedness of sovereignty through a social (national) contract (see Clark, 2005). The Treaty of Westphalia (and to a lesser extent the Treaties of Utrecht, signed in 1713–14) established the constituencies, not only of European nation-states but have for the first time regulated international equality among states and laid the foundation of the modern international state system (see for example Clark, 2005; Held, 1996). In this sense the Treaty of Westphalia has influenced the understanding of 'sovereignty' and 'legitimacy' within the international order – and the notion of a modern public-sphere concept where information sovereignty is, to varying degrees, regulated by the state.

Nancy Fraser has repeatedly made attempts to articulate core elements of the modern public sphere through transnational constructions of civil society, for example around issues of feminism as a 'non liberal', 'non bourgeois' 'counter' public *vis-à-vis* the Habermasian national form of public deliberation (Fraser, 1992: 115). In her more recent work, Fraser addresses the notion of what she calls a 'post'-Westphalian publicity as a model which incorporates multi-cultural societies, involving diasporic groups, migrants, non-nationals. It is a model where the public 'interlocutors' engage across distance and are, so Fraser notes, 'neither co-nationals nor fellow citizens' (Fraser, 2007: 16) in a national and transnational context. Such a revised notion of 'interlocutors' allows us to identify new forms of transnational public trajectories which, however, still need to be integrated into public constructions of the nation-state. In Fraser's argument, 'the "who" of communication . . . is often a collection of dispersed interlocutors, who do not constitute a demos. The "where" of communication . . . now stretches across vast reaches of the globe' (Fraser, 2007: 19). She argues that 'empirically' the national framework is being 'surpassed', and so 'the public sphere will simply be disempowered unless it is reconstituted on a different scale' and that the 'addressee of communication, once theorized as a sovereign territorial state is now an amorphous mix of public and private transnational powers that is neither easily identifiable nor rendered accountable' (Fraser, 2007: 19). In her work, the discursive concept of 'interlocutors' take on an important role, linking to the Habermasian framework of 'actors'. Fraser understands discourse as a sphere of 'publicity' where actors in the Habermasian model take on a public role. However, I would like to emphasize that Habermas also uses the term 'publicness' meaning the sphere of 'being public' and not so much 'making public' (often translated into English as 'publicity') which is a quite different form of communication (Volkmer, 2010). It seems that 'publicness', i.e. 'being public' not only relates back to the Kantian notion of public reason but allows us to identify normative deliberation along transnational spheres, such as in terms of gender (Fraser, 1992), religion (Zaret, 1992) or in contexts of a mass-mediated (national) subjectivity where 'self-unity' is considered a 'public value' (Warner, 1992). Despite these different approaches to transnational 'extensions' the modern, national sphere as a normative frame for conceptualizing communicative parameters of transnational public communication is still very much present in these conceptions or, as Fraser has noted, 'the Westphalian blind spot of public sphere is hard to miss' (Fraser, 2007: 14).

It should be mentioned, however, that a modern transnationalization of public discourse has also been addressed in relation to media, mainly in the context of television and the 'mediation' of 'co-presence'. Dahlgren argues that 'nationalism is a sort of mediated global . . . community' and claims 'it is apparent that tempo-spatial co-presence no longer has an automatic monopoly on orientational significance for individuals' (Dahlgren, 1995: 89). In these constructions, the ideal form of modern rational discourse is replaced by a diversity of 'texts' creating discourse between 'atomized individuals, consuming media in their homes' which 'do not comprise a public, nor do they tend to contribute much to the democratization of civil society' (Dahlgren, 1995: 19-20). 'Even if it is de-emphasized, no democratic order will work without some shared sense of commonality among its members. Talk both manifests and presupposes some kind of social bond between citizens' (Dahlgren, 1995: 20). Dahlgren views television as a 'televisual prism': an industry of audio-visual texts, and a sociocultural experience (Dahlgren, 1995: 25). What Dahlgren considered as 'private' spheres are now being integrated into a conception of the public which integrates both 'private' and 'public' space. Debates that also aim to raise new issues of equivalence between 'mass-mediated' and 'non-mass-mediated' publics refer mainly to Tomlinson's understanding of globalized media cultures (1999: 89). On a quite different note, Brian McNair argues that the public sphere has always been constituted by subspheres and that the 'rational' is a relative term. 'Subspheres' are organized by demography, political viewpoints, lifestyle and ethnicity' (McNair, 2006: 137). McNair also claims that the public sphere 'comprises even in its most primitive form a virtual, cognitive multiverse of spheres within spheres' (McNair, 2006: 137). However, globalization or global communication is characterized by new forms of decentralized 'inclusion'. Such ideas of fragmentation have also been identified as 'sphericules' (Gitlin, 1998) or 'micro-spheres' (Volkmer, 2002, 2011), *vis-à-vis* the national 'mainstream' as the 'macro' site of a national public sphere. These fractured publics are enclosed 'modular' spheres within the larger scale of hegemonic national majority spheres reflecting the public power domains of minority/ majority relations. Other approaches debate the transnational extension of national publics through globalized media forms in order to conceptualize a mediated global public sphere. However, pessimistic accounts note that global media are 'even more restricted in terms of access and participation than are the dominant state-limited media' (Sparks, 2000: 120). Sparks argues, that 'whatever definition of global media we take . . . they are very marginal . . . compared with the audiences for the older media bounded by the state system' (Sparks, 2000: 120). In fact, in Sparks' view, transnational media forms have led to an 'erosion of the state' from 'below' and 'above' through the 'erosion' of the state as the 'central regulator of cultural life'. An erosion of the state has been accelerated through 'the global movement of populations' and the development of 'global mechanisms of transmission', as well as 'complex patterns of international trade', with the outcome that traditional 'circuits of meaning production' are detached from the specific tastes of given and homogenous national audiences (Sparks, 2007: 145).

Transnational publics and political movements

A second stream identifies the conceptualization of transnational publics not only as a somewhat 'linear', 'extended' space along the lines of the Westphalian model of national sovereignty and legitimacy but as a 'disembedded' national space begun in the context of political trans-border movements. Since the late 1960s, political movements emerged around issues of human rights (see Guidry, Kennedy, Zald, 2000: 15) as an early transnational deliberative sphere *vis-à-vis* the normative form of national publics (in plural!). Forms of mediated activism emerged through a transnational centrality of thematic publics which was possible in the mass media age, by creating spectacular transnational events and capturing the attention of the international news media, for example by NGOs such as Greenpeace, anti-nuclear movements in the early 1980s, anti-globalization and anti-capitalist movements today. Tarro and McAdam (2005: 140) argue that the transnational 'diffusion' of these social movements are often related to a specific 'strategy of brockerage', that is 'information transfers that depend on the linking of two or more previously unconnected sites' or, in other words, establishing links between transnational 'nodes'. For example, Sikkink assumes that, transnational actors 'access the political systems of their target state' through a 'two-level' approach, i.e. 'concentration on a chief negotiator or head of government' as 'the linchpin' mediating 'between the international and the domestic' (Sikkink, 2005: 154).

However, in other contexts of activism, transnational publics are characterized by a 'lifting out' of the national space of communities of 'fate' and represent an approach that is quite different from the Habermasian model. These are 'disembedded' communities, for example, forced migrants or mobile communities of a nation without a state, which often engage in a public sphere *vis-à-vis* the (ontological) centrality of crises. Gilman-Opalsky uses the example of the Mexican Zapatista movement who cannot rely on 'institutions with a formal responsibility to legitimate themselves and their actions in the opinion and will of these communities of fate' (Gilman-Opalsky, 2008: 129). He positions 'unbounded' publics in such a public terrain 'of fate' in which nations have lost 'a degree of autonomy and sovereignty'. He further argues that 'non-bourgeois public spheres have always been driven to transnationalize, for structural and material reasons, bourgeois public spheres have not shared the same impetuses. Today, the enduring tension is represented by the fact that bourgeois public spheres have supported capitalist globalization whereas nonbourgeois public spheres remain at the losing end of these processes' (Gilman-Opalsky, 2008: 139/40). Other debates address publics of transnational activism as an 'activist web sphere' (Bennett, 2005: 222) and as a 'public interface' for a variety of publics. He notes that 'publics are beginning to fragment in most modern societies, while media channels are proliferating . . . activists can "be the media"' (Bennett, 2005: 222), 'shifting the brokerage process . . . from organizational leadership to dense interpersonal relationships' (Bennett, 2004: 224). Furthermore, globalized NGOs have after the Second World War begun to influence national publics through specific transnational information polities such as Amnesty International and PR event spectacles. Today, NGOs establish their own transnational thematic publics through the use of social media. These forms of publics constitute new fractured transnational communicative terrains which are, for example, described as 'reference publics' where 'supranational organizations increasingly provide new arenas for the articulation of claim' (della Porta and Krieso, 1999: 16–17).

Transnational publics and the cosmopolitan paradigm: deterritorializing universal political identity

The third conception is built upon a notion of cosmopolitanism which, however, rarely includes communication and media spheres. It opens up the 'state – but does not incorporate the globalized scope of media and communication. Transnational publics are, however, in vague terms, also addressed in the cosmopolitan paradigm which de-constructs the "paradox of bounded communities"' (Benhabib, 2006: 18) through the 'disaggregation of citizenship' (Benhabib, 2006: 46). Benhabib's work in particular relates to understanding cosmopolitanism as a 'philosophical project of mediations' (Benhabib, 2006: 20) and articulates the emptying out, for example, of national territoriality and 'boundedness', in the larger context 'issue of hospitality' as 'a right that belongs to all human beings insofar as we view them as potential participant in a world republic' (Benhabib, 2006: 22). In this sense, a 'universal community' emerges 'where a violation of rights in one part of the world is felt everywhere' (Benhabib, 2006:

150). Recent approaches position cosmopolitanism in a nexus of dis-junctures (see Held, 2010) in the centrality of nation-states through 'overlapping communities of fate, where the fates of nations are sig-nificantly intertwined' (Held, 2010: 36). In this sense, cosmopolitanism in contexts of the *Realpolitik* of a transnational political community, could be understood as a framework that, based on Kant's idea of universal rights, identifies specific formations of such a universal community. For example, Held suggests relating cosmopolitanism to the 'ethical and political space which sets out the terms of reference for the recognition of people's equal moral worth, their active agency and what is required for their autonomy and developments' (Held, 2010: 49). In these spaces, as Held argues, 'public interconnections' establish the 'consent' principle which 'constitutes the basis of non-coercive collective agreement and governance' (Held, 2010: 71).

Another set of approaches identifies cosmopolitanism through the lens of 'cosmopolitan nationalism' (Beck, 2006: 48). Beck's approach of 'modern' cosmopolitanism does not reflect on public communication but rather, in more general terms, on the global public sphere as a temporal 'space', as a 'cosmopolitan moment' (Beck, 2007: 56). Beck argues that 'the framework of the nation is not overcome' and he notes that 'the foundations and cultures of the mass media have changed dramatically and concomitantly'; all kinds of transnational connections and confrontations have emerged. As a result, 'cultural ties, loyalties and identities have expanded beyond national borders and systems of control. Individuals and groups who surf transnational television chan-nels and programmes simultaneously inhabit different worlds.' (Beck, 2006: 7) In consequence, the notion of a 'reflexive outlook' constitutes a 'sense of boundary-lessness' and 'the longing for re-establishing of the old boundary lines' (Beck, 2006: 8). In Beck's terminology, the cosmopolitan 'outlook' configures the ontological departure from nation-state boundedness, emerging as the 'unreality of the world of nation-states' (Beck, 2006: 21).

Concluding this review of these three paradigmatic areas which 'extend' public-sphere conceptions, we should now take these debates further. I argue that it is not only the transnationalization of national public spheres, the 'sense of boundary-less-ness' of the nation-state but specifically the process of *de-bracketing* of the society-state nexus 'as such' through supranational 'public discourses' has, in consequence, 'reciprocal' implications on state formations. Such a 'de-bracketing' process could be understood as a 'fracturing' of public communication, which is not only characterized by the transformation of publics, from national 'mass' media spheres to complex structures of interactive transnational 'networks' but by the 'fracturing' of public communication within large-scale processes of transnationalization in contexts of civil society formations. These processes are enhanced by new discursive technologies and emerge as scalar processes across diverse modern, weak and failed states. Departing from traditional lines of transnational 'expansions' or linear processes of transnationalization, public communication is not only positioned, depending on the paradigmatic angle within structures of transnationalization or internationalization and this is a characteristic of what I describe as *advanced* forms of global communication but, de- *and* re-territorialization within process of Network developments and globalization processes, 'the expanding scale, growing magnitude, speeding up and deepening impact of transcontinental flows and patterns of interaction' (Held, 2000) have implications for the formation of public communication within such a post-territorial sphere, a radicalization of spatial 'flows' in new forms of dense 'directedness' towards societies. De-territorialization of publicness is not only a structural component where public density emerges as a space and an epistemic process in the dichotomy of disembedding/re-embedding. It is an epistemic sphere based on processes of 'disconnections' of what are, as Held argues in a different context, 'broken links' between 'territory' and 'political power' (Held, 2000: 11). These 'broken links' appear as 'disembedding' of public communication from the 'territory' of national publics and its communicative traditions and rituals and the re-embedding of such a transnational public communication in the resonant space of subjective locality.

From transnational extensions to post-territoriality as a public domain

After having assessed the attempts to conceptualize the transnational pathways of the 'extension' of modern public-sphere activism and cosmopolitanism, we should now seek an understanding of the post-territorial sphere of deliberation and legitimacy. It seems that this new area of implications for the public is only marginally addressed in the traditional debates about public-sphere conceptions. Although traditional forms of national 'space' have for some time been absorbed into larger structures of global governance, civil society, legitimacy (Clark, 2005) and cosmopolitanism, recent debates – interestingly in political science – focus more generally on political 'spaces' as a new political territory where 'national space dissolves as the dominant form of political space' (Albert, 2009: 18). These processes are also described, for example as 'spatial turn' (Albert et al., 2009) in the social sciences. Ferguson and Mansbach suggest we consider such a 'remapping' of 'political space' altogether as the 'new frontier' of global political theory (Ferguson and Mansbach, 2004: 1). Whereas transnationalization is still tied to the paradigm of 'national' structures, the term 'post-territorialiy' suggests a radical paradigm shift towards the increasing spatial component of public communication. Post-territoriality reflects what we have described earlier as 'disembedded' forms of public taxonomies or 'trajectories' shaping global civil society. Both the 'anytime/ anywhere' mode of communication and discursive post-territorialization within the context of a global civil society context create the main challenges for public communication in our time.

I describe these post-territorial spheres as the 'debracketing' process of the state–society nexus. This process has often been addressed in macro-structural terms in globalization theory where, in the 'trans-modern' globalization paradigm, proposed for example by Robertson, Scholte and others, conceptions of 'post-territoriality' have already been in focus. Post-territoriality, for example, relates in Robertson's globalization approach to an understanding of the world as a whole, in its differentiation. Scholte's work critically reflects upon the 'methodological territorialism' that describes 'the social conditions of a particular epoch when bordered territorial units, separated by distance, formed far and away the overriding geographical framework for a macro-level social organization' (Scholte, 2000: 57). Arjun Appadurai's (1996) conception is another example, which has highlighted 'ethno', 'eco-' and 'media scapes' as phenomena of a deterritorialized global social structure. However, the breaking up of the state–society nexus reveals not only the limitations of modern conceptions of territorial state/society relations but at the same time leads to the opening of a new epistemological stratum as a sphere of loyalties, identities and civic engagement.

De-bracketing, reflective extension and post-territoriality

Ulrich Beck has highlighted the emerging globalized epistemological sphere and considers this 'epistemological shift' to be the signifier of a form of social, economic, and cultural 'dialectic' in an advanced globalization debate within the social sciences (Beck, 2006: 17). In these contexts, the conceptualization of modernity as a 'reflexive' form has implications, and Beck has identified these, for subjective 'world' epistemologies but also (but only in general terms) for public spheres. In this sense, we could argue that Beck's sphere of 'reflexive' practice not only relates to identity shifts, such as subjective biographies and social structures and also (as a side effect of his approach) constitute the dialectic dimension of deterritorialized public communication. In this sense, Beck's analysis allows us to draw a connection between these new spheres of 'reflexivity' as a globalized epistemology transforming normative discourse culture of (national) 'kinship' into broader 'reflexive' structures of modern nation-state publics, this is in effect, 'disembedding'. It goes without saying that this process is closely linked to the formations of transnational media spheres not only of 'linear' delivery (as was the case in the mass media age) but of 'disembedded', 'deterritorialized' communication. Satellite communication had already began in the 1960s to 'fracture' national mass media in Western countries through new forms of public 'geographies'. For example, whereas national print and broadcasting delivered political information within the 'linear' boundedness of national territory, it was satellite technology that emerged as a communication platform in the 1960s and delivered radio and television content in an 'asychronous' transcontinental 'footprint' mode which often only partially covered state territories. From the first 'live' broadcasts of 'world events' in the 1960s, satellite communication has become today a highly 'authentic' and de-territorialized political communication sphere and, with Internet and mobile phone platforms constitutes the macro-structure nexus of transnational discursive geographies.

These dense communicative formations no longer merely 'fracture' but dederritorialize public communication and through this process create layers of public discourse at the same time *within* and *beyond* national public formations. This is the change from previous forms of public culture to a public space through to post-territorial 'linking' often via trans-territorial 'interlocutors'. The dialectical relationship between these 'public trajectories' de- and reterritorialize public discourse and constitute an advanced – to use Habermas' term – 'post-national constellation' (Habermas, 2001a) of public communication. Whereas a decade ago, these de- and reterritorialized post-national public constellations emerged around 'universal' themes, for example, around environmental risk communication as well as human rights, today these de- and reterritorializing trajectories of public communication constitute transnational public spheres that are no longer tied to the normative epistemological sphere of a nation-state and arise not only in contexts of 'reflexive modernity' but 'reflective globalization';

these intensify notions of 'risks' and in a broader sense, densities of public 'world' consciousness. Not only the public sphere *within* national contexts has been transformed but the often overlooked traditional modern 'coordinates' are drawn into the open space of an unprecedented transnational discourse terrain. Occasionally, we see this emerging 'dialectic' of public sphere of de- and reterritorializing terrains surfacing in social-science debates, for example, as an 'endogenous' public formation where the political agenda is not only set but deeply challenged by transnational public discourses. This phenomenon is related both to the national ad hoc reciprocity of globalized forces, a process that Ulrich Beck calls 'risk communication' and to the constant discursive overlap where the transnational political, environmental, social and cultural public arena shapes national discourse (see Robert Cox, 2006, 2010). Other examples are deterritorialized 'mobile subjects', embedded in a sphere of 'multi-location' as 'place-polygamists' whose 'coming and going, being here both here and there across frontiers at the same time, has become a normal thing' (Beck, 2000: 75). Whereas Beck refers to these phenomena as the 'globalization of biographies', Bayart, more recently, describes these processes as a political economy of 'global subjectivation', which also includes the 'transnational and ethnicized subjectivity' (Bayart, 2007: 171) of migrant communities from Amsterdam to Sao Paolo. Other recent debates in the social sciences revolve around broader issues of deterritorialization suggest a conceptualization of both the 'territorial and "aterritorial" communication and spheres' (Gripsrud and Moe, 2010: 11).

In particular, debates in political theory have in recent years 'mapped' the shift towards a conception of transnational polities and governance structures *beyond* a conventional modern state-centric model. These conceptions in political science begin to frame this emerging post-territorialized space ithrough a number of different paradigmatic lenses: through the lens of civil society (Kaldor, 2003), through the lens of a post-international world or – to use a German term – 'Weltstaatlichkeit', as 'world statehood' which understands the national or the territorial state *itself* as a sphere of globalization (Stichweh, 2007: 27). Both traditional 'Westphalian' states and 'failed' state models are incorporated into such a model. Ferguson and Mansbach argue that, overall, 'state-centric theories and models . . . account for only a small part of what happens in the world, and, at worst, are deifices built on sand' as the 'interstate epoch is drawing to a close' (Ferguson and Mansbach, 2004: 4). The authors note that the boundaries 'that separate territorial states from one another' no longer 'demarcate political spaces based on economic, social, or cultural interests' as each of these 'has its own boundaries that in the face of localization and globalization are less and less compatible with the border of states'. They argue that the 'conception of political space as largely synonymous with territory poses a barrier to theory-building in global politics' (Ferguson and Mansbach, 2004: 74). Although the digital divide debate suggests that various world regions are on the passive end of technology access (which is often measured in 'Western' parameters of Internet access), in terms of public communication, it could be argued that activist groups or other 'multipliers' are engaged in these emerging public spheres.

Also, the often overlooked phenomena not only of diaspora and expatriate discourse that is the linking back to 'countries of origin' shows various models in which transnational communication 'resonates' as deliberation is achieved through these forms of post-territoriality. Post-territoriality could be considered as not only a new public geography but rather as the emerging of new dense and 'authentic' formations of public communication, establishing, arranging and organizing sometimes ad-hoc community-related collectives of shared interest without the obligation of a 'before' and 'after' continuation of communicative engagement. It is the relationship between global governance and public communication 'which stimulates a criss-cross of broader public deliberation in which policy choices (reported and discussed, e.g. within national media) are exposed to public scrutiny' (Nanz and Steffek, 2005: 192). Such a process not only opens up a space of transnational public 'accountability' but identifies the role of civil society as the 'transmission belt' between 'deliberative processes within international organizations and emerging transnational public spheres' (Nanz and Steffek, 2005: 199). These taxonomies are often particularly visible in public terrains of crisis situations; for example, the post-election crisis in Iran where transnational taxonomies delivered 'real time' information which created national 'resonance'.

It is quite interesting to note that debates in particular in political science and sociology have captured the contours of the power shift from the (nation-)state and international order towards post-territorial political terrains.[5] These debates reveal new formations of political territory which are no longer congruent with a nation-state. Political space is not a new concept but has already been discussed in the context of modernity where political space is a space where individuals and groups 'incessantly jar against each other – colliding, blocking, coalescing, separating' (Wolin cited by Ferguson/Mansbach, 2004: 74).[6] Beyond these formations, Scholte argues for a broadening of traditional international relations to include the interdependence of transnational spheres of social relations. He identifies a 'shift of conceptual focus from the parts to the whole in the study of social change'. It is in this context that forces of transformation emerge in such a 'totality', 'where the "world" encompasses local contexts, national settings, international circumstances and, with equal significance, the interpenetration and mutual constitution of those sphere within a systematic whole' (Scholte, 1993: 31). Scholte concludes that is 'is no small matter to make this move to a non-territorial, non-national conception of society.' (Scholte, 1993: 31). In this sense, the 'structural' imbalanced power of these transnational interdependencies in the sphere of transnational actors 'and cross-border activities, too, are structured in terms of gender, race, class, nationality or whatever other organizing principles might prevail in social relations' (Scholte, 1993: 87) involving unequal 'opportunities' (Scholte, 2000: 29). Such a globalized sphere, in Scholte's view, deepens 'arbitrary social relations'; however, in the role of undermining the national governance '. . . territorial mechanism like the state cannot . . . secure democratic governance of supraterritorial phenomena such as global communications' (Scholte, 2000: 32).

Beyond these fractured disciplinary debates, the transformation of social structures through connectivity has become one of the crucial characteristics of globalization. Castells (1996) was the first to outline the transformative imperatives of global 'flows' as a paradigmatic structural approach for the conceptualization of these new communicative forms, across modern and non-modern societies, not only in their implications for states but also for the 'self'. Following Castells, nuanced implications of trans-border networked communication for social macro-structural analysis have been addressed as a particular new phase of globalization in the paradigm of a 'network society' (Hassan, 2004; Benkler, 2006). These approaches reveal the complex implications of networked technology on structural societal 'taxonomies' – reaching not only across traditional late 'modern' but across various non-modern societies as well. Castells' notion of a network society in such an inclusive sociological theory relates not only – and this is often misunderstood – to technological phenomena, such as digital network access but distinguishes effects of this deepening 'resonance' of technological networks on societal macro-structures. It is this communicative 'resonance' sphere which is not only a simplistic technological 'space of flows' but in fact a sphere of 'network identity' (Castells, 1996) that conceptually opens up not only the 'digital space' but the overall communicative networked sphere in its imbalances and 'resonance' on traditional societal structures. In this sense, network communication is not only the 'fundamental spatial configuration' (Castells, 1996) but constitutes spatial 'places' formed of 'nodes' and 'hubs' – networks which constitute not just 'circuits' but spatially defined places of (communicative) 'territoriality'. This approach has shifted the sociological debate about globalization away from the interdependence of modern and global structures to an interdependence of networks and territory – opening up a new discourse terrain of globalized connectedness, along with 'hierarchical' sets of network-node relations. This process – as Sassen (2006) has shown, has severe implications for the understanding of 'territory'. Both, Castells and Sassen have transformed the debate about 'networks' and 'territory' from cultural spheres into the core of social theory. It is this macro-structural understanding of spatial 'flows' which helps to identify the arising space as a 'reflexive' interdependence *between* national (normative) and globalized discourse spheres which constitutes the deliberate sphere of public 'connectivity'.

These debates highlight important parameters of 'de-bracketing' processes of the (not only modern!) state–society nexus. However, what such a 'de-bracketing' process reveals is the 'opening' up of a space for public participation and deliberation. The relativistic embeddedness of public communication within such a transnational communication sphere shifts national public deliberation into a new discursive terrain and makes it impossible to relate to the ideal of a modern national public when attempting to 'map' these emerging structures. It is the post-territoriality enabled through this sphere of simultaneous public proximity that is a new layer of public 'connectivity'. Recent political crisis, for example in North Africa revealed this simultaneous public proximity through a discursive participation of trans-territorial publics, for example, through uploading of images and comments. As one Egyptian protester during the Arab Spring noted 'We use *Facebook* to organize ourselves, *Twitter* to coordinate and *YouTube* to let the world know.' Transnational communicative spheres are, on the one hand building transnational public networks, and have, on the other, severe implications for communication within states. Public communication is situated as an 'intersection' in the emerging gap between these two traditionally congruent principles of deliberative democracy.

These spheres include 'engaged' subjective reasoned discourse among networks of multiple 'interlocutors' in transnational contexts (Fraser, 2007) and also constitute in themselves forms of public agency. These emerging structures place the subject *within* 'intersections' of deliberation. In this sense, the distinction between a transnational and a 'national' public is obsolete. In the advanced process of globalization it is a merging of these two spheres that not only creates challenges for the key public institutions but also for public participation. The dialectic of disembedding/re-embedding constitutes new forms of deliberation in the spaces between the transnational and the state. This is the emerging space that also establishes new spheres of influence for institutions and organizations. These are the new localities or places within a transnational public that shape the taxonomies of public communication.

It is about the dense 'within' and not the 'stretched' 'across' that distinguishes the advanced sphere of globalized public communication between networks of centrality and the centrality of networks and distinguishes public communication from earlier, for example, mass media phases. These transnational public communicative territories have also severe implications for the definition of legitimacy. Legitimacy understood in this enlarged scope means that political space is understood as a contextual form of expressing loyalties among adherents to various polities that are distributed and related, where 'territorial space is only one of these possibilities' (Ferguson and Mansbach, 2004: 67). In times of advanced globalization no longer large scale, not so much the macro-structural globalizing spheres but rather the fine-grained spaces have globalized implications or, as Held notes: 'In a world of complex interpendencies, the actual prospects of people depend more on forces that are external (rather than internal) to the nation-state' (Held, 2010: 18).

The complex globalization debate in sociological and political science discourses emerging already in the early 1990s has never fully been adopted in the area of media and communication. Tomlinson's (1999) work on cultural globalization centres around transnational forms of 'mediated' proximity. I have discussed the emerging sphere of transnational political 'mediation' (Volkmer, 1996, 2003) and Rantanen (2005) has conceptualized 'mediated globalization' as a framework for the inclusion of new transnational communicative phenomena. Globalization has for a long time been critically perceived in a neoliberal framework that has led to quite specific debates about globalizations often based upon a comparative approach of methodological nationalism. Debates revolve around neoliberal imperialism (Sparks, 2007, Hafez, 2007), post-colonialism, 'hybridity' and more recently, of digital network cultures in contexts of journalism. What is striking is that media and communication theory never really incorporated interdisciplinary approaches and methodologies of globalization. However, such a transdisciplinary 'outlook' is necessary to capture 'fractured' forms of globalized communication. It seems, as it has recently been argued, that media and communication as a discipline has lost 'touch' with other disciplines (Ekecrantz, 2009; Rantanen, 2010; Hamelink, 2012).

The unfolding communicative interdependence of national (normative) and globalized discourses is visible in many of today's political crises and forms of transnational political activism. I argue that the de-bracketing of the state–society nexus emerges in three dimensions through the increasing 'resonance' space of post-territorial public communication which draws the main 'pillars' of modern society into crises.

Post-territoriality and the crisis of legitimacy

The public process of achieving legitimacy is traditionally understood as 'social action' towards and within a 'legitimate order' (Weber, 1968: 11). The assumed 'normative' consent as an outcome of public discourse relates to conceptions of legitimacy closely linked to 'kinship', articulated through national collective identity as an 'alignment' with the 'complementarity' of communication habits (Deutsch, 1953: 101). However, such an 'alignment' is continuously re-enforced through communication, maintaining ontologies of 'kinship' through information 'stored in living memories, associations, habits, and preferences of its members', and, as Deutsch points out 'these elements are . . . sufficiently complementary, they will add up to an integrated pattern or configuration of communicating, remembering, and acting, that is, to a culture' (Deutsch, 1953: 97). Although 'legitimacy' is a political terrain of sovereign states as a normative sphere of consensus, it is understood as a 'dual' practice: as an 'inward' looking sphere, meaning the 'credentials' of international society and 'outward' looking, meaning how members of international society 'conduct themselves' (Clark, 2005: 25).

This 'dual' practice model could also be used to identify the ways in which transnational communicative spheres relate to the deterritorialized re-formation of national legitimacy. The 'inward' and 'outward' looking sphere was quite distinctly mediated in the mass media age where national media were the main source of (foreign) information. Often Western media contributed to the 'inward' looking sphere, delivering – in Clark's model – the 'credentials of international society' but also to the 'outward' looking sphere which, again following Clark (2005), conveys the way in which 'members conduct themselves', for example, often involving the (Western) coverage of political and humanitarian conflicts of regional disaster zones where these zones did not have an international voice. Early forms of such an 'inward' looking sphere consisted of, depending on the preferred paradigmatic angle, 'propaganda', 'public diplomacy' or 'soft power' (Nye, 2004), that is, a 'linear' delivery of a 'legitimate order' via shortwave radio to international regions. For example, during the Cold War the propaganda campaigns of both the USA and Russia competed for influence on national public opinion particularly in developing nations, with ideological frames of legitimacy. These early forms delivered a 'counter legitimacy' *vis-à-vis* local governments of the targeted region which, it should be added, were not always authoritarian and also *vis-à-vis* other forms of political organization, such as on the community level from abroad.

These forms of transnational influence were followed in the mid 1980s by direct-to-home satellite channels which began to deliver particular angles on transnational political crises often *vis-à-vis* national mass media coverage. CNN's international channel created a different form of communicative legitimacy, through the delivery of 'live' and 'breaking news' images of international conflicts, such as the student protests in Beijing and of the Gulf War which influenced the perception of legitimate foreign policy among national publics. It is not surprising that the former Secretary General of the UN Boutros Ghali famously remarked that CNN is the sixteenth member of the UN Security Council. CNN International, as a US news outlet, often attempted to cover conflicts through local angles which, at times, challenged nationally 'bounded' legitimacy formations of, for example, foreign policy. Through advanced network communication this deterritorialized space has widened on the one hand, but, become more dense, on the other. Citizen journalism, through interactive communication via mobile phone cameras and threats, is only one form of individual engagement that not only creates 'public opinion' but rather directly engages in discourse across national territories. In this context, individuals take on roles as 'policy entrepreneurs' who set 'an issue on the transnational agenda, formulate policy solutions, or use windows of opportunity to promote their political projects in global governance systems' (Breitmeier, 2008: 48). Communicative legitimacy engages not only nation-states but reaches across other state formations. In these contexts, it has been argued that the growing 'de-hierarchization of the global legal order creates immense problems for democratic legitimacy' (Brunkhorst, 2007). The 'effectiveness' of democratic legitimacy functions in Germany but is is vague in 'nominalistic' constitutitional states, such as Argentina . . . symbolic constitutions.. or failed states (Brunkhorst, 2007: 77).

Post-territoriality and the crisis of sovereignty

In advanced globalization processes, the communicative 'spatiality' extends not only in a 'horizontal' sphere of communication 'flows', that is, 'extending' into transnational spatialities but, in addition, in a vertical (connected) sphere that intensifies public communication not only within macro-structural but subjective micro-structural networked densities. Public territories are no longer limited to the boundedness of state formations but rather overlap, interact, connect within diverse spheres of political spatialities, laying out new patterns of communicative 'symbolic power' (see Thompson, 1995: 17; Taylor, 1997: 20) in transnational contexts. The public sphere is no longer a national territorial space within the compounds of (national) sovereignty but rather is due to complex networked 'layerings', a communicative 'resonance' sphere spanning across multiple discourse territories.

Recent debates, however, highlight an additional emerging space of sovereignty besides the unilateral and multilateral polities of methodological territorialism (Agnew, 2009). Instead, Held and McGrew argue, the 'contemporary era has witnessed layers of governance spreading within and across political boundaries' (Held and McGrew, 2000, 2006: 11). Furthermore, the modern state is often seen as increasingly embedded in 'webs of regional and global interconnectness', permeated by quasi-supranational, intergovernmental and transnational forces, and 'unable to determine its own fate'. It is a process that creates new deterritorialized geographies of sovereignty or, as Castells notes, the 'network state' where 'agencies that previously flourished via territoriality and authority' are now in 'synergies' with other agencies elsewhere (Castells, 2010: 43). In addition, the (national) conception of information sovereignty is also being challenged by detachments of information sovereignty as a territorial policy and governance framework.

In such a post-territorial public terrain, loyalties are dispersed–constantly shifting and 'agency' is bundled in post-national forms of public subjectivity. Ferguson and Mansbach articulate such a process in political science and argue that there is no 'single substitute for the role of the Westphalian State' and no 'institution' is able to 'command authority' or even 'demand loyalties'. Instead, so the authors claim, 'different authorities must compete for these loyalties, and individuals will look for guidance and rewards from a variety of institutions depending upon issue and context' (Ferguson and Mansbach, 2004: 25).

This dynamic formation of 'floating' loyalties, detached from sovereign territorial 'bounded-ness', is described in even stronger terms by Strange who notes that these detached loyalties 'sometimes' relate to the state, sometimes with 'a firm', or 'a social movement operating across territorial frontiers', at other times with a 'family', we might add, a tribe, a 'generation', 'fellow-members of an occupation or profession'. Strange's main point is that we are faced with a 'new absence of absolutes' and that 'in a world of multiple, diffused authority' our 'individual consciences are our only guide' (Strange, 1996: 263-4). Others argue that, indeed, for decades, for example, modern societies have been incorporated into various transnational networks, sub-national governments, professional societies, political parties, transnational organizations who 'compete, conflict, cooperate, or otherwise interact with the sovereignty-bound actors of the state-centric world' (Cusimano, 2000: 27). Furthermore, these are processes of 'technological openings' that undermine 'sovereign authority, decentralized power and opened markets and societies' (Cusimano, 2000: 22).

The notion of 'floating' loyalties as one form of 'de-bracketing' sovereignty terrain occurs in parallel with processes of 'disaggregation' or 'fragmentation' of public accountability in the increasing sphere not only of intergovernmental collaboration and intergovernmental decision making. The lack of public accountability mechanisms in such a sphere is related both to intergovernmental organizations *vis-à-vis* states and to powerful intergovernmental 'interdependencies' that emerge in distinct ways across continents: in the Middle East where the Arab League is taking on a more active role since the regime change as an outcome of the 'Arab Spring', in Central Africa mainly in contexts of the UN and in Europe where the EU, WTO and the IMF take over core areas not only of sovereign governance but accountability measures not counteracted by national or larger European public spheres. Due to these forms of intergovernmental collaboration, what Slaughter has called 'disaggregated sovereignty' and a 'networked global order' (Slaughter, 2005: 37), it becomes easier for executive power to withdraw from democratic commitments.

Because of such a global 'interwovenness' it has become increasingly easy for executive governments to withdraw from democratic commitments and responsibilites. Such an 'emancipation' from democratic rights then 'increases the pace of transnational connections towards new centres of imperial and hegemonic power' (Brunkhorst, 2007: 74).[7]

However, such an interdependence between state power and a regional or international intergovernmental 'order' is taking on more and more sovereign governance terrains – without putting in place appropriate public accountability frameworks. It is this interplay that, in the long term, constitutes the crisis of sovereignty. This is the process currently taking place in the European Union, where in the context of the European sovereign debts crisis increasingly intergovernmental decision making begins to replace sovereign governance and creates a situation of a 'post-democratic' constellation (Habermas, 2011). Sovereignty is historically linked to the Westphalian model of sovereign rights over territory, including information sovereignty. However, sovereignty includes not only trans-border flows but – in modern societies – the sphere of public deliberation (as a fourth Estate) as well as public accountability.

In the European context, the crisis of sovereignty is not only caused by the increased influence on core sovereign terrains within European nations and, by the lack of a European wide public sphere of accountability, which constitutes a democratic deficit. Where national public spheres are eroding, governance is relocated to intergovernmental structures, a European public has not been established as a much-needed 'unified' space of a trans-sovereign public. As Koopmans and Erbe note: 'If one looks for a genuinely transnational European public sphere, there is not much to be found' (Koopmans and Erbe, 2004: 99) – despite the increasingly multi-cultural societies in European nation-states. However, the Europeanization of public spheres is often misperceived as the territorial space of a somewhat homogenous public, almost as a transfer of the constituencies of the national public into such a transnational sphere; for example, as a sphere where 'the same themes' discussed and 'the same frames of reference are available and in use in the various public spheres in Europe' (Risse, 2010: 119). Furthermore, national media are often considered as the main sites of European publics whereas transnational, mostly non-European satellite channels are rarely incorporated into European public contexts. The transnationalization of the European public is framed by the process of European policy formations through transnational-horizontal and nationally vertical 'mediated' legitimacy or journalistic spheres (see, for example, Koopmans, 2007; Heikkilae and Kunelius, 2006).[8]

Post-territoriality and the crisis of power

The crisis of power, or to be precise, the loss of state power, has been discussed in contexts of larger spheres of globalization; however, less in terms of public communication. Sassen's term the 'loss of control' underlines the particular way in which territorial exclusivity of states is 'reconfigured' in the process of (economic) globalization (Sassen, 1996). In her conception of contexts of economic globalized territory, 'central functions' are located 'disproportionally' in developed nation-states.

The shifting of state power in contexts of territorial public communication also reveals a concentration of corporate media organizations in developed countries. For example, a global media policy is needed in order to address multilaterally the shifting of media policy in contexts of neoliberal globalization. In such a sphere, communications policy is no longer 'made' at a clearly defined 'location' but is rather an 'informal mechanism', across a 'multiplicity of sites. "Specific policy issues, such as copyright, or rules governing property transactions migrate from one level to another, often typifying the flashpoint of conflicts between jurisdictions"' (Raboy, 2002: 7). Among these 'sites' are intergovernmental organizations, such UNESCO, International Telecommunications Union (ITU), the World Intellectual Property Organization (WIPO) and World Trade Organization (WTO). These organizations have taken on the regulation of harmonization of 'transborder' communication, for example, mobile communication, content regulation, and other services with implications for the policy frameworks of domestic media and communication. These intergovernmental organizations (and various others) multilaterally regulate particular spheres of a state's territorial information space.

States still aim to retain influence on the complexities of information inflows; for example, states protect their information space, enforced through what Price describes as 'defensiveness', 'protection of domestic producers', 'territorial integrity' and the 'strengthening of citizenship' (Price, 2002: 19) as the 'relationship between media and borders is always in transition' (Price, 2002: 19). States also interfere with communicative spheres of other states. Both of these strategies are tied into efforts to maintain sovereign power over information space. The way in which these efforts are conducted, however, differs among various state types. There are numerous examples of processes of state control over terrestrial information sovereignty that have emerged already in the radio age. Trans-border influence began with shortwave radio delivery where Russian and US shortwave radio for example targeted developing nations during the time of the Cold War. Trans-border flows of neighbouring terrestrial broadcasters are another model of early forms of deterritorializing processes, for example between neighbouring Western states and between state regimes. This terrestrial transborder space is carefully regulated in European nations, located in a tight multinational terrain where information sovereignty – despite other forms of regional collaboration – is considered to be a national imperative. These policy models of terrestrial trans-border spheres are rarely discussed in contexts of international media policy, although these forms emerged as early powerful international communication spheres not only in Europe but also between the USA and Mexico, and in Asia and South America. Media policy, for example in various European countries, aims to structure a national distinct public along the lines of these forms of terrestrial 'mediation' where national media, such as public service broadcasting and also commercial media are regulated within such a legally constructed normative national public space. The tremendous problems in the incorporation of new forms of transnational satellite television and transnational networked communication reflect the conceptual clash between a modern and a networked public. This is also an issue in the communication policy of the European Union, where satellite communication and mobile communication are regulated through national policy frameworks. These forms of extra-territorial 'extension' of sovereign information space have been followed by satellite communication since the early 1990s, which established a new phase of communication space spanning not only across vast geographical regions but also across geopolitical terrains and territorial state regulated spheres.

Satellite communication with digital platform capacities and direct-to-home technology has intensified this deterritorialized sphere of influence and this is often overlooked. It constitutes today, surprisingly, relatively unregulated communication territories overarching sovereign information spheres. Satellite 'footprints' are not congruent with state borders and cover, for example, only sections of a state and thus sometimes intentionally create unregulated information imbalances even *within* a state's territory. Lisa Parks argues that footprints should be considered as geopolitical communicative spaces alongside political alliance, trade relations or intercultural campaigns (Parks, 2009: 140). Satellite communication, however, is also a contested space. Even authoritarian states seem to lose influence in the shielding of information territory and attempts to jam incoming satellite signals seem to be a sign of such a 'loss of control'. For example, the BBC's Persian signal was jammed by Iranian state authorities during the coverage of the events in Cairo. Besides, the BBC World Service, *Voice of America*, *Deutsche Welle* and *Al Jazeera* are regularly jammed by various state authorities in order to censor incoming information. Another example is the jamming of the London-based satellite channel *Lualua TV* that delivers programmes to opposition members in Bahrain.

The disentangling of territorial and information sovereignty becomes more complicated as these two strategies are increasingly amalgamated with other attempts at state influence. Some states attempt to influence not only the media space of other states but, for example, expatriates within states and communicative spaces of 'de-bordered demoi on the transnational level' (Breitmeier, 2008: 17), opposition leaders, activists and so on. Since the emerging of new geopolitical conflicts in the aftermath of September 11, a number of state-owned satellite channels was established in order to deliver particular frames of world conflicts to a somewhat globalized audience. In addition, the 'loss of control' is related to what might be called transnational formations of 'subnational' communicative spheres. *MED-TV*, a Kurdish satellite, is an example, as this channel aimed to provide a political platform for the Kurdish population living in Turkey but also in Europe and the Middle East and creates what Sakr has famously described as 'Kurdistan in the sky'. The channel was accused of being the 'mouthpiece' of the radical Kurdistan Workers' Party (PKK). In consequence the broadcast licence was revoked in 1999 by the UK (where the satellite channel was formed); the channel, now named *MEDYA* moved to Belgium and linked with the programme in France where the licence was also revoked in 2004. The channel has been renamed as *Roj TV* and links up with a television programme from Denmark. Turkey has made attempts to influence European states to revoke the licence, a process that could be described as 'the extraterritoriality of state sovereignty': 'Ankara unleashed its coercive forces to prevent the reception of the airwaves within Turkey, whereas in Europe, it used diplomatic power, espionage, jamming, and various forms of intimidation to stop the emission of television signals. Since MED-TV was licensed in Britain and its studios were located in Brussels, Berlin and Stockholm, a number of European Union countries and even the United States has been drawn into Turkey's satellite war. Ankara has also tried to mobilize satellite service providers, both private and state-owned, against the channel' (Hassanpour, 1998: 53). The *MED-TV* case is only one example indicating the 'loss of state control' of communicative territory that emerges in quite different ways across North Africa, in Asia, in North America, in the Pacific and in Europe. These processes contribute to the debracketing of the state–society nexus where sovereign information spheres 'collide' in deterritorialized spaces.

The Internet further deepens these processes of state control and takes on new complex forms of shielding the domestic information space. In regions with tight government insulation, such as China, Singapore and Malaysia, the control over networked information space becomes porous. Attempts are, for example, exercised by the Chinese government, to replace US-based sites that constitute a transnational network centrality in many parts of the world with Chinese sites. These have become relatively tightly controlled but popular domestic platforms; *Baidu* is the name of the Chinese duplication of *Google*, *Weibo* the duplication of *Twitter* and *Renren* is the name of the duplication of *Facebook*. However, despite these attempts to force *Google* to self-censor sites, access to servers located abroad still allow the retrieval of communication beyond these controlled environments. The re-routing of communication across transnational servers permits access to otherwise restricted information. This was the case throughout the protests in Cairo, which allowed protesters continuous communication via *Twitter*, although the national Internet was closed down and server space was made available in California for voice messages to be converted into *Twitter*. These intersections between traditional conceptions of information sovereignty and formations of networked spheres between the national and the 'transnational' are the interesting processes where the public 'site' of political engagement becomes not only 'the local' in an advanced transnational public sphere, but integration into other forms of public sites creates not only national or transnational but often subjective 'public networks'.

It would be misleading, however, to reflect only on the transformation of publics. In fact, nations and state formations are transformed by globalization. However, the transformation of the national public to a globalized public where the nation is a space in global public communication will be the key challenge in the next decade. It is a complex new territory where conventional terminologies and conceptual frameworks require new conceptual approaches as the static construction of nations and states does not allow us to capture these new forms of transnational civic deliberations. Citizenship has become a mediated practice where conceptions of national belonging and civic practice are constantly reflected. In this sense, we could argue that Beck's notion of self-reflexivity could be refined as reflexive citizenship *vis-à-vis* such an emerging transnational public discourse.

These spheres of globalized reflexivity are articulated through an emerging dialectical space between modern and globalized forms and, in a sense, between national territory and the deterritorialized fractures of globalization. These distinct forms of 'relativity' identify varying spheres of dialectical 'reciprocity' which, through this debate, began to loosen up the 'boundedness' of social theory of what Scholte has labelled 'methodological territorialism' (Scholte, 2000: 56). Scholte argues that the 'territorialist method means formulating concepts and questions . . . and drawing conclusions all in a territorial spatial framework' (Scholte, 2000: 56), which emerged with modern social theory and mainly included the modern geography of national territories. The communicative role of globalization has not been a core theme in globalization studies, nor in communication studies themselves, and global governance formations operate to some extent without conceptions of public accountability. Transnational public formations are still a grey area. In particular the inclusion of non-modern forms of globalized deliberation is difficult to theorize. The lack of conceptions of public deliberation in a globalized context constitutes a 'risk' in itself.

2

Post-Territoriality in Spheres of 'Public Assemblages'

As discussed in the previous chapter, it seems no longer possible to understand the public sphere solely in the normative framework of deliberative civic communication, which emerged in the traditions in the European model of modern nation-building. A model of public space has been suggested that situates the dialectic of public space between networks of centrality and the centrality of networks. Keeping this model in mind, the previous chapter has assessed some of the openings in the boundedness of 'the state', through the lens of globalized structures as articulated in sociology and political science. In this chapter I will take these openings further; I will discuss not so much 'digital' and 'web-based' public connectivity but rather the ways that these are embedded in larger structures of 'public assemblages' as a sphere of public space between networks of centrality and the centrality of networks, overarching societies. I will develop this term through a comparison of the historical evolution of trans-border communication in different world regions since the time of the printing press in order to relate today's phenomena to historiographies of local public cultures becoming trans-border.

Layers of what we might call transnational public 'densities', dense discursive structures, not only crisscross but overarch the 'bounded' national model of deliberation. Densities are highly specific discursive networks of public space, from 'activism' to thematically focused communicative 'layers', delivered via satellite channels and/or across social media sites within subjectively chosen peer-to-peer networks based around human rights, climate change and political crises. Since the 'Occupy Wall Street' movement, specific digitally delivered forms of political organization, 'digital activism', enhanced through social media mobilization, which have exercised a specific form of re-appropriation of public space, for example of urban space in the centre of global cities (see Bennett and Segerberg, 2013; Castells, 2012). Despite these forms of digital activism, which are driven by digitally enabled forms of power such as acceleration of content and the initiation of viral 'ripple' processes across social media spaces, numerous other examples could be used to identify new structures of 'densities' which, through connectivity to national actors and their overarching presence 'across' societies, establish a space of deliberation through specific forms of re-appropriation. One example is crisis mapping, and globally dispersed crisis mappers who, situated anywhere in the world, provide sites for local activism. We have seen crisis mapping in the aftermath of Fukushima, where citizens in Japan take on the role of finding 'proof' of radioactive contamination and provide it via sites in English to a world community, challenging the official governmental information strategy. From digital activism to crisis mapping and conflict coverage, these diverse layers of networked actors and, in this sense, deterritorialized discourse, are specifically linked and have 'vertical' implications for public discourse. Such a specific 'verticalization', the 'anchoring' of networked public space, has implications for governance legitimacy transnationally 'ventilated' from Nairobi to Tonga, from Cairo to Berlin, from Moscow to Sao Paulo. However, 'networked publics' are often perceived as an entirely 'spatial' sphere, for example, in a techno-centric perspective through 'the growing availability of digital media production tools and infrastructures' providing 'traffic in media across social connections and networks' (Avle, 2011: 16). Other conceptions of 'networked publics' are mainly outlined in public communication as a digital space in relation to particular digital spheres, such as *Facebook* (Valtysson, 2012) and, more recently in the context of the role of *Twitter* in political conflicts, as a sphere of (conflict) 'appropriation' of public space (Gerbaudo, 2012). Beyond these more content-oriented approaches; Castells' term 'mass self-communication' serves as an approach to capture the structure of a geographical 'geometry' of relationships between globalized actors (Castells, 2010: 36). He argues that the transformation of nation-states in contexts of networked 'mass self-communication' deconstructs the nation-state towards network spheres. Although the term 'mass self-communication' bears an ambiguity, as the prefix 'mass' could be associated with the outdated paradigm of 'mass' media, Castells uses this term to identify a communicative model that addresses the transformation of the traditional institutional political systems through the increasing power of 'local civil society', and NGOs embedded in networks of a global civil society. His model also directs us to a new institutional political system related to social movements via 'networks of action' and what Castells calls the 'movement of opinion', using 'ad hoc mobilization' by means of 'horizontal, autonomous network communication' (Castells, 2010: 41). Castells has captured the macro-structures of these transformations, which emerge through a new space between the 'self' and communicative flows.

Appropriation, verticalization – and spheres of public resonance

The sphere of public 'densities' is based on these larger spheres of con-nectivity, but at the same time incorporates dynamic contraction through 'intersecting' points, the verticalization of these globalized horizontal networked formations as local 'resonance'. This is a reso-nance terrain which Ulrich Beck, in his work on reflexive modernity, and more particularly on cosmopolitan sociology, describes in broader contexts as an example of what we might call here vertical 'anchor' points or 'nodes' of transnational public communication. For example, Beck relates the debate about 'human rights regimes', a specific tran-snational polity sphere, to 'on the ground' implications for states, as these polity regimes become 'so-called domestic affairs' of a state and, through this 'domestication', even 'everybody's affair' (Beck, 2007: 65). Another example of such a globalized polity 'domestication' is, again in Beck's view, the way states engage in state terrorism against their own citizens, a process which could 'trigger' even 'intervention and . . . preventative action' based on a transnational justification of 'world citizenship rights' (Beck, 2007: 66).

While from a sociological viewpoint such a transnational polity sphere might constitute a universal rights regime, in the context of public communication, Beck's examples help to assess the layer of public discourse that is not only a horizontal sphere among civil society advocates or activists but, according to Beck, a cosmopolitan sphere. In the context of public communication, these examples point towards an emerging moral sphere of public justification that is not only deeply embedded in values of a global civil society, but deeply embedded vertically in local public communication. The linking with transnational polity spheres contributes to the debracketing, the opening up, of the state–society nexus through the localization of these public justifications. In this sense the networked public links up to the vertical 'anchor nodes' of diverse society types, where transnational horizontal spheres of justification are amalgamated with local vertical polity spheres.

Despite the assumption that most world regions are incorporated into a 'network society', the conceptualization of public communication through local public resonance allows us to address shifting scalar differences in the extent of 'local' engagement with transnational public communication across world regions. These differences are often defined in technological terms; however, a broader understanding of networks incorporating all forms of communicative platforms, such as television, newspapers, mobile phones, social media etc. allows us to acknowledge what might be called cultural network asymmetries in communication networks across localities. Whereas in some world regions networks consist of complex forms of multiple platforms, IPTV, satellite television, mobile phone applications, enabling engagement in the cross-platform complexities of public discourse, in other regions the Internet, accessed not through landline connections but in Internet cafés or schools, constitutes the main link for political communication (for example for a political elite and/or activists). This link is also being drawn into local public space, as could be observed in the time of the Arab Spring.

In other localities, for example in many African countries, national public media forms are 'networks of centrality' in public communication and digital platforms, for example through mobile connections serving mainly as social and, if necessary, conflict platforms. Despite the parallel existence of public and private media in so-called 'developing' regions, a recent survey of sixteen post-authoritarian countries in Africa has shown that public media are in most countries the networks of trust, and what we might understand as 'networks of centrality' for political information (Moehler and Singh, 2011); however, other media forms serve as platforms for engagement. The authors argue that 'because the government's position is so strong, the private media cannot function effectively as a counterweight to the power of the ruling party unless they are trusted more than official sources' (Moehler and Singh, 2011: 277).

However, the trust in those media closely connected to governments characterizes a 'transitional' public culture that has been transferred from an authoritarian to a post-authoritarian regime. There is also a transformation of public cultures from the history of north, south, west and east African regions where transnational communication has been associated with complex and diverse forms of imperial and, later, post-colonial public structures. It is interesting that in the context of the 'microcosm' of urban public cultures in some African countries, such as Kenya, societal development is strongly associated with the educated youth generation and emerging middle classes who enjoy digital connectivity (Graetz, 2011: 286). However, digital platforms are perceived as opportunities for active communicative integration into a 'global world' (Graetz, 2011: 287). These connections of public space have, as Avle (2011) points out, implications for what we might call local network 'ecologies'. These local network ecologies are another example of what we have described earlier as 'vertical anchor nodes'. Local websites hosted in Ghana are increasingly interwoven with transnational spheres as a space for active engagement of expatriates and national citizens. In other world regions, such as southeast Asia, governments often tightly control the public sphere of the state; however, digital public spaces are less monitored and serve as sites for 'alternative' public communication. In other parts of Asia, like China, as Li argues, the transition of the Chinese online public space 'is characteristic of highly organized centralization and a vibrant proliferation of popular discourses and folk narratives, as well as narrowing space for rational deliberation' (Li, 2010: 74). These diverse examples of networked space reveal scalar transnational public formations across horizontal and vertical public networks; as I have argued earlier, these require an inclusive approach in order to identify the 'links' between the transnational and the local, and to conceptualize a relativistic approach of networked public space.

For this reason, an understanding of these multiple scalar layerings of different networked public cultures might help to overcome oft-drawn distinctions between so-called 'mass' and individual media, between national television and 'digital' media, and conceptualize the merging densities of public networks across different societies. Such an approach allows us to assess particular notions of 'world horizons' not so much by simply overcoming the 'container model' of modern social theory (Beck, 2000) but rather by suggesting an ontology of public network texture as a 'resonance' sphere in the densities of advanced globalization. This approach captures the sphere of 'relativistic' connectivity in transnational contexts as transnational layers interwoven into national public spheres but also of networked interdependence of deliberation across societies in such a post-territorial communicative space.

Deterrorialization and debracketing: Opening up the 'resonance' spatiality

It is quite difficult to overcome the limitations of the well-established normative nation-state paradigm when addressing these emerging communicative layerings. Whereas in many media and communication debates, the nation-state seems to prevail as a core unit of analysis and comparison, a phenomenon which I have described as a 'methodological paradox' (Volkmer, 2012), in sociological debates the dimensions of the transformation of the nation-state have been in focus for some time. It is useful for our discussion here to address some of these arguments regarding the transformative 'parameters' of the nation-state in contexts of supra-national new structures of interdependence. As early as the 1990s, Scholte suggested an interdisciplinary approach for the understanding of historiographies of social transformation across what he calls globalized 'connections'. Scholte reminds us that Durkheim and Mauss (Durkheim and Mauss, 1913) at the beginning of the twentieth century already understood international social relations as an 'interdependent system' (Scholte, 1993: 21),[1] which laid the groundwork for the focus on 'international relations' in sociological debates. Approaches of 'world-system' analysis (Wallerstein, 1974) even suggest conceptualizing the situated-ness of the nation-state, still the core unit of analysis, in larger spheres of transnational capitalism, knowledge economies and culture. Wallerstein's conception of 'world system analysis' does not so much undermine the nation-state but help to identify supra-national 'relativistic' relations, with serious implications for (modern) centre-periphery paradigms (Wallerstein, 1974).

In addition, the relativistic globalization debate emerging in the 1990s began to identify the neoliberal construction of globalization and the diversity of globalized forms – that is, processes of 'differentiation', 'relativity' and 'interdependence' – as particular side effects of globalization, influencing polities, governance and accountability (see Held and McGrew, 2003). These processes have implications for the nation-state. More specifically, it is the globalized 'horizontal' relation through a 'relativistic' approach that understands globalization as a 'disembedding' process (Giddens, 1990). Globalized, horizontal spheres are also perceived in relativistic globalization debates as what Robertson describes, for example, as the 'universalism of particularism' and the 'particularism of universalism'. Such a conception of interdependence suggests distinct spheres of the 'global' and

the 'local', and identifies the dialectic sphere as 'glocal', a key characteristic of differentiations (Robertson, 1992: 100) within a 'global
age' (Albrow, 1996). Other spheres of globalized interdependence
are addressed, for example in Appadurai's well-known distinction
between globalized symbolic terrains of 'techno-' and 'mediascapes',
representing terrains of transnationalization; less so as a trans-border
'extension' than through scales of an 'overlapping, disjunctive order'
(Appadurai, 1996: 32). These cultural, economic and political transformations of interdependencies overcame the boundedness of globalization theory in the paradigm of (the first) modernity. Tomlinson,
for example, argues that globalization equals deterritorialization and
that globalization in its 'rawest description', relates to the 'proliferation of complex connectedness across distance . . . deterritorialization
refers to the reach of this connectivity into the localities in which
everyday life is concluded and experienced' (Tomlinson, 2006: 152).
These are overlapping disjunctures that capture post-modern forms
of 'centre-periphery' relations as flows in a globalized context, mainly
identifying 'horizontal' spheres of globalized 'polarization' *beyond* the
nation-state level. Going further, Beck argues that the density of the
sphere of global risks 'forces us to confront the apparently excluded
other'. Global risks, so he argues, 'tear down national barriers and
mix natives with foreigners' (Beck, 2009: 15). In consequence, Beck
argues that these processes relate to 'reflexivity of uncertainty', for
example the 'cosmopolitan moment' (Beck, 2009: 47) and 'subpolitics',
which he understands as being a core component of a 'global public
sphere' (Beck, 2009: 81).

These diverse paradigms identify very particular openings in the
state–society nexus and an increasing porosity in the boundedness of
states in *advanced* globalization; however, these 'openings' no longer
relate mainly to forms of horizontal interdependence and local connectivity, but – and this seems to emerge in contexts of public communication – to reflexive formations in contexts of horizontal 'risks'
and to reflectively connected resonance. Vertical resonance spheres
emerge, and I consider these to be characteristic of the increasing (also
subjectively experienced) communicative densities of *advanced* globalization, in *tight* 'overlaps', in connected fine lines of 'layered' spheres
of public communication. In this sense such a vertical resonance sphere
relates not so much to transnational communication *across* localities
but to vertically *interweaving* network 'contractions'. It is through *this*
dialectic of disembedding/re-embedding that subnational, national,
and transnational public communication can be understood as a reflectively interdependent process. Through this process not only the

nation, the state, the locality, but the 'lifeworld' becomes a site of globalized public communication. Such a process where subjective communication spaces are incorporated into and amalgamated by dense globalized civil society spheres, breaches the state–society nexus. This shift of public communication between subjective forms and a globalized civil society influences new logics of deliberation and legitimacy. Public communication is no longer embedded within the private/public nexus of nation-states but is, rather, a layered reflective space, emerging *within* transnational intersections. In such a conception of public resonance space, the transnational and the national are no longer separate side-by-side terrains but incorporated into a vertical public spatiality.[2]

Such a public resonance sphere as a debracketing mechanism of the state–society nexus is further manifested by processes of the deterritorialization of political space. These processes were addressed some time ago in the context of international relations in political science. Some debates suggest to more vigorously articulate international relations in the paradigm of post-international politics (Rosenau, 1989). Rosenau justifies such an approach by arguing that 'the world is not so much a system dominated by states and national governments as a congeries of spheres of authority . . . that are subject to considerable flux and not necessarily coterminous with the division of territorial space' and further suggests that no longer will nations, but 'spheres of authority' constitute 'the analytic units' of such a 'new ontology' (Rosenau, 1989). It is remarkable that Rosenau and other scholars of international relations had already assessed these significant paradigm shifts by the end of the 1980s; however, they are rarely incorporated into discussions about public deliberation. Furthermore, Ferguson and Mansbach, from the viewpoint of political science, argue that political space is deterritorialized in the sense that boundaries which 'separate territorial states from another increasingly *do not* demarcate political spaces based on economic, social, or cultural interests.' The authors also claim that 'each of these has its own boundaries that in the face of localization and globalization are less and less compatible with the borders of states.' Ferguson and Mansbach conclude, 'thus the conception of political space as largely synonymous with territory poses a barrier to theory-building in global politics today' (Ferguson and Mansbach, 2004: 74).

Through the lens of such a framework, deterritorialized forms emerge where political space no longer 'coincides with territorial space as defined by an interstate system' (Ferguson and Mansbach, 2004: 74).

Political space is already 'disembedded from the normative' and it is through this process that these spatialities not only deterritorialize but also debracket the ontological configuration of the state–society nexus. These are processes which, in consequence, relate to new forms of civic subjectivity. As Ferguson and Mansbach note:

> Citizenship and nationality hardly begin to define who we are and where our loyalties lie, and those allegiances may lie far down our identity/loyalty hierarchy. The question of who is inside and who is outside the boundaries of civic and moral obligation is regaining an importance for political theory and global politics not seen since the birth of the Westphalian State. (Ferguson and Mansbach, 2004: 23)

These are important conceptions of political spatialities as deterritorialized densities which overarch but are not congruent with, territorial boundedness. The core of Ferguson and Mansbach's work is significant for a mapping of the broad parameters of political space, while the core subject of mine is the 'disembedded' density of public space. This is not about digital space as such but the coming into being of new communicative links. This occurs between transnational densities through reflective resonance spatialities, and describes public space in contexts of advanced globalized interdependence; it allows a reconfiguration of cosmopolitan world society and points towards the parameters of global governance in the context of (transnational) accountability in local forms of transnational public space.

Spheres of public 'assemblages'

The term 'assemblage' – with connotations to the term 'assembly', representing a traditional form of deliberation – is useful for the description of multilayered, multidirectional densities of public space. Assemblage as a dynamic spatial configuration captures these public spaces in new forms of non-bounded demarcation. Deleuze and Guatarri (1987) understand assemblage as a 'continuous self-vibrating plateau', and Ong argues that assemblages constitute 'knowledge ecologies' where 'technology and politics not only create their own spaces, but also give diverse values to the practices and actors thus connected to each other' (Ong, 2005: 338). Although both of these conceptions deconstruct the specifics of these supra-national dimensions, it is Sassen's term use of the term 'assemblage' which helps to fully understand the dynamic, active, continuous production site of transterritorial public layers across network centralities. In this sense, Sassen's discussion of 'assemblage' might serve as a framework here to further explore the 'layering' processes of public interdependence. It should be noted that Sassen uses the concept of 'assemblage' as an analytical tool to construct nations as sites of globalization.

I suggest a slightly different approach, however; that we understand the debracketing process of the state–society nexus in terms not only of the (modern) nation-state, but across diverse state formations; for example, the authoritarian as well as the so-called failed states. As discussed earlier, such an inclusive model is often abandoned in a normative focus on Western traditions of nation-states which excludes diverse cultural- and societal-specific conceptions of public communication. In this sense, Sassen's term 'assemblage' and in the context of this work, 'public' assemblage, allows us to map the reach *across* the 'supranational' or the reach *within*, the 'subnational', and relates to formations we have discussed earlier: the densely layered forms of public spatialitiy that are vertical 'nodes'. In this sense, the term 'public assemblage' captures a holistic formation of public space which appears as a fractured 'micro' public on the national level while gaining deliberative momentum as a 'macro' public in a supranational space. Sassen's conception of 'assemblage' – which she unfolds across spheres of authority, territory and rights (Sassen, 2006) – is a very helpful model for the analysis of the dialectic of public densities within new forms of public space. I will briefly outline Sassen's line of argumentation before taking this further into the communicative structure of public terrains.

Sassen understands assemblage as a combination of two spheres that are formations of 'transboundary' centrality: 'spatialities' and 'temporalities'. These are produced in various networks and domains. However, the crucial mechanism of these spatialities is that they do not simply stand outside the national. Sassen uses the term 'assemblage' to describe globalization processes, which 'take place deep inside territories and institutional domains that have largely been constructed in national terms in much of the world' and notes, 'what makes these processes part of globalization even though they are localized in national, indeed subnational, settings is that they are oriented towards global agendas and systems' (Sassen, 2006: 3). Assemblages are partly 'inserted' into, 'or arise from, the national and hence evince complex imbrications with the latter' (Sassen, 2006: 378). In this sense, Sassen's concept helps to shift away from older 'hierarchies' and other modern conceptions of the nation-state within a globalized order of inside/outside, domestic/foreign, real/virtual, and in my context, majority/minority publics and other 'ordering' relicts of modern social theory centralized around the nation-state. This conception of assemblage identifies not only new shifting orders across networks but rather new dynamic centralities of public space, which in times of advanced globalization have reciprocal implications not only for the nation-state but for various forms of state formations.

Sassen captures this reciprocal sphere of assemblage formations as a 'highly disruptive insertion into the national as container of social life' and continues, 'neither the national nor the global represents a fully stabilized meaning today' (Sassen, 2006: 378). Assemblages constitute 'analytical borderlands' as an 'inbetween type' of 'spatio-temporal order' (Sassen, 2006: 379). She argues for a 'thickening of the global' (Sassen, 2006: 382), which unfolds in numerous spheres which she understands as an 'analytical borderland' – 'geographies' across territories (Sassen, 2006: 386), where the horizontal and vertical intersect in particular ways. For example, 'localized struggles by actors who are not globally mobile are nonetheless critical for the organizational infrastructure of a globally networked politics; it is precisely the combination of localized practices and global networks that makes possible a new type of power for actors who would be seen as powerless in terms of conventional variables' (Sassen, 2006: 383). For this reason, she argues, it is important to understand the 'specific interactions – analytic borderlands – where actors or entities from two putatively different spatio-temporal orders intersect precisely on the question of velocity.' (Sassen, 2006: 385).

However, assemblages are hybrid spatialities as they not only debut reterritorialize; or, in Sassen's words, 'unbundle' the 'traditional territoriality of the national', in 'partial, often highly specialized ways' (Sassen, 2006: 389). Sassen argues that assemblages are not exclusively national or global but are 'elements of each' and they 'bring together what are often different spatio-temporal orders, that is, different velocities and different scopes'. In particular, Sassen's understanding of assemblage in its role of unbundling the 'traditional territoriality of the national' (Sassen, 2006: 389) is important for the discussion of public spatiality. It is the hybridity of assemblage and this unbundling feature of assemblage that makes this term so relevant to the debate and allows one to configure a public spatiality between space and national spheres.

Furthermore, Sassen's term 'assemblage' allows us to capture fully the vertical resonance spatiality of public space. Assemblages, Sassen argues, are related to the national as a 'more complex site for the global', and 'the specific and deep histories of a country become more, rather than less, significant and hence produce distinctive negotiations with the new endogenous and external global forces' (Sassen, 2006: 229/30). It is the relationship between 'territory' and the state that is shifting: 'critical components of authority deployed in the making of the territorial state are shifting towards becoming strong capabilities for detaching that authority from its exclusive territory and onto multiple bordering systems. Insofar as many of these systems are operating inside the nation-state, they may be obscuring the fact that a significant shift has happened. It may take a while to become legible in its aggregate impact.'

Sassen further claims: 'At its most extreme this may entail a shift of capabilities historically associated with the nation-state onto global digital assemblages; given their extreme form, such assemblages may make the switch more visible than other types of transformations that might be foundational' (Sassen, 2006: 419/20).

I would even go further and argue that the epistemic architecture of these spatialities and temporalities is defined by differentiation *through* 'connectivity'. In this sense it is not so much the fact that global networks 'connect and disconnect all the time', rather that connectivity opens up technological macro-structures and – in an advanced stage of network *Realpolitik* – constitutes an epistemic sphere. I use the term 'assemblage' as a working term here for identifying interdependent scalar spheres of public assemblage as increasing 'thickening' layers of network communication. The term public assemblage allows the highlighting of this layering as spatial 'territory', which is invisible in linear, sometimes one-dimensional, terminologies of international, transnational or global communication. Sassen defines globalization as the simultaneous frame of 'spatiality' and 'temporality'; however, I understand globalization in relation to public communication, or 'public density', as a deliberative space that incorporates both of these forms in the context of public assemblages. Using this approach allows one to identify diverse forms of transnational density as public spatialities; the space of 'simultaneous temporality', the space of 'micro-spheres' and the space of 'mediator'.

Public assemblages as spaces of simultaneous temporality

We could argue that 'simultaneous temporality' as a public density emerged as a deliberative space with early forms of 'live' satellite television. CNN international's live coverage of international political and other events, which were either rebroadcast 'live' by national broadcasters or received by transnational audiences directly through rooftop satellite dishes, created an early form of public space of simultaneous temporality. Such a simultaneous temporality, between the transnational and the national sphere, became a powerful form of public agenda setting in the early days of satellite news channels. CNN's dominance of 'live' coverage of the first moments of the Gulf War in January 1991 was an 'historic first' (MacGregor, 1992: 26) but its subsequent live reporting through satellite links established a new form of transnational instant war journalism. The public density of 'simultaneous temporality' was the basis for what has been labelled 'media diplomacy' in the context of humanitarian crisis communication, such as in the coverage of the civil war in Somalia in 1991, or the NATO initiative in Kosovo in 1998, where live images led to foreign policy shifts in the USA. Despite the implications of such a coverage for contesting news frames (Wolfsfeld, 1997) and national agenda-setting processes (Livingston and Eachus, 1995), the simultaneous temporality of transnational satellite delivery created an early form of transnational media-state relationship where live coverage (often with a US perspective) has influenced the public agenda in other countries as well. Such processes even sidelined diplomatic and other forms of political negotiation. Other public formations through simultaneous temporality are contexts of 'pity' in processes of mediating morality through television images. These forms of mediated moral engagement have been described as 'distant suffering', as a space of 'pity', in terms like 'denunciation', 'empathy' or 'aesthetization' of suffering (Boltanski, 1993, 1999; Ibrahim, 2010), related to 'action-at-a-distance' and forms of cosmopolitan publics (Chouliaraki, 2006).

Whereas in earlier decades of satellite live coverage, temporal density was closely linked to territorial spaces – terrestrial broadcasting delivered political information in its own temporality, for example – temporal density of public communication is increasingly interrelated not only in contexts of large-scale conflicts or humanitarian crises but also in national conflict situations. As Maekinen and Kuira's (2008) study of the Kenyan post-election crisis and similar studies of the crisis in Iraq reveal, these crises, delivered via Internet sites, have engaged national citizens and in particular expatriates in transnational, simultaneously engaged 'community publics', interacting in the same temporal space as those actually engaged in the protests in Kenya and Iraq, and expatriates abroad. In the Kenyan crisis, particularly, the simultaneous temporality in a transnational context was also created through production of interactive tools, by blending two Internet applications to deliver up-to-date information. A combination of *Google Maps* that allows users to 'zoom in' and 'a tool for users, via mobile phone or Internet browser, to report incidents of violence on the map, add photos, video and written content that document when and where violence occurs' (Goldstein and Rotich, 2008: 6). Simultaneous temporality as public density in *advanced* networked contexts shapes 'live' proximity among transnational and national audiences in public demands for political foreign-policy initiatives, and is a simultaneous deterritorialized form of collective networked action. It is in these contexts that a temporally condensed simultaneous form of public communication emerges where publics are not only connected in technological terms but are discursively and instantaneously connected. The world climate conference in Copenhagen in 2009 and the protests around the world economic forum in Davos in 2010 have revealed new forms of temporal density where platforms are used for creating a transnational debate. This allowed simultaneous temporality of protests, organized by activist networks.

With micro-blogging sites the texture of temporal density increases, particularly in crisis situations, as a new form of simultaneous public space which, although related to a geographical place, emerges in a deterritorialized space. The live delivery, and simultaneous communication via linear and networked forms, characterize this emerging sphere of transnational public communication, where casual posting on micro-blogs sets the agenda for transnational broadcasters and the narrative frame for the audience. Micro-blogging postings about post-election demonstrations in Tehran are simultaneously accessed wherever *Twitter* access is possible. The simultaneously delivered minute-by-minute subjective assessments of conflicts were available in Tehran, Europe, the USA and Australia. The *Facebook* site, *Tahir Square – Today we are all Egyptians*, was used to deliver immediate information which, when combined with a Blackberry and iPhone app in Cairo and a transnational public, led to a continuous coverage in international mainstream media. For example a *Twitter* posting '1 hour ago' provides authentic accounts of protests in Syria: 'Tank, navy attack on Syria's Latakia kills 26', and someone else posts the request to 'Please help spread the hashtag "Syria bleeds" in support of Syria today.' Postings which organize protests in Iran simultaneously within a transnational community deterritorializes public engagement and creates a close temporal density. The 'retweet' mechanism allows further ventilation of these postings within the transnational space and even accelerates the perception of simultaneous temporality. Another example is the type of simultaneous temporality in relation to the transnational 'Occupy Wall Street' protests and 'Acta' activism. Temporal density creates a transnational 'centrality' of public space, where transnational protests relate to organized campaigns and national activism. The simultaneous temporality of these protests in more than 900 cities in 80 countries across Latin America, Africa, Europe, Australia, New Zealand and the USA creates a new form of temporal, dense public space, enabled through networked communication and a new form of transnational public deliberation: a public space which is, in itself, covered by national news media.

These forms of simultaneous temporality seem to represent a public acceleration of what Virilio describes as the 'real instant'. Virilio has quite early on argued that globalization is no longer 'the global' versus 'the local' or 'transnational' versus 'the national' but rather the 'sudden temporal switch', the 'real instant' that characterizes 'dromoscopic proximity' (Virilio, 1997) within a globalized territory. It is the 'dromoscopic proximity' of fractured publics, which to some extent has always existed but has remained mainly invisible. It seems that public life is characterized by new forms of density, of simultaneous temporality, 'magnifying' public attention in a transnational context. Advanced global communication magnifies what Beck describes as 'cosmopolitan moments' (Beck, 2007). The magnified moments constitute public density through their transnational nature and through 'connectivity', 'relational' discourse spheres and their temporality; that is, their temporal density (Virilio, 1997: 385).

Public assemblages as the space of micro-spheres

Another formation of public assemblages is constituted by transnational 'micro-spheres' (Volkmer, 2002, 2011), which are quite different from what Dahlgren calls 'issue publics' (Dahlgren, 2001). Microspheres are thematic publics which are assessed from multiple geographically dispersed places. They represent authentic 'counter-flows' to mainstream coverage and 'create an extra-societal global public space' (Volkmer, 2002, 2011: 313). A study, conducted in 2007, investigated transnational satellite channels and concluded that mainly major 'Western players' such as CNN and BBC have a 'global reach'. However, the authors also highlight the 'increasing stream of contra-flow' to the Western world – the growing population of non-Western diasporas within most Western states. 'Mobilizing linguistic and cultural ties, a number of satellite channels from Asia and the Arab-speaking world are expanding beyond their region', and news channels from India and China are increasingly available in the markets of the USA and Europe' (Rai and Cottle, 2010: 63). Beyond these spheres of locality, the authors also highlight the formation of authenticity. Besides identifying these new satellite cultures, it is also interesting to note that these are often related to other similar spheres. For example, transnational television for Arab communities began in 1991 with the *Middle East Broadcast Centre* (MBC), London, followed by *Al Jazeera, Al Arabiya, CNN Arabic,* in addition to multiple national Arabic channels. Most of these channels are delivered into the Arab region, and via the *Hotbird* satellite into Europe. Since Rai and Cottle's study, political information channels via satellite are multiplied and represent a new 'ecology' of satellite political information channels; they should be perceived as a 'layer' of micro-sphere formations. Today there are an increasing number of satellite channels with close to worldwide distribution; among these are *Abu Dhabi TV* (Arabic), *TV Globo* (from Brazil), *Televisa* (Mexico), *VT4* (Vietnamese), and *Zee TV*, providing Indian content in Hindi. Although it is interesting to note how many highly specialized satellite channels are available, it is not simply the availability but the public space in which they are incorporated that identifies the public micro-sphere. Such a public micro-sphere not only provides 'authentic' political information but also creates transnational forms of public deliberation. Micro-spheres can be accessed from various world regions; however, often overlooked, they 'resonate' in particular ways in local and national contexts. For example, they resonate very differently in the USA, compared with North Africa and the Arab region. Micro-spheres are no longer isolated spaces, but they are incorporated into a public identity.

Besides these 'trans-local' micro-sphere assemblages, however, other forms relate to new spheres of social movements which are, as Tennant notes, increasingly situated in relationships between 'technosocial' and 'institutional' transformations in governance in national states and movements, 'enabling new forms of contentious collective action' (Tennant, 2007: 120). She argues that neither the 'spatial aspects of these transformations nor the consequences for the way in which local, "micro" processes are articulated into broader national or transnational movements has received systematic attention' (Tennant, 2007: 120).

Public assemblages and mediators

The transformation of the public actor, delivering not only 'discourse' but 'mediation', represents a third form of public assemblage. The sphere of public mediator is also a deliberative sphere as 'voices' are increasingly forming an 'aura' of public communication. Built into Fraser's notion of subaltern counterpublics and the 'widening contested discursive space' (Fraser, 1992) the role of a 'mediator' gains an increasing relevance in transnational publics. The 'blogosphere' as a network of individual mediators has, over the last years, established itself as a 'fifth' estate (Cooper, 2006). As a transnational assemblage it represents different forms of 'mediation'. In the early phase of the blogosphere individuals, such as *Salam Pax*, the 'most famous blogger in the world', gained international prominence. *Salam Pax*, based in Baghdad, posted individual accounts of the final phase of the Sadam Hussein regime and the allied invasion of Iraq in 2003. This was the early phase of authentic conflict mediation in a transnational context quite unique, and counterbalanced the media images of the invasion. Since that time, the blogosphere has become a complex public universe of highly specific accounts and discourses. The following image visualizes the transnational scope of the blogosphere.

Despite the fact that blogs can be accessed in many world regions, a recent statistic, produced by Technorati, an organization that continuously indexes and 'maps' worldwide blog sites, reveals that in 2011, the most active bloggers were based in the USA, followed by Europe, Oceania, Latin America, south Asia, east Asia, the Middle East and Africa (most of the blogs are posted in South Africa). In order to provide support to bloggers in developing regions, an organization like *Global Voices*, a non-profit organization based in the Netherlands, operates as a public service blog aggregator. The organization translates and lists blogs and in particular provides advocacy for blogs from countries where governments practise censorship. However, sites also emerge that focus on political blogs in developing regions, such as Africa, the Caribbean or Asia, but also incorporate Europe and Australia. One such site is called *The Nahmias Cipher Report* and is a platform aggregating reports by individuals from these regions. Besides aggregators, operating as mediators of thematic blogs which are, in the case of Global Voices, 'formatted' for specific transnational users, individual, highly specific blogs are targeting a transnational user sphere as well as governments and politicians. An example of such a model is the highly specialized blog by Yanis Varioufakis which, posted from Sydney, Australia, focuses entirely on the Euro crisis and creates an international debate about various sectors of European governance and polity. These phenomena are also related to a globalized interdependent public. As Bruns argues, the public sphere is 'decentralized across the network itself'; it is a 'shifting terrain which dissolves the boundaries of the public sphere and extends public participation from society' to a 'pan-societal environment experienced and enlivened by citizens themselves' (Bruns, 2008: 69).

These examples of public assemblage create a particular density which is slightly different from Sassen's approach. Sassen situates assemblage on the axis of digital, global and national spatialities. However, I suggest considering public assemblages as layers of 'interdependence', since this dimension allows the capture of fine lines of transnationally connected discourse spheres. Although not much work exists which positions transnational communication in a historical context, I argue that such a historical lens is important in order to understand the specific forms of today's trans-border formations. It is such a historical depth which allows us to understand the way in which spheres of interdependence have emerged in different shapes and 'geographies' since the time of the printing press. Since then, public assemblages have taken on quite different shapes of interdependence as particular trans-border publics. Communication technology which allowed the extension of large-scale communicative geographies beyond territorially bounded states emerged in the nineteenth century with the telegraph. However, trans-border – the term 'border' is used here in a broad sense of territoriality – communication emerged much earlier (Innis, 1951; McLuhan, 1962). It is quite surprising that only a few authors reflect upon the historical foundations of these formations of trans-border communication. These historical accounts mainly relate to ways in which 'globality' began to unfold in the nineteenth century and mainly contrast contemporary globalization processes with older forms of trans-territoriality. For example, Held identifies ways early forms of trans-border communication in the eighteenth and nineteenth centuries, such as 'trade routes and empires' which link distant populations together through quite simple networks of interaction (Held, 2006). Further accounts relate to the assumption that 'globality had little existence outside the mind' as 'supraterritorial communications, markets, production . . . were absent' (Scholte, 2000: 65), and other debates associate trans-border communication with either the first industrial use of trans-border technologies or the role of the telegraph and transatlantic cables in establishing hierarchies of the colonial territorial order of (governance) centrality and (public) peripheries (Mattelart, 2000).

A historiography of constructions of public territory as a dialectic process of deliberation between the transnational and the local *across* the 'shifting centrality' is a useful approach here. Ruggie (1993) remarks that the distinction between the 'domestic' and 'foreign' boundedness of modernity did not exist in the understanding of the 'spatial extension of the medieval system of rule', which, instead, was structured by a 'non exclusive form of territoriality' where 'authority was both personalized and parcelized within and across territorial formations'. According to Ruggie, prior to the thirteenth century only conceptions of 'frontiers' existed, but not in the modern sense of 'borders' (Ruggie, 1993: 150). In the modern era, two 'demarcations' occurred, 'between public and private', and this is of importance for the discussion here of 'internal' and 'external' realms (Ruggie, 1993: 151). Ferguson and Mansbach also state that in medieval times a clear distinction between 'domestic' and 'foreign' realms, between 'inside' and 'outside', was lacking, 'the absence of which made it impossible to distinguish clearly between public and private property, private and "national" interests, or between war and crime', it was 'rule over people' rather than territory (Ferguson and Mansbach, 2004: 76 and 77). The authors also relate these medieval conceptions of rule over people to pre-colonial Africa (Ferguson and Mansbach, 2004: 78).

This is a quite different concept from what is meant by territoriality in the context of public-sphere discussion. It is an important point that constitutes a demarcation of non-national, non-Westphalian forms of public sphere, and the positioning of public spheres in the dialectic of internal/external terrains. This dialectical space of public spheres across internal/external relations is not addressed in Habermas' public-sphere conception, which develops the public sphere exclusively in the frame of public/private (national) realms and less across historically shifting internal/external demarcations. This is an important distinction, as it allowed Habermas to develop rational discourse and deliberation exclusively through the idealization of an intersubjective 'speech' situation, through a conception of public discourse built on intersubjective (physical) proximity in the dialectic of public/private realms *within* territorial boundedness – beginning with the Greek city state, and moving on to feudal regimes and the nation-state. It is important to note that the internal/external dialectic which evolved historically – see Innis' (1951) important work in this context – and which outlined the historiography of communicative boundaries in relation to technology is not addressed in the Habermasian approach of the public sphere, which is entirely conceptualized in a territorially bounded public/private dialectic. It seems that Habermas' approach has overlooked the complexities of evolving trans-border, trans-territorial communicative space since the time of the printing press. Since the invention of the printing press the dynamic of internal/external dialectic has produced a new sphere of trans-territorial communication. The historical dynamics of such a dialectic are often over-looked in today's discussion of public spheres, which are often related to the Habermasian model. I would argue that such an inside/outside dichotomy has developed historically in different forms across world regions and this historicity constitutes an important sphere for an understanding of transnational spheres of world regions. It is the 'unbundling of territoriality' (Ruggie, 1993: 165) and, in contexts of public communication, the spaces that emerge through such an unbundling of public territory, and of demarcations of inside/outside, which lay the grounds for a deeper understanding of transnational public communication. Trans-border flows have historically played a role in the formation of supra-territorial political agency, from independent trading organizations, colonial state structures where communication was directed from the centre to the periphery, and back to authoritative states where propaganda came through the formation of various forms of trans-border spheres. It is quite interesting to compare the specific networks which have influenced the methods and circuits of trans-border assemblages. An analysis of the formation of public assemblages in the context of diverse technologies over the last few centuries reveals that 'connectivity' and 'resonance' emerge as layers of deliberative trans-border space. In particular, it is the nexus of trans-border public connectivity within these public assemblage formations that constitute the resonance terrain of reflective public communication in a transnational context, with implications for state publics. *This* is the space of public deliberation emerging as discursive taxonomies, *beyond* the container model of the state–society nexus but still influencing it. In this context, it is no longer the structure of 'transnational' or 'national'; these epistemic forms of public communication collide in the sphere of public assemblage.

Historiography of layers of public assemblages

Trans-border densities evolved through what might be called 'cultures of publicness' not as a rational discourse sphere of deliberation but as a discourse sphere of imagination – of narratives, of representations of the 'world', of 'the foreign', of 'the other', often through paintings, poems, novels. Public communication was local, taking place on public squares, in markets, bazaars, tea houses and streets, and through these local practices, citizens engaged in early forms of assembly. However, early forms of trans-border flows created a perception not only of the 'world' but of particular forms of public culture, and emerged in visual art where imaginings and representations of 'the other' as 'the foreign' have existed in paintings for centuries. The conception of assemblage in an analysis of the layering of trans-border interdependencies, helps not only to identify the broad sphere of international or linear centre-to-periphery communication but trans-border communication as historical 'scales' of complex 'public geographies'. Conceptions of the history of trans-border communication relate mainly to the 'nation' as a container model of public discourse. This approach overshadows non-national, non-linear 'trans-border' communication, which existed for centuries and created historical assemblages as layers of trans-border public connectedness across world regions.

The printing press and early networks of trans-border assemblages

Despite these various forms of local public culture, it was the printing press that enabled the production of imaginations and narratives in a deliverable format and, through this process, the establishment of early forms of what we might call, in a broad sense – and in acknowledgement of Ruggie's (1993) remark that 'borders' did not exist – trans-territorial public culture. Although 'trans-border' means something different in the early period of the printing press, an inside/outside dichotomy existed around other forms of territorial boundedness. The printing press, as invented in China, created a very particular conception of 'public'. Chow explains that the word 'gong' means 'to make public' through the process of printing a text but also painting. 'Public' in this tradition mainly designates a space 'outside the family', and is 'the opposite of private or personal' (Chow, 2004: 15). According to Chow 'to make something *gong* was to print it' for the 'reading public'. By the sixteenth century, all major methods of publishing, including woodblock and movable type, were in use in China (Chow, 2004: 22). Furthermore, by the late Ming phase, the cost of printing had become so low that literati often published their writings. Books were one of the most widely available and affordable commodities during this time (Chow, 2004).

The printing press has already created quite different spheres in Europe. Spheres of 'centrality' and 'periphery', for example, which McLuhan (1962) described (following Innis) as the 'Gutenberg Galaxy'.

As opposed to the inclusive acoustic space of 'sound', the linearity of the printed word, the alphabet, created distance, exclusion and the power of centrality. However, the printing press has also created centrality and periphery across emerging public spheres:

> In the fifteenth and sixteenth centuries, the printing press began eroding . . . distinctions between classes: in transferring responsibility for disseminating knowledge from scribes in the monasteries to printers in the cities, it furthered the shift in written communication from a language available only to the elite (Latin) to more common tongues (the vernaculars). But as the sixteenth century progressed, the press began creating the bases for new class distinctions: the plethora of books it churned out, while helping to enlighten many of the previously unenlightened, also expanded exponentially the information available for the learned to learn and the ignorant to remain ignorant about (Stephens, 1988: 128)

With cities developing into important trade centres in Europe, they also became spaces for diverse forms of public communication. Eisenstein notes that printers' workshops would be found anywhere in Europe in 'every municipal centre by 1500' (Eisenstein, 1979: 44). Although the sphere of book trade might be understood as a local sphere, books already conveyed the imaginings of the 'other', and foreign 'worlds' and in this sense, created centrality and periphery in a trans-border space: 'The work of the letter writer, agents and nouveallanten of sixteenth-century Europe helped sustain an image of an international society that transcended national boundaries; it gave legitimacy to the great empire without an emperor in which international trade and finance functioned' (Stephens, 1988: 77).

Furthermore, Stephens argues, 'The international community of trade and finance in the sixteenth century was in effect another super-society – an imperial order in which but a small percentage of the inhabitants of any local area had citizenship. The bulk of the population not only lacked the capital to participate in this community, it could not afford news of this community. For written news is among the most expensive' (Stephens, 1988: 77).

The printing culture began to spread in various local centres across Europe and the following examples show that this was not at all an inward looking world imagination. In Venice printers created publications that imagined the foreign world and 'maps and accounts of voyages to exotic places', published in 'four languages' (Briggs and Burke, 2009: 48). Amsterdam began to turn into one of the most 'cosmopolitan cities in Europe' (Stephens, 1988: 157). A printing house, for example, promoted its publications through this phrase: 'You may buy books cheaper at Amsterdam in all languages than at the places where they are first printed'. Books were published in Amsterdam as the cosmopolitan centre in a variety of languages, such as Russian, Yiddish, Armenian and Georgian (Briggs and Burke, 2009: 49). Furthermore, by 1619 a second weekly newssheet was printed and by 1645 'at least eight different weeklies or biweeklies were for sale . . . supplied merchants and other readers not only with news of Italy and Germany and the battles of the Thirty Years War but with news from America, Africa and Asia' (Stephens, 1988: 157).

However, besides these early forms of local imaginings of the foreign world, foreign news appeared in local publications and allowed an early version of what we might describe as trans-regional interdependence, creating a trans-border public of book readers diversified around languages and themes; newsletters and early versions of newspapers began to build a quite different trans-border public culture. These processes coincided with the emerging role of cities as centres of trade and governance, and hence political centres. Cities were already of significant size and some had a population of 25,000 (Wuthnow, 1989), such as Antwerp, Amsterdam, Strasburg, Nuremberg, Augsburg, Magdeburg, Cologne, Ghent, Vienna (Wuthnow, 1989: 56). Furthermore, it is often overlooked that these urban trade centres were linked through regular news couriers 'with cities as far away as London and Seville' and Wuthnow notes that the 'larger merchant houses maintained envoys in all the major cities and sent messages back and forth by horseback or boat concerning contracts, economic conditions, and other news' (Wuthnow, 1989: 56). Beyond these imaginings of the 'other', foreign news appeared in the weeklies mentioned above and trade routes served as communication routes. The Silk Road in Asia was one of these routes that also served as communication routes, and in Europe the Hanseatic League from the twelfth to eighteenth centuries constituted an important network of about two hundred cities stretching across northern Europe. In Europe, the Hanseatic League, a trade-city league network across northern Europe, constituted, along with city-states (for example, in Italy), political alternatives to the territorial state (Ruggie, 1993).

One of the phenomena of trans-border public assemblage relates to early trans-regional formations, which evolved through networks of trade centres. These networks were supported and maintained through the trans-border delivery of newsletters, an early form of newspaper addressing political news for the trans-regional trade community around a common interest. One of the most influential newsletters was the one established by the house of Fugger, financiers based in Augsburg, Germany. The *Fugger Newsletter* created a trans-border community across Europe which might serve as an early example of a form of public assemblage in the sixteenth century, building a public interdependence across territories where these trans-border spheres created a common community among traders, independent of their locality.

> Through the news they shared, the wheat traders of Venice, the silver traders of Antwerp, the merchants of Nuremberg, the financiers of Augsburg, and their trading partners around the world, were being drawn together into a society based on this new sensibility; on common interests – the fate of some ships sailing from India to Lisbon; on common values – a belief in the rights of capital. (Stephens, 1988: 77)

The Fugger Newsletters contained news from various foreign Fugger partners, sent as private notes about political and other events relevant to the financial world and then made available to Fugger clients. This trade community could be described as an early form of public assemblage through interdependence – of financial activities for example – related within political contexts through trans-border communication.

> The written news – resolutely cosmopolitan in perspective – that flowed into and out of Europe's trading centres enabled business people like Fugger to share a perspective, to share a view of a large and coherent, if not predictable, world – a world in which it was possible to imagine cargos arriving, interest being paid, profits being made. (Stephens, 1988: 77).

The House of Fugger had already established a news-reporting agency in all the major trading cities in Europe, such as London, Paris, Antwerp and Venice. The newsletters contained written letters from each of their foreign partners and through this process their famous 'Golden Counting-House' in Augsburg became 'cognisant of all the happenings in the known world' (*The Fugger Newsletters*, 1924).

An example shows the degree of detail contained in international reports relevant to their international trading community: 'Further news coming in and considered correct is that the Spanish fleet has already built a strong fortress at the most important point on the Arabian Sea, whereby the navigation of the Turks is entirely blocked. This has been pointed out to the Sultan, who has held a long consultation with the Grand Vizier. A Pasha is to be sent to Cairo, so that with all that he requires, especially wood which will be sent from here, he may build on the spot a powerful fleet for use against the Spaniards. The English and French ambassadors have, as they publicly admit, relaxed somewhat in their dispute until their masters, on receiving their reports, communicate with them as to their behaviour in future' (*The Fugger Newsletters*, vol. 2, 1926, 1970: 112).

The newsletter was followed by weekly newssheets, which are early forms of newspapers, targeting a broader audience. 'Venice constituted the most important centre of information at the beginning of the sixteenth century . . . Merchants and diplomats brought news into Venice, and they made it their business to collect news while they were there . . .' (Stephens, 1988: 151). News about wars dominated these newssheets. For example, one of the major continuing news stories in Europe in the sixteenth century was the war with the Turks; the siege of Vienna was printed across Europe in French, German, Italian and Latin (Stephen, 1988: 93).

However, it is important to keep in mind that these developments of technology and public communication emerged in the European context in a very particular way. Forms of public trans-border interdependence could also be described in other world regions – for example, in the Arab region, where newspapers appeared quite late – and other forms of interregional interdependence were deeply embedded into the public based in religious culture. As Briggs and Burke argue, there was some resistance to print in Muslim regions. The authors claim that 'Muslim countries have been regarded as a barrier to the passage of printing from China to the West', and Briggs argues that in 1515 a decree was issued 'punishing the practice of printing with the death penalty'. Briggs and Burke remark also that in the early sixteenth century 'the sale of non-religious printed books in Arabic characters' was allowed, which 'were probably imports from Italy'. The authors suggest that the reason for such resistance was that print 'struck right at the heart of person to person transmission of knowledge which was fundamental in the world of Islam' (Robinson, cited by Briggs and Burke, 2010: 14).

The role of public dialogue within the particular notion of public sphere is described by Eickelman and Anderson (2003): 'Public dialogue has long held a special place in the Muslim world. A religious public sphere of learned scholars, schools of jurisprudence, and their supporters was often autonomous from the official sphere of rulers in the early Islamic centuries. . . . The result was to strengthen the role of men of learning . . . in the public sphere from the third Islamic century through the modern era. Subsequent caliphs and other temporal rulers intervened in this sphere only with caution, and in general left it alone' (also Hurvitz, 1997: 6: Eickelman and Anderson, 2003: 2).

The first printed periodical newspaper appeared in 1816 and the first Arab daily in 1873. Lebanon and Egypt were early centres of newspaper publications. In Australia, newspapers also emerged quite late and were closely related to the trans-border connections of the colonial public. Webby, for example notes, that from 'the seventeenth century onwards, European navigators and sailors began bumping into the west coast of Australia' and also carried printing technology. In 1788, an old wooden screen press, a small selection of used type and some paper and ink began operating in Australia. These technologies were used for administrative purposes; for example, the earliest extant production is a government order, dated 18 November 1796. A few years later, the first Australian newspaper, the *Sydney Gazette and New South Wales Advertiser*, was issued on 5 March 1803 (Webby, 1996: 22).

In Canada, the process by which remote territories were incorporated into a modern nation was more complex. The development of a periodical press played a significant role, as periodicals served as political tools, 'in the creation of representative government in the provinces, in the establishment of a press free of political censorship; in the creation of a unified nation . . . in the creation of distinct cultures, both local and national, and in the promotion of innumerable other religious, commercial, and special-interest causes' (Distad and Distad, 1996: 62). In Canada, newspapers began to proliferate at the turn of the nineteenth century (Distad and Distad, 1996: 68).

India is another example of this model, where newspapers and the periodical press emerged as late as the end of the eighteenth century. In India, a local place such as the market served, and still does today, as a community sphere where the locals gather 'to listen to and exchange information with the tradesmen, caravans, pilgrims, and wandering vagrants who come from neighbouring towns and from as far as Persia and Afghanistan' (Chaudhuri, 1996: 175).

> The speed with which important news travelled in India was a mystery in itself. It was surprising that the news about a disaster in Manipur in eastern India in 1891 was talked about in the bazaars of Allahabad and other places in the north long before it reached the general public through the newspapers. (Chaudhuri, 1996: 175)

The first newspaper was founded in 1780 in India. During this time, the British administrators were already aware that the press could eventually lead to political consciousness among the Indian population. It was even prohibited to publish the newspaper 'until it shall have been previously inspected by the Secretary to the Government or by a person authorized by him for that purpose' (Chaudhuri, 1996: 177). In fact, Jesuits brought the first printing press to India in 1550 (Natarajan, 1962:

4). Until 1816, as Natarajan remarks, there were no Indian proprietors or editors of newspapers. Between 1816 and 1820, only one Indian-owned newspaper was published weekly in Calcutta (Natarajan, 1962: 29). As noted in the *Queen Victoria Periodicals*, 'the native newspapers are generally not much thought of', and 'very few of them are ever read by those Englishmen who rule the destinies of India. The native under-stands the Englishmen better than he is known by the latter; but neither of them knows the other sufficiently well for the furtherance of their common interests. Misunderstanding has been the cause of India's ruin' (Chaudhuri, 1996: 182).

This sphere of international interdependence began in South Africa even later. Cape Town was until 1831 regarded as the site where news-papers or periodicals were produced. The first newspapers at the Cape were published in 1824, but tied to colonial communication, which was enhanced by the telegraph and the utilization of telegraph lines for political communication, a process which created a powerful colonial public sphere (Vann and VanArsdel, 1996).

The formation of foreign journalism, reporting events from foreign regions, established new forms of interdependence not only for a small elite group but for trading classes and larger social classes. Foreign journalism established a new agency system around colonial struc-tures. The news agency Reuters is an example of such a colonial news agency (Boyd-Barrett, 1980) and foreign journalism in its traditional form produced a national view of the world and contributed to the formation of international interdependent publics.

News agencies and networks of assemblages across extra-territorial centres

The nineteenth century could be perceived as what Chase-Dunn and Niemeyer call 'the emergence and growth of an overlayer of regional and increasingly global formal organizational structures on top of the interstate system' (2009: 41). They define political globalization as 'the relative strength and density of larger versus smaller interaction net-works and organizational structures' (Chase-Dunn and Niemeyer, 2009: 42). The authors note that the 'waves' of international political integration began after the Napoleonic Wars early in the nineteenth century. For example national newspapers (and news agencies) deliv-ered conceptions of the centrality of the nation-state through concep-tions of periphery, which either related to other (European) nations but also to peripheral colonies. This is a phenomenon that is often debated around imperialist or post-colonial approaches.

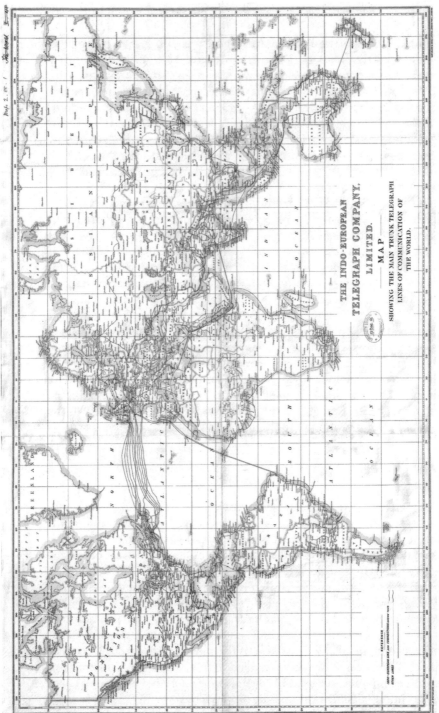

Figure 2.1 World cable network in the 1880s.
From Read (1992) *The Power of News*, pp. 74–5.

Newspapers in Africa, Canada and Australia evolved at a time when the notion of a trans-border assemblage of interdependence related not only to the domestic and foreign interdependence of emerging European publics – where the dichotomy of domestic and foreign created national identity – but to the context of colonialism where domestic and foreign related to colonial centres and (colonized) peripheries. These formations of trans-border public territoriality were further enhanced by the particular structure of the telegraph network in the nineteenth century. The first underwater telegraphic cable connected Calais and Dover in 1851, in subsequent years across the Atlantic, and two decades later to Asia and China, Australia, the coasts of Africa and the Caribbean. Subsequently, similar networks were established in South America. As Thussu notes, 'The British cable of 1874 was joined in 1879 by a new French cable across the north Atlantic, with a spur to Brazil, and by a new German cable from Emden to the Azores to Morovia on the African coast. And from there to Recife. By 1881, a network along the pacific coast from Mexico to Peru was in operation. In the 1880s France established a series of links along the coast of Indochina and Africa, with networks in Senegal' (Thussu, 2000: 16). This cable network in combination with the telegraph created a network of public trans-border interdependence, connecting European nations to their colonies and, on a more abstract level, could be described as a network of interdependence across extra-territorial centres.

The telegraph, as overland and undersea telegraphic cable line, was the first communication technology which, as James Carey famously remarked, separated 'communication from transportation' (Carey, 1989: 203). It enabled the formation of an international communication network of powerful information routes across a newly formed international communication territory. The International Telegraph Union (ITU) was created in 1865 as an intergovernmental agency to determine standards and procedures between member countries, and, ultimately, to create a 'first unified electric sphere' (Mattelart, 2000: 8).

Britain had, in 1892, a global share of 66 per cent and in 1923 of 50 per cent of the world's telegraphic cable network (Headrick, 1991; Thussu, 2000: 19). The interdependence across extra-territorial centres relates to forms of centre-periphery communication along a hierarchic scale of colonial communication: 'The rapid development of the telegraph was a crucial feature in the unification of the British Empire . . . the telegraph allowed the Colonial Office and the India Office to communicate directly with the Empire within minutes, when, previously, it had taken months for post to come via sea' (Thussu, 2000: 14). Within the British, French, German and other European colonial powers, the telegraph served as a network of sovereignty and interdependence across extra-territorial spaces. This interdependence across extra-territorial centres – a form of trans-border communication – during this time was further enhanced by the establishment of news agencies serving the new and increasing forms of national public sphere in Europe and in many of the colonial regions (see note above). News items were selected and framed from the viewpoint of colonial powers and delivered to clients in colonies and dominions.

For example, the main news agencies of the nineteenth century, Reuters, Wolff and Havas were 'indirectly linked to their respective governments' and 'their news services reflected their respective national interests' (Boyd-Barrett, 1998: 23) and constituted an early network of foreign correspondents who created trans-border news flows to national media outlets which then filtered this foreign news according to a national agenda. News agencies began to mediate not only between 'retail media, state and capital' (Boyd-Barrett, 1998: 3) but through influence on local news agendas to shape a particular world perception. Newspapers relied on news agencies for trans-border information, which was framed in colonial centres. However, among the emerging news agencies of the time, such as AP of New York, Havas (Paris), Wolff (Berlin), Reuters was the most powerful agency and Reuters' editorial office in London was the 'clearing-house for most news originating from outside Europe' (Read, 1992: 59).

Concerns about a similar dominance were raised in Australia, where the main Australian daily newspapers agreed reluctantly to take on news from the Reuters agency as they feared that Reuters aimed to dominate the press,[3] which was already the case in India where Reuters 'came to dominate the supply of news not only to and from India but also within the country' as a 'counter-part of that in London' (Read, 1992: 63). Another example is Egypt, an important trade centre for Britain, where the local press was weak and could not afford to subscribe regularly to Reuters news. In consequence, Reuters published 'its news directly in the form of bulletins . . . delivered by hand' (Read, 1992: 62). These news items for the various international press outlets were produced from a British perspective and 'its loyalty was most clearly demonstrated in its coverage of wars, large or small, in which Britain was involved'. Reuters reported defeats as readily as victories; but the British cause was always assumed to be 'right', and British troops to be 'ours' (Read, 1992: 67). Guidelines for Reuters journalists, such as those in China, suggested that 'only the murder of Europeans should normally be reported to London' (Read, 1992: 107). Although national news agencies were founded throughout the 1970s, the

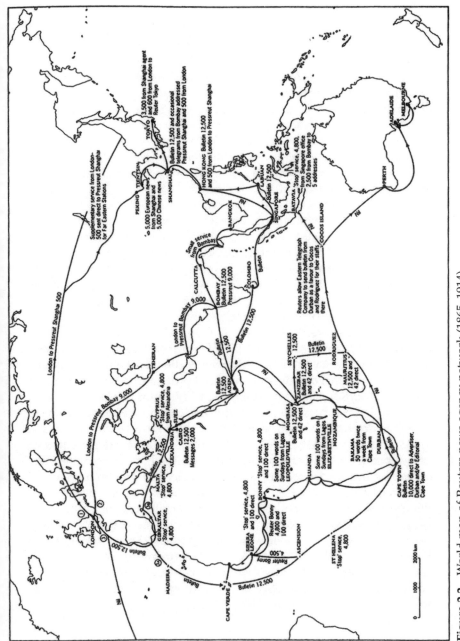

Figure 2.2 World map of Reuters news agency network (1865–1914).
Source: Read (1992), *The Power of News*, p. 77.

influence of the 'big four' remained. Rantanen (1998) has outlined the complex relationships between these and local agencies, which were often used as entry points into national markets. A study reveals that in Latin America's 'most important source of foreign news', 23 per cent of foreign news is delivered by Reuters and Agence France Presse and 10 per cent by a national agency; in western Europe 11 per cent by Reuters, 10 per cent by a national agency and 49 per cent by 'own journalist'; in Africa 37 per cent by Reuters and AFP, 33 per cent by a national news agency and 20 per cent by 'own journalist' (Pietilaeinen, 1998, cited by Boyd-Barrett and Rantanen, 2004: 33).

While news agencies remained crucial networks of trans-border flows of political information, shortwave radio emerged as a new network sphere of interdependence across extra-territorial centres. Shortwave radio began to target audiences internationally, beginning to create new forms of centre and periphery. This is – to borrow a term from Thompson (1996) – the 'symbolic power' of the national media of emerging nation-states shaping the relevance of national public life within the dichotomy of centres and peripheries of transnational public interdependence. Radio Moscow, the first shortwave radio station, delivered programmes in 1920; BBC's Empire Service in 1932 and then Voice of America. By the 1960s, Moscow Radio was the world's largest single international broadcaster and aired programmes in 84 languages (Thussu, 2000: 30). These were followed by other forms of radio service, for example US services to eastern Europe, creating overlapping layers of public networks of interdependence across extra-territorial centres. What Thussu called the 'war of airwaves' represented networks of interdependence built around a political centre. For example, the *Voice of America*, headquartered in Washington delivered programmes across local transmitters: Bangkok for southeast Asia; Poro and Tinang in the Philippines for China and southeast Asia; Colombo for south Asia; Tangier, Morocco, for North Africa; Rhodes, Greece, for the Middle East; Selebi-Phikawe in Botswana, for southern Africa; Monrovia in Liberia for sub-Saharan Africa; Munich, Germany for eastern Europe and the former Soviet Union; Woofferton in England for the former Soviet Union; Greenville, USA for Latin America; Punta Gord in Belize for central America (Thussu, 2000: 32).

National media and networks of assemblages

Quite different types of networks of interdependence emerged as spheres of public assemblage with radio and television broadcasting, which were considered to be national (that is, territoria) media with implications for conceptions of domestic and foreign news in public communication. This had to do with the fact that the regulation of terrestrial airwaves is considered a matter of state sovereignty. The flow of foreign news in emerging spheres of television was a continuation of the influence of news agencies, and each of the agencies – Reuters, AP, Agence France Presse (AFP), TASS and UPI – served as the provider of foreign news. In addition, foreign news was selected and 'domesticated' by national news outlets. Going beyond news agencies, satellite platforms, such as *Intelsat* and *Panamsat*, delivered live events to national broadcasters who framed these live images in national narratives. Despite these types of foreign news 'flow' platforms, political information from broadcasters was incorporated into the sovereign sphere of a nation, with regard to both domestic and foreign news. Eickelman and Anderson describe this process as a 'control of the broadcast and printed word to foster common, shared, and modern identities at least as much as to deny these means to potential opponents. The central asymmetrical structure of mass media is a product of this; states see these media as vehicles of consolidation and standardization. When recast as differences between senders and receivers, distinctions between centre and periphery become far more ambiguous and porous as the senders become multiple and shifting' (Eickelman and Anderson, 2003: 3). This approach relates to news and political information, whereas other programme formats are in some countries privatized. The Westphalian model of sovereignty, in this case as a sovereignty of information space, relates in some regions to government control of political information and in others to the selection of news frames, which create certain foreign news profiles. For example a study by Semmel (1976) of US newspapers revealed that 'the image of the global system presented by the prestige US press is basically Eurocentric, big-power dominant, and Western-oriented. In this news map of the world, only a few countries are important or deemed to be of interest; those societies outside the mainstream of prevailing American world perspectives receive minimal attention or no attention at all' (Semmel, 1976: 731).

When discussing the internationalization of media in the time of the Cold War, a perspective of centrality reflects not only the geopolitical interest spectrum but larger macro-structural processes of the Western dominance of non-Western media cultures in developing regions. Dependency theory identifies these as 'the sum of processes by which a society is brought into the modern world system and how its dominating stratum' is pressured to 'promote' the values and structures of the 'dominant centre of the system' (Schiller, 1976: 9).

Processes mainly relating to the US media system that began in those days to influence emerging mass media cultures in various world regions, as Thussu notes, promoted an 'American way of life' through 'mediated consumer lifestyles' (Thussu, 2000: 62). The UNESCO Mac-Bride Report revealed in more detail the imbalances in information flow. It is important to distinguish these macro-structural developments from the micro-structures of public trajectories of interdependence, of public conceptions of and public connectivity to trans-border worlds. In general terms, these fine-grained trajectories of public interdependence are – because of geopolitical interests and political loyalties – related to 'dependency' processes; however, they show a somewhat more precise profile.

Although a number of studies investigated the foreign coverage in national news in the early decades during the main phase of the 'Cold War', one of the first international comparative studies was Gerbner and Marvanyi's study, which investigated the flow of foreign news and the representation of world regions, or the 'similarities and differences of "the outside world" which each society projects for its members' (Gerbner and Marvanyi, 1977: 52). The study, undertaken in 1970, analysed foreign news from leading newspapers in nine countries: among these were the USA, UK, West Germany, Soviet Union, Hungary, Czechoslovakia, Ghana, India and the Philippines. Results showed that the publicly owned press had a larger number of foreign news items than have commercially operated newspapers. However one of the main outcomes of this study was the construction of 'foreign news worlds' which reveal interesting patterns of trans-border territorialities of public interdependence. Results showed public 'worlds' in third world countries and the Soviet Union, followed by south Asia and the Far East, western Europe, North America and Latin America (Gerbner and Marvanyi, 1977: 60). Furthermore, the Soviet audience received more news about the USA and eastern and western Europe than readers in those countries received about the Soviet Union (Gerbner and Marvanyi, 1977: 60). The authors concluded that Africa, Australia Oceania, China, Mongolia and north Korea were barely visible and that western Europe rather than the USA was the region which most appeared in the news across the diverse countries involved in the study (Gerbner and Marvanyi, 1977: 60).

The first study to compare newspapers and television internationally was Stevenson and Shaw's study of news flow across seventeen countries, ranging from Latin and North America, Africa, the Middle East, Asia to western and eastern Europe. The study identified detailed accounts of foreign world representation in national media. Revealing an internationalization of the national public sphere, the study is of further interest in that it identified characteristics of news actors in those days. Stevenson and Lash showed that the main actor in foreign news stories was the executive branch of government. 'Chief executives usually are charged with responsibility for foreign affairs and when they travel or speak, their words readily lend themselves to national stories. For the moment at least, they are the nation' (Stevenson and Shaw, 1984: 138). Although they included nations with a free as well as restricted press system, this outcome is surprising, given the lack of foreign news stories around activism and other forms of civic engagement.

A more recent study reveals examples of the trans-border public through the international news coverage – in forty-four countries on all continents – which identified 'the most important country mentioned in a news story' (Wu, 2004). One of the countries with the longest list of international regions represented during the two-week study is Iran, where the USA was mentioned the most often by far, followed by the UK, Russia, China, Israel, Germany. In Kenya, other African countries were mainly covered, followed by the USA, UK, France, India and Bosnia. Although in this study the frequency of main countries in a foreign news report does not reveal the core of a story, it does show the transnational news profile and the degree of public interdependence provided by national news media.

Assemblages as spheres of connectivity

New layers of trans-border public assemblage emerged with satellite spheres. Satellite technology, and in particular direct-to-home satellite delivery, represents a new layer of a public which is broadly interdependent; that is, it relates through the domestic/foreign dichotomy of national news outlets to the outside world and in this sense creates a larger international public interdependence. It is interesting to note that there were some attempts to regulate this new transnational sphere of satellite delivery as a spatial communicative form. For example, the Soviet Union made an attempt 'to obtain a United Nations sanction for a prohibition on the use of direct satellite transmission of television without prior permission of target nations' (Stevenson, 1984: 12) and to keep 'signals beamed more or less to one country' (Stevenson, 1984: 32).

Direct-to-home satellite delivery has created a new layer of transborder publics which directly connects to authentic, fractured political information and through this process, creates public 'proximity'. In the early phase of globalization (in the early 1990s), the live delivery of conflicts and political crises and the emerging proximity and density of public communication in the context of international events determined the legitimacy of foreign policy decisions (see Robinson, 2002; Gilboa, 2002; Michalski and Gow, 2007). This type of public assemblage creates a particular kind of inside/outside deliberation through direct access to conflicts delivered live, such as in the first war in the Persian Gulf in 1990–91. CNN played a dominant role in the first Gulf War by agenda setting not only in the USA but in various countries worldwide. These new trans-border layerings of direct access and connectivity were not only delivered by narratives but also images with powerful implications (even in public memory) for public spaces. This first phase of major Western satellite channels as transnational forms of political information – BBC World, *Deutsche Welle* – was soon broadening, involving other Western and non-Western direct-to-home satellite platforms for political information in what Cushion describes as a 'race for transnational reach and influence', which, in Cushion's model is followed by a third 'regionalizing' phase (Cushion, 2010: 15). Although I agree with Cushion in characterizing phases of satellite 'interpenetration', in terms of understanding these specific spheres of satellite communication in their role of public communication, the role of public connectivity between 'supra-' and 'subnational' spheres constitutes a new form of the inside/outside dialectic where connectivity and subnational implications emerge as new terrains. Direct-to-home satellite platforms opened up the territorial public which was, in the early 1990s, otherwise still dominated by national media. Satellite platforms began to provide thematic and highly diverse political information and create a space for public deliberation through a new dialectic of supra- and subnational spheres.

In the advanced phase of globalization, satellite communication is no longer a communicative sphere of global reach but a sphere which targets an increasingly globalized density of local political satellite channels, as post-territorial 'layerings', stretching across world regions. Over the last years, increasingly regional and national channels, as Rai and Cottle argue, reveal a satellite ecology with 'multifarious flows and formations that can both span across regions stimulating greater global integration and convergence, and concentrate and intensify within regions engendering localization, regionalization and even fragmentation' (Rai and Cottle, 2010: 75). Such a post-territorial 'ecology' of advanced satellite connectivity about the formation of deliberative supra- and subnational publics communicates across various territories through highly authentic forms of political information. These new spaces of public deliberation via direct connectivity are under-researched. However, the region where satellite communication and the role of political information have been mostly studied is the Arab region. In this region, where various governments have exercised control, satellite communication has enabled access to political information and to particular forms of public deliberation. It is the fact that satellites from Europe, such as *Eutelsat*, share the footprint with the North African continent – *MBC* started in 1991, *Al Jazeera* in 1996 as the second transnational Arabic channel – which creates a particular form of deliberation in the inside/outside dialectic. Sakr describes this space of deliberation through connectivity in North Africa where 'a small number of Algerians started to receive satellite television from France in the late 1980s, via France Telecom Satellite . . . Algerians seized the initiative in gaining access to satellite programmes through improvised neighbourhood cable networks . . . that allowed large-scale sharing of a single satellite dish' (Sakr, 2001: 11). And, she notes, as 'the violent conflict between Islamist extremists and government forces escalated and censorship was tightened, French-speaking Algerians turned en masse to the news and analysis available by satellite' (Sakr, 2001: 11). Sakr argues that Eutelsat capacity 'was crucial' to broadcasters who, 'for political reasons, could not hope to transmit from Arabsat' (Sakr, 2001: 14).

Sakr describes this process in North Africa:

> The new satellite viewing in communities was configured more broadly than the readerships of national or even pan-Arab newspapers. They incorporated people who, whether for reasons of sex, illiteracy, remoteness from newspaper distribution circuits, or disinterest in overt government propaganda, were previously left out of the media loop. More and more people therefore would appear to have become enmeshed in a process where 'images, values and ideas flow ever more swiftly and smoothly across national boundaries.' (Sakr, 2001: 25)

Traditional forms of satellite channel are increasingly bundled to new 'themed' digital platforms delivered to particular world regions, which increases what might be called the 'authentic density'. For example, *CCTV* (Chinese Central Television) not only operates an international channel dedicated to political information but also a television platform which includes channels in Chinese, French and English delivered via *Eutelsat* to South Africa. Digiturk is another platform delivering 142 channels, many of which send political information across Europe, North Africa, the Middle East, Saudi Arabian Peninsula, Turkey,

Somalia and the east African region. Another platform, Hi Tv, delivers about sixty channels, among them BBC World News South Asia, Sky News and Fox News, as well as *Al Jazeera* English to central western Africa.

Reviewing these diverse processes – which could only be outlined here – reveals the increasing densities of interdependence in transnational communication. The examples reveal an increasing degree of transnational reach and 'verticalized' transnationalization, with is further sustained through networked communication and, in our context, network centralities.

We will next take this process further and address the spaces of deliberation as they emerge in the new densities of reflective public space.

3

From 'Reflexive' Modernity to 'Reflective' Globalization: The Public Space of 'Inbetween-Ness'

The previous chapter has described 'public assemblages', which are not congruent with national boundedness and national sovereignty principles. Public assemblage constitutes not only transnational but non-bounded structures of publicness that are difficult to conceptualize in the way in which these dynamic, shifting and 'dense' layers of publicness facilitate deliberative communication. It is not surprising that, despite these new 'unbounded' formations of 'public interdependence', the modern dialectical 'order' of deliberation still serves as the core framework for our understanding of deliberation in these new spaces.

The underlying model of this deliberative discourse principle is the centrality of modern democracy. Depending on the choice of paradigms, civic deliberative discourse is articulated from the utilitarian perspective of the nineteenth century as a participatory 'corrector' of representative 'enlightened' government as suggested by John Stuart Mill (1865); from the libertarian perspective as a sphere of 'justification' (Rawls, 1999); and from the perspective of critical theory as a powerful 'normative' sphere of public reason, enabled by an ethical framework of discourse procedures (Cohen, 1988; Fishkin, 1995; Habermas, 1999). These diverse conceptions of deliberation from Mill to Rawls to Habermas have positioned deliberation as a discourse space of 'inbetween-ness' – between civic spheres and democratic institutions. It is a discursive space where judgements about the 'common good' are negotiated between 'citizens' and 'the state' and a dialectic of space enables a 'bounded' imagination of a public sphere but also of 'bounded' 'information. Fishkin writes that a 'collective process' of deliberation 'occurs in which the group has a reasonable chance to form its collective, considered judgements – to give its public voice'. In addition, arguments 'on rival positions get an extended hearing' and in this sense, 'the same information is available to all. They also participate, in a context which is small enough that each can credibly believe that his or her individual voice counts' (Fishkin, 1995: 34). In more general terms, this definition situates deliberation in the general scope of discursive practice, where final subjective and collective positions are subject to change through such a deliberative practice and only those norms, rules, or decisions resulting from reason-based agreement among citizens are considered to be legitimate.

The core territories of this traditional dialectical 'order' are challenged by a public interdependence where 'the common good' is shifting towards a transnational horizon, of the more generalized 'human condition' (Robertson, 1992). A concern for humanity was suggested in the early phase of globalization but given the increasing densities of *advanced* globalization it led towards a quite specific 'commonality'. The discursive process of negotiating 'individual' and 'collective' judgements as 'reason-based' agreements is no longer related to a 'bounded' civic collective but fluctuates across thematic spaces and loyalties of broad unbounded communicative spheres, which suggests the articulation of new 'normative' structures. Public deliberation is embedded in these fluid public interdependent geographies of dynamic, asymmetrical networked spheres where communicative 'centralities' and 'peripheries' continuously shift around communities, 'events', and conflicts. Deliberative spheres seem to emerge in a new sphere of 'inbetween-ness', not as in the modern deliberative paradigm between 'citizens' and the 'state' but in what we might call a 'transnational deliberative' paradigm, enabled through public interdependence, between 'networks' of choice and lifeworld 'locality'. This is a deliberative space that is not exclusive to the modern nation-states but through the 'connectivity' of loyalties, of agency and relational spaces of public interdependence is increasingly embedded in other state formations, for example, even in authoritarian states where centralizd forms of censorship are increasingly porous and political actors engage with transnational spatial communities. However, such an interdependent dimension of public communication is not 'only' a space of 'social media' or digital communication as it is sometimes perceived in debates of digital publicness but a multi-layered spectrum of subjectively chosen 'authentic' communicative forms, incorporating traditional (e.g. local) dimensions of deliberative cultures that are, however, embedded in public practices *across* geographies of network spheres. Such a public interdependence constitutes an increasingly important frame for deliberation across world regions, political regimes and society types. The 'resonance' space of such a public interdependence, i.e. the way in which such a public interdependence is 'anchored', reflected in deliberative civic spheres is, however, quite different in Bangkok, Mexico City, Paris or New York.

Processes of 'disembedding' deliberative discourse

When assessing public deliberation in spatial networked discourses, Western approaches are either generalized in larger contexts of international communication (see Hamelink, 2012), deliberation is situated in the national institutional order, or they are segregated along regional clusters of Western and 'other' modernities, for example in the discussion of the 'Asian' or the 'Arab' context. We have not yet identified the ways in which deliberative practices and deliberative cultures take on diverse shapes in public spaces of 'reflexive,' 'second' or 'compressed' (Beck, 1992) modernities, in particular in non-Western world regions. What is interesting is that Western and, in Beck's sense, 'reflexive' modern public cultures provide a framework for assessing interdependencies; however, these debates have rarely been related to new forms of communicative public deliberation. Calhoun has recently pointed out that 'social and political theory relies heavily on tacit incorporation of Western historical patterns into seemingly universal categories' and argues that, for example 'social theory needs history' for a more systematic assessment of 'tensions and contractions' in 'historical patterns' which would help to overcome the assumed 'seemingly universal categories' (Calhoun, 2010: 603). Such an approach would allow the assessment of important regional distinctions and we have outlined historical conceptions of trans-border space across geographical regions in the previous chapter. In the contexts of our debate, we should go even further and 'contextualize' the inclusion of these local historiographies *within* the larger scope of public interdependence, to make them visible, give voice within contexts of public engagement in unbounded communicative forms of social media, satellite television, mobile communication and the multiple platforms of the Internet.

Public discourse is 'spiralling' across continents through thematically centred, 'self referential' discourse networks, which combine layers of different media forms. Such a 'viral' publicness relates to

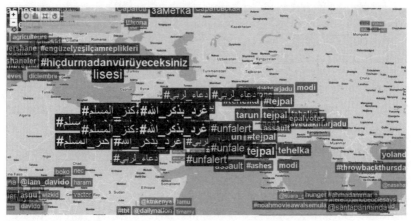

Figure 3.1 Trendsmap global.
This map visualizes the 'live' density of *Twitter* feeds across the world. The size reflects the frequency of these terms being tweeted or retweeted.

the inclusive, thematically authentic structure of discourse, connecting multiple fractured publics, floating across specific discourse cultures of transnational 'localities'. This sphere of interdependent publicness transforms conceptions of international or 'transnational' communication where quite often, the 'transnational' is perceived as a side-by-side model of the national. For example, in journalism studies, the 'foreign' and the 'domestic' are often used as two independent 'units of analysis'. Dense public interdependencies are not 'linear' but 'clustered' 'patches' of 'viral' communicative 'layers' stretching across national territories. Local 'ecologies' of deliberative cultures are absorbed by public densities in networked spaces that are accessible in any world region with advanced mobile (smart) phone technology and Internet connection. Increasingly these are deliberative forms 'connected' across continents and set a transnational political agenda in national contexts. For example, protests against rising fuel prices are transnationally connected and take place simultaneously within one week from Albany, New York, Tel Aviv, Madrid, Jarkarta to Kathmandu, Nepal; however, local protests in these cities engage in very particular regional specific debates and address slightly different local political discourses within the scope of the transnationally interdependent discourse. Furthermore, these local debates remain engaged in the larger transnational discourse space, creating a new 'reflective deliberative mechanism.

Despite these new deliberative 'reflective' spatial appropriations 'across distance' of civic communication, the modern paradigm of deliberation seems still to be used in contexts of those public network spheres which are not 'bounded' to modern Western regions but take shape across a spectrum of society formations. We are so used to assessing 'national' or 'regional' 'territorial' forms of deliberation that specifics of spatial, 'relational' structures across spheres of public inter-dependence are only on the periphery of debates. The particular 'reflec-tive' dimensions of public deliberation of post-colonial publics situated in network structures have only recently become the focus of debates by African scholars. The increasing role of urban places in so-called 'developing' regions not only as a 'world' or 'media' cities (Sassen, 1991; Mcquire, 2008) but as dense local sites of deliberative public practices, engaged in very particular ways in a transnational discourse sphere and through access to public interdependence create a new 'reflective' site of transnational deliberation. Transnational urban centres have been created, for example, in Jordan, the United Arab Emirates and Egypt with the intention of attracting 'knowledge-based industries'. According to Abdelhay, during the second half of the 1990s particularly, new technology networks provided sites for debates between citizens, scholars and associations about the principle of the freedom of the press and the promotion of an independent, free and pluralistic Arab media and, as a result, 'local regimes could no longer imprint their so-called "national values" upon their subjects' (Abdelhay, 2012: 532).

A change of perspective from the nation to the urban centre in con-texts of communicative 'connectedness' can be quite illuminating and help to identify 'reflective' local spheres of deliberation. Only very few studies address these new sites of public interdependence in regions rarely included in research. *Facebook* produces a weekly updated, quite interesting statistic (October 2012) which maps *Facebook* connec-tivity rates not only of nations but of world cities, which maps a quite different communicative landscape beyond the procedures of meth-odological nationalism. This statistic reveals that the most 'connected' city worldwide is Bangkok with 8.6 million users, followed by Jakarta with 7.4 million and Istanbul, 7 million. Other top ten *Facebook* cities are Bogota, Sao Paulo, Mexico City, Santiago and Mumbai. London is the only 'Western' city among the top ten. Although *Facebook* consti-tutes a multifunctional platform, the degree of 'connectedness' across these world cities to the transnational universe of social and other media (for example, news feeds) reveals that no longer are urban centres in developing regions 'disconnected' but rather in the top ten

Table 3.1   List of top 20 cities on *Facebook*, 2012.

Ranking	City	Country	Users	Penetration %
1	Bangkok	Thailand	8682940	104.74
2	Jakarta	Indonesia	7434580	34.10
3	Istanbul	Turkey	7066700	62.98
4	London	United Kingdom	6139180	73.79
5	Bogota	Colombia	6112120	82.15
6	Sao Paulo	Brazil	5718220	29.88
7	Mexico City	Mexico	4294820	23.30
8	Santiago	Chile	4129700	73.35
9	Mumbai	India	3700460	18.95
10	Buenos Aires	Argentina	3533840	28.52
11	Rio de Janeiro	Brazil	3487300	194.72
12	New York	United States	3420380	17.03
13	Los Angeles (CA)	United States	3405600	23.12
14	Kuala Lumpur	Malaysia	3328240	60.85
15	Paris	France	3062020	29.36
16	Bangalore	India	2931460	44.02
17	Singapore	Singapore	2662680	61.64
18	Ankara	Turkey	2551160	66.96
19	Caracas	Venezuela	2503940	93.78
20	Lima	Peru	2480220	32.00

Source: www.socialbakers.com

for social media use. Although it should be noted that the degree of *Facebook* connectivity does not necessarily relate to new spatial forms of deliberation, it indicates the 'reflective' potential for such a deliberative mechanism. However, as could be observed in the past, specific deliberative forms of this public interdependence rupture as 'viral' publics.

This change of perspective from the nation to the urban centre is quite helpful as it shifts away from the narrowness of the nation as the dominating unit of comparative analysis; a unit of analysis that 'hides' these important new 'vertical' network structures emerging in urban centres of all world regions. A recent study of the 'glocal' media space in Kuala Lumpur has produced interesting insights into the specific ways in which local and transnational news organizations, co-located in Kuala Lumpur, engage with specific public 'densities' of transnational network spaces in this mega city (Firdaus, 2012; Volkmer and Firdaus, 2013), revealing a 'reflective' sphere of journalism organizations. In Malaysia, as Firdaus argues 'political contestation and public discourse largely occurs online through blogs, social media, citizen journalism news sites, and other forms of user-driven networked platforms'. In consequence 'a global surge in social networking media, coupled with a burgeoning of networked young citizens and the rise of a new breed of social media-savvy politicians has expanded Malaysia's political and public spheres to include a networked user-driven media sphere'. This also means that, 'from a journalistic perspective, this development expands the professional journalist's 'news net' . . . to subsequently gather information online, connect with networked news sources, and download content that can be used as news material' (Firdaus, 2012: 101). Another example is the Tunisian uprising in 2011 and the subsequent 'viral' public network created during the Arab Spring, through dense spatial inter-dependence of a social media 'hub' in Sidibouzid, a small town in Central Tunisia, which was 'accelerated' and made densely 'viral' by foreign-educated youth, familiar with the specifics of spatial discourse mechanisms, located in the urban centre of Tunis which, in conse-quence, mobilized deliberative publics as well as transnational news organizations through spatial 'density' existing across Tunisia and beyond (Alqudsi-ghabra, 2012). These are only a few examples of diverse 'reflective' public-sphere 'places' of non-Western regions that engage with a multiplicity of other transnational/spatial public 'nodes' and, often unnoticed, seamlessly overcome the paradigmatic ideal of 'bounded' modern linearity of deliberation.

Reviewing diverse approaches that conceptualize forms of medi-ated deliberation, also reveals processes of fine-lined 'disembedding' of the traditional modern, bounded space of 'inbetween-ness' of deliberation between citizens and democratic institutions that have been articulated in the context of national mass media cultures. For example, Thompson suggests in 1995 that 'mediated publicness' is a dis-embedded space of 'the visible' which is a 'non-localized,' 'non-dialogical' and 'open-ended space'; a space in which 'mediated symbolic forms can be expressed and received by a plurality of non-present others' (Thompson, 1995: 245). Thompson situates such a 'non-localized' space of the 'visible' in the context of electronic mass media where 'producers' and 'recipients' of mediated symbolic forms are 'generally not engaged in a dialogue with one another' (Thompson, 1995: 246). Although, strictly speaking, Thompson's approach is related to the sphere of national mass media as a 'non-dialogical' form of mediated discourse, the term 'mediated publicness' is important here, as it highlights the appropriation of communicative space through, for example, 'action at a distance' where publicness of the 'here' and 'now' imagines absent 'viewers' (Thompson, 1995: 103). Related to crisis 'media events', such 'action at a distance' causes 'concerted responsive action' (Thompson, 1995: 114; Dahlgren, 1995). This appropriation of symbolic public space constitutes in Dahlgren's terminology, 'despatialized simultaneously' where the 'experience of a shared now is uncoupled from the imperatives of physical proximity' (Dahlgren, 2009: 115). This despatialized appropriation of deliberation resurfaces as radical democracy, digital publicness, counter publics and – this is a more recent term – connective activism.

The paradigmatic limitations of the nationally 'bounded' conception of modern 'inbetween-ness' of deliberation are also surfacing in the increasing ambiguity of the scope of political regimes imposing national civic inclusion/exclusion – 'citizens' with a passport and 'exclusion' of 'residents' with a visa. The bounded model of public deliberation is rarely addressed in these contexts where migrants who reside in a country for several years but do not hold citizenship are excluded from formal deliberative mechanism, such as voting, public office and quite often, are excluded from public voice in mainstream national media. However, the politics of inclusion/exclusion in a national terrain is undergoing rapid change. Spichal predicts that 'in the future, the majority of citizens of a nation-state would be non-residents who moved to other countries, and the majority of residents would be non-citizens' (Spichal, 2012: 153); in consequence he suggests that 'taking the democratic principle seriously' makes it necessary to acknowledge that 'the ranks of those who should be entitled to participate in decision making should run even beyond resident non-citizens and non-resident citizens' and within such a mobile modern society of the twenty-first century 'normativity' should 'include all those outside the state's boundaries who may be impacted by the state's decision' (Spichal, 2012: 153). Ambiguities of inclusion/exclusion in not only multi-cultural but transnationally mobile societies are considered as the 'burden of public reason in the liberal state' (Frohock, 1999: 40). In Frohock's understanding, phrased about twenty years ago and visionary at the time, deliberation needs to include the way of reconciliation of claims originating in political differences 'among persons who may have nothing in common except membership in the political system' (Frohock, 1999: 40). However, the assumption of membership of a national community still constitutes the main source of legitimacy based on collective judgement of the people. These examples suggest that the 'internal' boundedness of deliberative discourse not only *vis-à-vis* an assumed 'national', collectively perceived territoriality but also *vis-à-vis* a centrality of modern deliberative democracies is 'shifting' and 'dissolving' in the context of borderless public communication (see also Bohman and Rehg, 1997; Taylor, 2004). In this context, 'the' national public sphere is only one terrain of deliberation within multiple fractured, highly specific 'ad hoc' – publics as dynamically changing inclusive sites not necessarily engaging national citizens but integrating diverse forms of 'communicative action', which is not necessarily based on communication in direct speech but through other forms of 'utterance', and this could be considered as the outcome of a transnational culture of mediation. A culture of mediation of an advanced 'space of the visible' where not only news 'events' but a spectrum of representations, narratives, rituals, images, of ontologically loaded icons and diverse forms of narratives are entangled in a viral form of deliberation in a transnationally interdependent publicness – a dense public 'cluster' *across* layers of communicative networks of public interdependence, which – seamlessly – engages with 'interlocutors' of *diverse* society types. As Couldry notes there are 'new kinds of individual political actors: no longer just the charismatic party or strike leader, or the authorized commentator on mainstream politics . . . but the individual – without any initial store of political authority – who can suddenly acquire status as a significant political actor by acting online' (Couldry, 2012: 121).

Transnational publics and 'fields' of deliberation

Not only deliberative democracy but the conception of transnational 'modern' deliberation seems also to be related to national boundedness *vis-à-vis* the 'centrality' of nation-states. Bohman whose work attempts to articulate new terrains of transnational publics argues for a widening of spheres from (national) 'demos' to (transnational) demoi and a 'distributive public sphere' as a space among publics of 'decentred' demoi (Bohman, 2007: 61). Despite these important extensions caused by decentring processes, his approach seems to relate to 'demoi' of modern nation-states. De-centred 'demoi' are situated in Bohman's approach in spaces of 'unprecedented extent, intensity', and 'speed of social interactions across borders' (Bohman, 2007: 22). As Bohmann has pointed out, the democratizing 'effect of publics' is centred around communicative networks which are as 'dispersed' and 'distributed' as the authority 'with which they interact' (Bohman, 2006: 61). However, these conceptions of 'decentred' publics mainly address the transnational of nation-states in the European context and the transnationalization of nation-state publics (Bohman, 2007).

A second debate situates transnational deliberation within global civil society, however, *vis-à-vis* national and intergovernmental institutions. In these conceptions, deliberation is 'bounded' to national institutional legitimacy and through this angle, engaged with transnational, i.e. intergovernmental institutions from the WTO to the UN and European Union. Such a transnational institutional boundedness or methodological nationalism of democratic legitimacy within the boundaries of a nation-state is often understood as 'international deliberation' (see Gastin, 2008).

A third set of conceptions addresses the transnationalization not so much of deliberation but rather of 'justification' in – what Walzer (1983) once called – 'spheres of justice'. For example, Gutman and Thompson suggest that, although deliberative democracy requires only that 'justifications be given to citizens who are bound by the decisions', citizens of foreign countries are often 'constrained to accept the consequences of the decisions that are the citizens who are legally bound by them' and the authors conclude that the distinction between 'being bound' and 'being significantly affected' begin to 'erode' (Gutman and Thompson, 2004: 37). In their view, the 'globalization of deliberation' (2004: 39) makes 'international institutions more deliberative' as 'domestic forums' in which 'public officials speak to the ordinary citizens of foreign nations'(2004: 39). In this context, 'the role of communication' through the media, the Internet, and international exchanges becomes 'even more important in the international sphere than it is in the domestic sphere' (Gutman and Thompson, 2004: 62).

Conceptions of nationally 'bounded' mediated deliberation, constitute a fourth approach, assessing, for example, 'deliberative conversation' among citizens (see Moy and Gastil, 2006). 'Deliberative conversation' is understood as a national 'problem-solving' conversation, for example in contexts of 'mediated' political conflicts. Early studies in this area focused on specific media forms and the degree of engagement in deliberative conversation, for example between 'public' networks of mediated and interpersonal local contexts. Other approaches address the role of 'agenda setting', mainly relating to a political agenda salience within a national and, less so, transnational spatial forms of agenda constructions and identify the role of parties and the visibility of political actors in mainstream media during election campaigns (see Semetko and Schoenbach, 1994; Hopmann et al., 2010). Others argue for a 'two-step web effect', which suggests an integrative approach to discursive platforms and mainstream media for national election mobilization. The formation of deliberation within 'online' and 'offline' spheres in a national, for example US context, constitutes an emerging research area. Beyond these forms of deliberation, the active engagement with political information in an increasingly complex political communication environment is addressed for example by Yuan (2011) who uses the approach of 'repertoire' (Hasebrink and Popp, 2006) to describe the processes of manoeuvring across new decentralized communicative landscapes, not only of news sources but also of practices and formations of 'convergence'. Hasebrink and Popp suggest a 'repertoire' approach that allows us to assess empirically 'patterns of selection', which incorporates sets of selective communicative processes and 'shifts the empirical approach to news consumption from 'single variables . . . to patterns of selections.' As Yuan argues that such an approach reshifts processes of public agenda setting, for example from national mass media to centralized digital platforms, (Yuan, 2011) and directly engages with the complex active role of the user in negotiating access and participation in diverse forms of mainly national public contexts in such a decentralized public environment.

It is quite interesting to note that deliberation is rarely associated with a move away from the modern bounded 'order' of deliberation. Deliberative spheres are situated between increasingly powerful intergovernmental 'institutional' formations and the 'state' for example, through specific 'thematic' transnational publics in broader spheres of a global civil society. Dryzek's conception of 'discourse democracy' is a broad approach to a 'shared set of concepts, categories, and ideas that provide its adherents with a framework for making sense of situations, embodying judgments, assumptions, capabilities, dispositions, and intentions' (Dryzek, 1990). Deliberation in this space engages with powerful pressure for political 'action', for example, in contexts of violence and genocide, and growing demands for 'justification' of state interference or – and I should add, this also becomes an issue of justification – of non-interference. Kassner develops an interesting argument that if a state's 'sovereignty depended on its proper respect for the demands of justice there would be no justice-based reasons for one state to interfere with the internal affairs of another sovereign state' (Kassner 2013). These moral 'adjustments' to the sovereignty of a state are particularly important as transnational publics deliberate on issues of injustice and 'make them 'public' with often moral implications for governance. The political and humanitarian crisis in Syria is an example for this macro-structure of deliberation where moral obligations to interfere emerge, however, non-interference is justified. 'Live' video footage reporting on violence and demands of 'justice' constitute magnified deliberative discourse beyond the traditional modern 'order' of deliberation.

In cases where approaches attempt to identify deliberative spheres in spatial contexts, these are considered as 'cyber-deliberation' (Siedschlag, 2007: 35). Quite often, these debates magnify the communicative deliberation within the 'virtual' space without identifying the linkages of these spatial forms of deliberation to not only national or even transnational public spheres. Siedschlag proposes a term 'digital deliberation' closely connected to existing public structures 'beyond the boundaries of the nation-state', and involving a broad range of actors (Siedschlag, 2007: 51).

Other approaches position the transnationalization of deliberation in the 'unbounded' complexity of a global civil society in an 'affective arena' (Basset and Smith, 2010: 414), which allows us to overcome the modern linear 'order' of deliberation through what the authors more openly describe as a space for 'critical reflection and affective expression', where discourse relates the co-existence of both 'reason-giving' and 'affect' (Bassett and Smith, 2010: 414). With the term 'affected arena', Bassett and Smith refer to the 'emotional impact' of 'verbal and non-verbal campaigning – pictoral, musical, narrative and the like', which they argue is becoming 'central' to the politics of a global civil society. In this sense, deliberative communication occurs within a global civil society whose members identify themselves 'first' and 'foremost' as members of a national public. The authors note that global civil society 'must encourage participants in transnational public spheres to view themselves as a public' (Bassett and Smith, 2010: 422).

'Public interdependence' is a network of dynamic densities 'across' diverse territories in advanced globalization and deeply (to varying degrees) across different society forms incorporated in the public communication of 'the state' (not only of the nation-state). In this sense even a state-controlled public is no longer an exclusive territorial public but constitutes a communicative 'layer', a 'node' within the horizontal 'interdependence' of public communication. The reality of public communicative practice is already 'disembedded' through what we might call 'fields of deliberation', which emerge in a new space of inbetween-ness, between networks of transnational public interdependence and 'localities'. One example of such a 'field of deliberation' is 'virtual activism' intensifying publicness by simultaneously enhancing geographically dispersed 'local' discourse across transnationally accessible platform-centred activism of resistance and engagement. An example is the virtual activism in the context of human rights abuse in China, emerging through social networking sites and intensively engaging through audiovisual clips on *YouTube* these as a consequence, re-appear in national 'mainstream' media in the USA as well as in highly specific blogs. The post-election conflicts in Kenya and Iran are other examples where discursive connectivity across diverse geographical sites resulted in a governmental change in Kenya and a transnational 'visibility' for local conflict in a region on the periphery of mainstream media. The 'Occupy' movement with its simultaneous protests across world regions is another example of a field of deliberation as is 'virtual Activism' a virtual platform registered as a NGO providing support and training for launching transnational campaigns.

A second example of a 'field' of deliberation between transnational public interdependence and locality is 'fluid' or 'direct' democracy, a form of virtual 'transparency', demanding day-to-day governance accountability through digital 'fluid' transparency. One example is the Pirate Party movement, founded in 2010 with the aim of promoting 'direct', 'liquid' democracy, freedom of information and open content. The Pirate Party movement operates, to illustrate the transnational scope, across about fifty countries including Argentina, Australia, to Greece, UK, Norway Tunisia, Ukraine, Uruguay, Venezuela etc. The Pirate Party is an example of a new form of political agency where decisions are reached less through traditional representational committees than through discursive and egalitarian online 'liquid democratic means', enhancing its influence through the strength of public interdependence across its transnational 'nodes'.

A third 'field' could be described as deliberative 'transparency', which also goes beyond traditional forms of 'publicness'. Deliberative 'transparency' relates to a non-discursive release of 'facts' and 'issues'. This field of deliberation' is often associated with *Wikileaks*, used in the context of new forms of civic deliberation. About a week after the outbreak of the post-election crisis in Kenya, a 'small group of concerned Kenyans, located throughout the diaspora, came together to launch an online campaign called *Ushahidi* to spread awareness about the violence devastating their country' (Goldstein and Rotich, 2008: 5). Besides SMS messaging and blogs, *Ushahidi* was incorporated into *Google* Maps and allowed 'users to zoom in and view satellite images of Kenya, with a tool for users, via mobile phone or Internet browsers, to report incidents of violence on the map, add photos, video, and written content that document where and when violence occurs' (Goldstein and Rotich, 2008: 6). As the authors note, this reporting of violence was a new form of public engagement by 'frustrated citizens', in Kenya and in the Kenyan transnational diaspora.

Subjective 'testimonies' posted on social media sites which – staged across multiplatform 'media events' – counterbalance and dispute official political structures, might also serve as examples of an increasingly influential, though invisible fourth field of deliberation. I will use the campaign of social network communication between Israeli and Iranian citizens as an example. This is an international discursive campaign on *Facebook* for peaceful reconciliation of the political conflict between the two countries, where Israeli and Iranian citizens are enabled to engage with each other. The campaign has been initiated by an individual, an Israeli citizen who began to counterbalance national media conflict frames between Israel and Iran by sending personal messages of sympathy to 'the Iranian people'; this initiated an anti-war campaign by Israeli and Iranian citizens and also by supportive from individuals in the USA and Europe in support. It is a campaign of direct discourse among Israel and Iran which is impossible through national media and has created a new sphere of direct civil society engagement creating a deliberative sphere beyond the state level. As a 'local' outcome of this transnational civic discourse of Israeli and Iranian anti-war sentiments, an initiative against war with Iran has been launched in Israel, accompanied by anti-war protests in Tel Aviv. This *YouTube* 'event' has created a 'live' discourse for about two weeks about the Middle East conflict between individual citizens as 'interlocutors', not only from Israel and Iran and other world regions. These are just examples of increasingly influential fields of deliberation in contexts of not only transnational communication in general but specifically of public interdependence.

Interdependence and 'reflexive' modernity

Despite the assumption of a 'universality' of deliberative discourse developed in the context of modern societies, the ideal that has become a normative model of deliberation is related to the Habermasian understanding of public discourse. However, Habermas' work – and this is sometimes overlooked – suggests a 'reflexive' sphere of debate through communicative action that is not necessarily devoted to a nationally 'bounded' sphere. Habermas argues that the public sphere can be 'best described as a network for communicating information and points of view . . . the streams of communication are, in the process, filtered and synthesized in such a way that they coalesce into bundles of topically specified public opinion' (Habermas, 1996: 360). He extends the scope of the normative structure of the public sphere by arguing that the public sphere distinguishes itself through a communication structure that is related to a 'third feature' of communicative action which refers 'neither to the functions nor to the contents of everyday communication but to the social space generated in communicative action' (Habermas, 1996: 360). A few years later he notes that traditionally 'established obligations rooted in communicative action do not *of themselves* reach beyond the limits of the family, the tribe, the city or the nation' but rather that 'the reflexive form of communicative action behaves differently' and 'argumentation of its very nature points beyond all particular forms of life . . .' (Habermas, 1999).

Habermas seems to address such a 'space' as a somewhat open resonance terrain of communicative action. However, in his work 'reflexive communicative action' is embedded in the paradigm of 'modern', discursive structures that create such a 'social space'. Habermas' notion of reflexive discourse is obviously tied to nationally 'bounded' modern deliberation *vis-à-vis* traditional public institutions, assuming the discourse ethic as the universal discourse principle and assuming that 'the practice of deliberation and justification we call 'argumentation' is to be found in all cultures and societies and that there is no functionally equivalent alternative to this mode of problem solving' (Habermas, 1999: 43). The conceptual embeddedness of such a 'reflexive form of communicative action' in a universal paradigm of modernity is also revealed in Habermas' attempts to situate communicative action in international formations terrains, i.e. between nations. For example, in frameworks of 'postnational' constellations of deliberation in a transnational European context. However, Habermas understands the 'modern' communicative constellations in a larger sphere of reasoned discourse and argues that 'bit by bit, they introduce us to *another* perspective, from which we see the growing interdependence of social arenas, communities of risks, and the networks of shared fate ever more clearly'(emphasis in original Habermas, 2001b: 55).

Habermas' notion of 'reflexive' communicative engagement across the 'growing interdependence' and 'networks of shared fate' is important here. It is important because it signifies the deviation from the traditions of discursive deliberation to reflexive deliberation that might serve in our discussion as a broad conceptual matrix for the understanding of public interdependence as a local, subjective perception of a reflexive resonance 'space'. A perception of interdependent space emerges *across* 'modern' and non-modern societies, between the 'national' and the 'transnational' as reflexive sites of deliberation in an advanced globalized public sphere and relates to 'local' communicative action.

This understanding of 'reflexivity' enables us to locate the resonance 'link' in the larger scope of an interdependent geography of deliberative communication. It is a reflexive 'reciprocal' link, producing networked interdependent forms of deliberation, not only through 'stretched' 'trans-border' formations but as a 'reflexive' deliberative 'local' sphere where, I argue, the national forms of publics constitute a 'node', one site among multiple others. Formations of 'reflexive' space constitute a deliberative global civil society 'arena' (Bassett and Smith, 2010) through an engagement with public terrains of diverse societies. These forms of 'viral' deliberation might relate to what Mary Kaldor defines in a global civil society context as 'zones of civility' (Kaldor, 2003: 6): communicative spaces between various (national) civic identities *beyond* and *within* the state. Globalization approaches, for example in political science and sociology, have addressed interesting terrains of 'deterritorialization' and a macro-scope of 'reflexive space'; however, have they have rarely reflected upon implications for national and transnational public communication.

Some recent debates in political science identify a broader spectrum of 'de-territorialization', political spheres of trans-boundedness that might constitute realms of 'reflexive' spaces of deliberation in non-national territories. For example, de-territorialization of governance emerges in such a sphere of reflexive 'inbetween-ness' through relations to increasingly influential transnational governance institutions such as the WTO and the EU. These spaces emerge without appropriate normative public legitimacy in the context of such a supra-national governance formation among democratic nation-states. The crisis of the euro has revealed the emerging legitimacy gap between national and supranational governance. These structures might relate to what is called a 'post-Westphalian order', refining national statehood in contexts of transnational 'entities'. Habermas has repeatedly pointed towards the gap in formal legitimacy and the lack of a European public sphere.

A second example for a new sphere of 'reflexive' space could also relate to a new transnational connected political class. Often over-looked, a new transnational professional class emerges across financial centres of all continents, including not only the traditional trading centres Frankfurt, New York and London, but also the new financial hubs of Dubai, Mumbai, Singapore, Kuala Lumpur, Beijing. The *Forbes* list of 'Emerging Global Cities' ranking is quite illuminating in this context of new reflexive spaces as it indicates 'global cities' with a high percentage of young, 'aspirational professionals', lists. Global cities are new 'hubs' in this interdependent financial network, such as Chengdu, China with a population of 10 million, Abu Dhabi, Curitiba, Brazil, as well as Tripoli. These emerging transnationally 'connected' sites of 'geo-governance' have increasingly significant implications on the political and economic development of the region. This professional class engages in a transnational interdependent public which shares the same values with peers in other world regions. These new 'non-national' public cultures are rarely addressed in nationally oriented debates of deliberation and have not yet been acknowledged in the emerging debate of public communication in 'developing' regions.

A third example which indicates 'reflexive' spaces of public delib-eration centres around cosmopolitanism and 'a post-Westphalian order in which sovereign statehood and territoriality are loosening their grip on modern political life' (Held, 2010). It is a focus less on the 'relativity' of the boundedness as a 'centre' of territorial 'legitimacy' (for example *vis-à-vis* the Westphalian order) but rather on the – what might be called – the 'normative' relativity of 'accountability' (Held and Koenig-Archibugi, 2005) which constitutes a new important aspect of a transnational interdependent public and, in such a broader context 'scalar' spaces of public deliberation. For example, Nanz and Steffek consider a transnational public accountability as an 'inter-mediate' sphere in contexts of international public organizations where, it is argued, an 'international public sphere – conceived as a pluralistic social realm of a variety of sometimes overlapping . . . publics engaged in transnational dialogue – can provide an adequate political realm with actors and deliberative processes that help to democratize global governance practice' (Nanz and Steffek, 2005: 197). These are just three examples where debates in political science address parameter of what we might call, 'reflexive' spaces of deliberation.

Sociological conceptions of globalization address the de-territorialization of the 'national' by conceptualizing new formations of 'relativistic' globalized spheres in order to further map broader sectors of 'reflexivity' which are also relevant for identifying a deliberative space, between the 'global' and the 'local'. For example, Roland Robertson has argued that 'we must return to the question of the actual form of recent and contemporary moves in the direction of global interdependence and global consciousness' (Robertson, 1992: 22). Robertson understands the 'globalization axis' through the dialectic of 'glocal' relations (Robertson, 1992) which constitute an important 'resonance' sphere for deliberative discourse,

The network paradigm (Castells, 1996) situates transnational trajectories of political, economical, social structures and capitalism in the space of 'node'-'space' relations. The dialectic of such a 'node'-space' relation, constituting, for example, civic identity through renegotiating the centrality and de-centrality of 'nodes' has not only articulated new forms of 'network space' but a networked transborder space of communicative 'depth'. In consequence, Castells understands networked power as a 'reflexive' form as 'the form of power exercised by certain nodes over other nodes within the network' (Castells, 2009: 419).

These network-centred constructions of dialectical relations between 'nodes' and 'spaces' underline the structural shift of societal 'relations' and globalization as 'relativistic interdependence' to the density of 'flows'. Flows, which, following Sassen, adhere with network formations as a 'social logic' (Sassen, 2005: 54) creating public agency through, 'participation of local organizations in global networks.' These processes shape, so Sassen argues, 'elementary forms of transboundary public spheres or forms of globality centred in multiple localized types of struggles and agency' (Sassen, 2005: 54). Sassen identifies the emerging communicative 'densities' through a model of 'multiscalar' processes which absorb local struggles into such 'a global electronic space' (Sassen, 2005: 55). Sassen understands as a consequence of this process – and this is a very important 'side aspect' – that localities constitute 'micro-environments with global span'. (Sassen, 2005: 55). It is what Sassen calls a 'rescaling process' which is incorporates not only transborder 'connections' but rather 'global micro-spaces' (Sassen, 2007b: 7).

Reflexive modernity as a 'bounded' sphere

Sociological debates of globalization address in particular the notions of 'reflexivity'. It is this approach of reflexivity which, although implications on political communication and the public sphere are rarely addressed, help to understand the scope of 'disembedding' and the 'lifting-out' of social relations of modern societies where 'local contexts of interaction' are restructured 'across indefinite spans of time–space ' (Giddens, 1990: 21), resulting in new forms of 'involvement' across 'distance' (Giddens, 1990: 64). Interestingly, the implications – if there are any – for political and public structures are only very broadly raised. Giddens only vaguely subscribes to the formation of 'deliberation' through political issues which 'flow from processes of self-actualization in post-traditional contexts, where globalizing tendencies intrude deeply into the reflexive project of the self, and conversely where processes of self-realization influence global strategies' (Giddens, 1991: 214). In consequence, he articulates the emerging dialectic of global and local relation as the space of 'reflexive' modernity. A reflexive process where 'not just the local community, but intimate features of personal life and the self become intertwined with relations of indefinite time–space extension' (Giddens, 1994: 59). Giddens understands 'reflexivity' as a necessary process as trust as the traditions of society are shifting away and the individual positioning, identity and biography requires justifications within the 'radical modernity' of nation-states. However, it is important to note that in Giddens' approach, 'life politics' as a reflexive subjective is a 'disembedding' process and deeply related to the boundedness of, I should add: the modern, the nation-state.

Modernity is the central 'axis' of this globalization approach which identifies the new dynamics of globalization affecting social life in modern nations where social practices are constantly examined and reformed in the light of incoming information about those very practices, thus constitutively altering their character' (Giddens, 1990: 38). In Giddens' view, reflexivity is deeply tied to modernity and 'constituted in' and 'through reflexively applied knowledge' but the 'equation of knowledge with certitude has turned out to be misconceived'. Giddens argues that 'we are aboard a world which is thoroughly constituted through reflexively applied knowledge, but at the same time we can never be sure that any given element of that knowledge will not be revised' (Giddens, 1990: 39). Giddens understands reflexive 'disembedding' of the self as a key process of modernity. In this sense, modernity 'breaks down the protective framework of the small community and of tradition' and in consequence, the individual 'feels bereft and alone in a world in which she or he lacks . . . the sense of security provided by more traditional settings.'(Giddens, 1991: 33/4). The term 'reflexive awareness' is used by Giddens to identify new terrains of subjective 'confrontation' between 'anxiety' and 'ontological security'. Practical consciousness 'is the cognitive and emotive anchor of the feelings of ontological security' (Giddens, 1991: 36). Giddens identifies an early form of 'reflexive' modernization *vis-à-vis* an early scope of what we might call 'relativistic' globalization in which through a process of 'constant' examining and reforming, the subject repositions itself 'in the light of incoming information' (Giddens, 1990: 38). In this sense, the word reflexive does not – and this is emphatically emphasized by Giddens (1994) and by Beck, 1994 – relate to 'reflection' but rather to the reflexive process of 'self-confrontation' (Beck, 1994: 5), that is, the confrontation of the modern self through perceptions of globalized risk.

> The type of confrontation of the bases of modernization with the consequences of modernization should be clearly distinguished from the increase of knowledge and scientization in the sense of self-reflection on modernization. Let us call the autonomous, undesired and unseen, transition from industrial to risk society reflexivity (to differentiate it from and contrast it with reflection). Then 'reflexive modernization' means self-confrontation with the effects of risk society that cannot be dealt with and assimilated in the system of industrial society . . . The fact that this very constellation may later, in a second stage, in turn become the object of (public, political and scientific) reflection must not obscure the unreflected, quasi-authonous mechanism of the transition. (Beck, 1994: 6).

Giddens' and Beck's conceptions of reflexive globalization are situated in early globalization processes where the 'release' of individuals from modern societies into a global 'risk society' emerged as a core theme of relativistic globalization. It is not only the 'release' of modern subjects (of modern societies) into an uncharted globalized territory resulting in individualization as a form of modern reflexivity of a 'globalized' subject.[1] This process relates to a 'reflexive confrontation,' in particular in Beck's work with globalized 'risks' and, for example, a 'reflexive' view of the world through the horizon of, mainly, 'industrial society' (Beck, 1994: 8). In consequence, 'risk society' is 'by tendency' a 'self-critical' society (experts undercut by opposing experts etc.). 'Individualization' means 'first, the disembedding and, second, the re-embedding of industrial society ways of life by new ones, in which the individuals must produce, stage and cobble together their biographies themselves.' (Beck, 1994:13). In consequence, 'individualization' and 'globalization' are 'two sides of the same process of reflexive modernization' (Beck, 1994:14).

Beck argues that the 'framework' of the nation is 'not overcome.' In Beck's view, 'the foundations of the industries and cultures of the mass media have changed dramatically and concomitantly all kinds of transnational connections and confrontations have emerged. The result is that cultural ties, loyalties and identities have expanded beyond national borders and systems of control. Individuals and groups who surf transnational television channels and programmes simultaneously inhabit different worlds'. However, Beck builds his argumentation of 'self-confrontation' as a 'reflexive' sphere of globalization *vis-à-vis* the nation-state (and, for example, not other state formations) and does not provide a deeper insight into the transformative 'moments' of continuous networked communication on the sphere of 'reflexive' self confrontation in contexts of other state formations. Networked communication goes far beyond a notion of 'transnational television channels' and public implications of these new complexities of communication transform could be related to Beck's notion of 'reflexivity' and such a reflexive sphere repositions public communication.

It is quite interesting that the discussion of de-territorialization processes relate mainly to the modern 'nation-state' and less so to other state formations. The outcome of which is that mainly the nation-state is being reflected in increasingly entangled relation to transnational densities of globalized taxonomies and not other states as sites of particular and specific globalization structures. Examples are Beck's term 'sub-politics' and new forms of 'risk-politics' which are mainly conceptualized in traditionally national contexts of 'media publicity, citizen's initiatives, new social movements' (Beck, 1992: 222).

The notion of such a process of 'reflexive modernity' and in fact, the notion of the term 'reflexivity' itself highlight in Beck's context – and this point is important for our discussion – the limitations of modern globalization as it not so much conceptualizes the extension of modernity *into* a globalized transnational/non-modern sphere but rather reveals – what I would describe as – the *limitations* of modernity *within* such a globalized context. In this context 'reflexivity' is used as a paradigmatic 'tool' to address limitations of modernity in such a globalized multi-directional territory. In this sense the self-referential resonance of globalization on modern political institutions and civic identity[2] rare ways to address the nonterritorial, non-national space of 'reflexivity', such as the perceptions of 'global risks'. It seems that the emerging sphere of transnational political communication has, indeed, not only further shifted the process of 'disembedding' that is the 'lifting out' of local life from 'localized contexts' (Giddens, 1990, 53) but over time – and the advanced complexity is rarely addressed – transformed the conceptual parameters of a modern 'national' public through new structures of trans-border communication via continuous transnational, transborder or 'spatial' networked spheres of seamless 'flows'. In this sense, public parameters not only relate (and I am 'radicalizing' Beck's argument here) both to the 'disembedding' of individuals from the assumed traditional social – i.e. public – structures of modern nation-states and the rising awareness of global risks but rather the 'disembedding' of parameters of the modern conception of a normative public sphere.

I argue that today's advanced globalization radicalizes transnational 'connections' in such a way that these 'links' are becoming fractured and dense and reach deep into lifeworlds and – through this communicative mechanism – accelerate and intensify the discourse of 'self-confrontation'. This is a self-confrontation that, in Gidden's and Beck's approach relates to reflexivity of identities. However, in today's advanced and communicatively increasingly dense globalized communication sphere such an identity is a discursive self confrontation embedded in a subjective public 'locality'. I would like to add that Beck's recent work begins to re-think 'self confrontation' in a terrain of transnational interdependence, less as a discursive 'acceleration' but rather as a globalized social structure through, for example, 'cosmopolitanization of lifeworlds' (Beck, 2006) and, more recently, a sphere of 'generational' experience (Beck and Beck-Gernsheim, 2009; see also Volkmer, 2006). However, it is Beck who at least constructed some link between 'reflexivity' and – in very general terms – the larger scope of the public sphere as the 'world risk society' creates 'the reciprocal relationship between the public sphere and globality' (Beck, 2005: 39). It is this, in my view, new form of 'reflexive' layering of globally interdependent subjective forms of reflexivity, and the 'locality' as a 'resonance' terrain of legitimacy which might have been invisible in the time of the early 1990s but which constitutes today a deliberative sphere of reflexive re-embedding. In this sense, it is important to understand globalized network formations not only as a transnational media form but in the larger conception of a continuous subjective 'public' self-confrontation *vis-à-vis* globalized communicative networks which in such a dialectic constitute a 'reflexive' form of public communication. This is a new 'reflexive' public space which relates to a re-thinking of deliberation beyond the modern conception.

It seems that Beck understands these increased forms of 'reflexive' proximity in larger contexts of an 'epistemological' shift in the globalization debate. This epistemological shift emerges through the disintegration of the national 'outlook' *vis-à-vis* what he calls 'cosmopolitanization'. Beck is right in pointing out – through this 'outlook' approach – that these advanced forms of globalization 'de-ontologize' (Beck, 2006:17) social structures. However, Beck's analysis does *not* reflect the role of transnational communicative spheres in the 'disenchantment' of categories of modern social theory, nor the power of communicative relations to reflexively re-ontologize social structures in a transnational context with consequences for the relationship between legitimacy and territoriality. Epistemological shifts of globalization are addressed in Beck's approach as 'cosmopolitan outlook', such as the 'glass world' of 'boundary-lessness' (Beck, 2006: 8), as cosmopolitanization, in a way an epistemological 'network', not only of transnational interdependencies but multiple 'loyalties', such as an increased engagement of 'non-state actors' and new forms of political institutions that are constituted and continuously constructed and reconstructed through communicative spheres. These processes help to understand formations of 'horizontal' 'spans', for example, institutional or civic interdependencies.

Interdependence as 'reflective' space of 'inbetween-ness'

We see phenomena of transboundary loyalties emerging in debates of citizenship and new forms of public agencies that not only suggest a political unbundling of what Beck calls 'methodological nationalism' and of 'civic territoriality. For example, in contexts of Western media and network cultures Mossberger suggests to understand public communication in the terrain of 'digital citizenship' (Mossberger et al., 2008). Such a 'spatial' civic territoriality is deeply embedded in the lifeworld not so much as public/private dichotomous sphere which is the Habermasian theme, but as a subjectivization of public life not as a somewhat passive 'exposure' to digital media but rather subjectively chosen discursive cross-referencing and cross-framing of information resources. In this sense, coming back to the more general discussion of deliberation in contexts of transnationalization, these processes reposition globalization not as a spatial extension, but as a spatial *contraction*.

Other debates reconceptualize citizenship in a 'post-Westphalian', non territorial context as communities of shared fate, for example, the mass protesters and activists. In this sense, citizenships of globalization seem to define the conceptions of community in terms of an inter-related sphere of action. We could argue that, historically, these communities of 'shared fate' were perceived as enhancing national collective identity (from Heidegger to Weber) and emerged around humanitarian contexts in early globalization debates. However, what has changed are the frameworks of the trans-territorial nexus of public community. This is the crucial point not only of global and local engagement and of public 'inbetween-ness'. These are the processes that have implications on statist and national publics which are related to a larger globalized public community nexus, 'reflected' in the space of inbetween-ness: a space of inbetween-ness between a public community nexus and the subjective discursive 'self-confrontation'. The nation-state and the different construction of the public with the (static) nation-state paradigm are less the crucial issues here than, arguing with Sassen, the 'embeddedness of the global in the national' and the 'renegotiation of national encasements' (Sassen, 2007a: 80), through such a space of inbetween-ness are important new spheres, reshaping public spheres in various society types, where the lifeworld sphere constitutes a reflective node of supra- and sub-national public territories. It is this lifeworld embeddedness that creates the new space of inbetween-ness of deliberation, not between 'the state' and 'the people' but between globalized public trajectories and local action.

Formations of the public dynamics of de-nationalized communicative 'flows' have been discussed for some time. Urry has used the term 'fluidity' in his critique of 'container' thinking (Urry, 2003); 'transcultural thickenings' is another term used to describe phenomena of 'flows' (Couldry and Hepp, 2012). Whereas these concepts are important in cultural contexts, the political implications of communicative cultures of such a 'fluidity' and 'thickening' for public discourse are rarely addressed. I would argue that these processes further enhance the de-nationalizing and the de-territorializing of public communication across the 'glass world' (Beck, 2006: 8) of 'horizontal' interdependent publics but, in addition, a vertical shift of this axis positions the sphere of public deliberation deeply in the 'locality' of the subjective 'lifeworld'. The subjectively selected appropriation of public spaces by citizens in Tehran, Hong Kong, San Francisco and Berlin, made by means of subjective choices of smart phone apps, *Facebook* news feeds, subjective choices of satellite television, subjective choices of social media and subjective choices of national news channels creates a discursive horizon where the 'national and the 'international' merge in the density of lifeworld specific public interdependence. In this sense, the traditional modern dichotomy of private and public dissolves in a subjectively perceived horizon of deliberately chosen public spaces. Due to these new communicative formations, public deliberation is no longer exclusively oriented towards the 'ideal' speech situation, which hides large scopes of deliberative discourse. The 'reality' of discourse across networks of public interdependence reveals a sphere of diverse forms of discursive 'representation', of narratives but also icons and images which constitute 'meaning' and 'relevance' in an advanced globalized media culture. Some years ago, Latour suggested that we understand public communication through 'objects' as new forms of representative 'assembly' in the 'res publica' of a public space (Latour, 2005). Couldry understands discursive rituals around mediation as a deliberative space that helps sufficiently to include the new structures of publicness and, through this, of public deliberation (Couldry, 2012).

The space of inbetween-ness constitutes not only a sphere 'contraction' – of disembedding/re-embedding across communicative layers but as a second dimension, a sphere of the de-bracketing of the state–society 'nexus', through the opening of disembedded-re-embedded-'ness' as an epistemological space of 'inbetween-ness' – not only between the global and the local or the nation as a site of globalization but between 'the world' and 'me' – which constitutes the 'reflective' dialectic form of deliberation in communicative globalization at the core of new forms of transnational publics. It is this 'reflective' dialectic that is at the centre not only of what might be called communicative globalization and transnational public deliberation. This process is the epistemological shift that relates to the macro-structural developments of deterritorialized spaces and the transformation of the nation to a 'local' site of globalization, but also to micro-structures of an emerging transnational public sphere as a crucial component of today's globalization process. It is less a 'global' extension than the 'resonance' of such an extension, which emerges as an important sphere of the transnational interdependence. It is the dialectical process of the global/local 'extension' of micro-transnationalization through the 'reorienting of national agendas towards global ones' (Sassen, 2006). In the dense dialectical spaces of 'contraction' transnational public communication reconfigures national/statist and, indeed, local contexts.

It seems that the networked structure of public discourse shapes 'zones' of 'self-confrontation' through 'reflective' contraction across a globalized public interdependence. The public space of 'inbetween-ness', located between subjective 'locality' and public interdependence, continuously 'reflects' the local/subjective lens back into the flows of borderless networks of (transnational) loyalties and political agency. In this sense such a 'reflective' or discursive 'mirroring' process is re-embedding territorial statist publics through a 'reflective' subjective 'place-ness'. Public deliberation is disembedded from the dialectical relation between global institutions and nations to globalized 'reflexivity' of 'local' contexts as a public epistemology. The density of public interdependence emerges in this 'reflective' context as a space of deliberation across world regions.

I use the term 'reflective' inbetween-ness for a communicative sphere in the dense nexus of advanced globalization. Such a 'reflective' sphere of inbetween-ness is characterized by four 'disjunctures': the first disjuncture relates to the opening up, the 'de-bracketing' of the normative modern 'inside/outside' – or 'domestic/foreign' – dichotomy and the 'linearity' of international communication. A second disjuncture relates to the reflective sphere of inbetween-ness as a shift away from 'reflexive' modernity because it allows the articulation of globally dispersed densities of public interdependence to become a communicative 'resonance' on diverse forms of subjective 'locality' – beyond the boundedness of society types. The third disjuncture positions 'reflective' inbetween-ness as reflective globalization because it shifts the axis of globalization from 'reflexive' modernity as a consequence of the loosening up of the horizontal boundedness of a national 'order' – this results in the self-repositioning of the subject in the 'vertical' sphere of 'reflective' public interdependence as an active discursive self-confrontation in the universe of network flows. A fourth disjuncture relates to subjectively selected public trajectories that merge in a space of 'inbetween-ness' as a reflective sphere, this, takes on different 'public shapes' across various society types and, thus, constitutes a disjuncture from 'the nation'.

Through such a density of public interdependence and the 'linking' of geographically dispersed interlocutors, the space of inbetween-ness opens up the state–society nexus as public density, released from territorial boundaries and embedded across the communicative spaces of a globalized civil society. This 'de-bracketing' process of the normative state–society nexus in the national public sphere allows us, for example, to 'reflect' the state from 'outside'. In this sense, globalized communication is no longer a process of time-distance 'stretching' relations where events are shaped but public interdependence is 'live' simultaneous discourse and engagement in worldwide subjective 'resonance' localities. This approach builds on Giddens' understanding of reflexive modernity (1994); however it takes this further as the state (and not only the modern nation-state), which is now 'reflectively' perceived from 'outside' from 'within'. Reflective globalization constitutes a communication sphere across public interdependence and allows us to identify exposure to a multiplicity of 'reasoned' public deliberation. Not only modern European nation-states but all societies are, however, through diverse formations, drawn into such a 'de-bracketing process' through forms of public interdependence. We are so used to the ordering of national communication spheres as methodological nationalism that have become increasingly problematic in social science research; for example, Held and McGrew argue 'By eroding the distinctions between the domestic and the international, endogenous and exogenous, internal and external, the idea of globalization directly challenges the "methodological nationalism". This is the crucial area of new formations of not only "digital space" but rather a "deliberative space", emerging between the shifting away of the normative "congruence" of "territoriality" and "legitimacy"' (Held and McGrew, 2006). The de-bracketing of media space is most visible through satellite footprints which stretch across regions, are

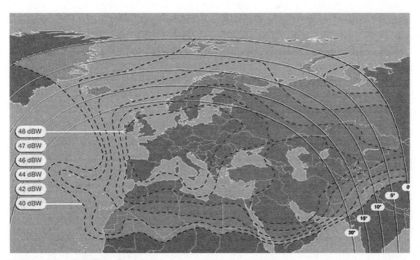

Figure 3.2 Satellite footprint.
Satellite footprints deliver the communicative spaces across landmasses and create arbitrary zones of communication. The European and North African 'footprints' merge into a common information space across central Europe to North Africa and the Middle East.

not congruent with national borders and, as shown on the image above, seamlessly merge European and African satellite communication into a 'common' information space.

Reflective inbetween-ness goes beyond globalized social forms of 'distant proximities' (Rosenau, 2003), which incorporate local sites of globalization but do not relate to the continuous dynamic reflection of 'distant proximity' within communicative spheres. The approach also goes beyond 'spatial relations', which, for example, have been addressed in early conceptions of what Tomlinson understood as 'deterritorialization' as the 'reach' of 'connectivity' into 'the localities in which everyday life is conducted and experienced' (Tomlinson, 2006: 152).

Reflective inbetweenness relates to a continuous communicative 'self confrontation' of the subject in contexts of public interdependence. Such an interdependence could be understood as civic 'links'. Ferguson and Mansbach (2004) conceptualize 'links', for example, as 'fates of people everywhere' who have become linked and suggest that in these contexts citizens' expectations are expanding in such a way that 'the demands they place on institutions are multiplying' (Ferguson and Mansbach, 2004: 28). Besides these civic 'links' raising political connectedness and renegotiating the relationship between citizens and institutions, Sassen's theory of 'links' relates to the 'embeddedness' of 'digital space' and highlights the space between the 'digital' and 'non-digital' domains, the 'destabilizing of existing hierarchies' and the 'mediating cultures which organize the relation between technologies and users/actors' (Sassen, 2006: 343). Sassen argues that 'the spatialities and temporalities that are produced in these various networks and domains do not simply stand outside the national. They are partly inserted in, or arise from, the national and hence evince complex imbrications with the latter' (Sassen, 2006: 378). She notes in more general terms that 'today's novel assemblages' can be a 'highly disruptive insertion' into 'the national as container of social life' (Sassen, 2006: 379). Sassen argues that 'the insertion of global projects, coming not only from the outside but also from inside of the national, produces a partial unbundling of national space and hence potentially the national spatio-temporal order' (Sassen, 2006: 381).

It is difficult to assess more deeply frameworks of such a space as inbetween-ness. What comes to mind is Habermas' concept of 'interpenetration' of 'lifeworld' and 'system' (Habermas, 1987), which causes the 'need' for forms of communicative action. Habermas understands interpenetration also as a link between lifeworld and world consciousness. Habermas argues that while 'participants in interaction turn "towards the world", reproduce through their accomplishment of mutual understanding the cultural knowledge upon which they draw, they simultaneously reproduce their memberships in collectivities and their identities' (Habermas, 1987: 139). It is the cultural reproduction of lifeworld where the 'continuity and coherence are measured by the *nationality* of the knowledge accepted as valid' (Habermas, 1987: 140, emphasis in original). 'Centred worldviews that do not yet allow for a radical differentiation of formal world-concepts are, at least in their core domains, immunized against dissonant experiences . . . in the experiential domain of normatively guided interaction, however, a social world of legitimately regulated interpersonal relations detaches itself only gradually from the diffuse background of the lifeworld' (Habermas, 1987: 133). The discursive density of public interdependence is no longer a 'system' as in the times of mass media and the early forms of transnational satellite communication, not only deeply interwoven into the lifeworld but rather situating the lifeworld in trajectories of networked communication. Whereas in the Habermasian context, 'these contexts of relevance are concentrically ordered and become increasingly anonymous and diffused as the spatiotemporal and social distance grows' (Habermas, 1987: 123), the sphere of interpenetration is situated between de- and re-embedding. It is such a 'reflective public' which merges not only the Habermasian private/ public dichotomy but the national and the transnational to a new form of subjective public 'localism' where not only different media forms amalgamate but where network places represent new forms of public community.

The axis of public interdependence is no longer the nation, rather the 'lifeworld' as a space of the communicative 'reflection' of multiscalar globalized networks. It is *this* space where public communication emerges as a space of deliberation as a 'public space of inbetween-ness'. Such a space of inbetween-ness opens up a discourse space which involves transnationally dispersed interlocutors as new forms of public agency. These forms cut across traditional public agency and institutions and create communicative loyalties that have implications for notions of national identity, citizenship, political legitimacy and constructions of 'the other'. These phenomena are not only characteristic in the Western world but also in other world regions. For example, youth in Morocco, perceive web chats not only as liberating because they are not allowed to express certain opinions in the national public sphere and as providing 'access to the world' (Braune, 2008: 82). However, as Sassen has argued, localized struggles by actors who are not globally mobile are 'nonetheless critical for the organizational infrastructures of a globally networked politics: it is precisely the combination of localized practices and global networks that makes possible a new type of power for actors who would be seen as powerless in terms of conventional variables' (Sassen, 2006: 383).

Whereas developing regions are often perceived in a Western perspective through the 'digital divide', media imperialism or post-colonialism debates that are relevant for assessing the particularities of transnationalization, more recently debates focus on new areas of public engagement in contexts of communicative networks. Over recent years, more attention has been given to political engagement in networked structures in non-modern societies where, for example, 'new media' 'supplement' but do not 'supplant' old media, and it is argued that 'a majority of African countries are still locked in systems of political-communicational centralization (Banda, Mudhai and Tettey, 2009: 3). Without overly generalizing the diversity of African nations and undermining the digital divide and the fact that large segments of citizens in the quite diverse African nations are not 'connected, it seems to be important also to address the cultures of connectedness and gain an understanding of the local implications of globalized communicative spheres, to assess the dimensions of 'resonance' of transnational public interdependence on deliberation. As Frere and Kiyindou point out in contexts of francophone Africa, despite the fact that only a minority of the population is engaged in these new global networks, 'their contribution to democracy cannot be underestimated (Frere and Kiyindou, 2009: 79). The authors argue, that in the context of francophone Africa, access to a supranational digital sphere is considered crucial, as is the ability to constitute virtual communities and engage in cross-border networks (Frere and Kiyindou, 2009: 77). Furthermore, the state monopoly of monitoring the inflow of 'foreign' news is no longer possible, African governments have 'hardly any grip on the choices of the Internet user-consumer, who can freely choose the information that is interesting or useful and decide to join a particular 'virtual community' (Frere and Kiyindou, 2009: 78). The particular reflective 'resonance' sphere in Frere and Kiyindou's account of the digital transformation seems to reconfigure local political engagement through engaging with transnational discourses. As the authors note, 'the Internet has given more capacity to local civil society associations and organizations to exchange concerns and ideas with counterparts abroad. Pressure groups, including cultural minorities, have become more visible and, therefore, generally are more able to make themselves, heard, thanks to the web' (Frere and Kiyindou, 2009: 78). In this sense it reinforces civic consciousness locally, but it is also a tool of globalization that leaves less and less power within local civil society to influence decision makers (Frere and Kiyindou, 2009: 85). 'It allows a growing input from the diasporas into local debates and processes' (Frere and Kiyindou, 2009: 85). As outlined in this account, we might argue that the public interdependence between citizens and 'expatriates' seems to reposition civic deliberation in larger transnational contexts, disembedding the local community.

Other recent debates address the implications of transnational publics for generational specific engagement. This is another example of the 'resonance' of public interdependence in 'developing' countries with large youth segments. This youth generation, particularly in cities, is 'connected' and increasingly actively involved in public spaces and transnational activism. The Mexican sociologist Reguilo describes the implications for 'local' deliberation through such a globalized engagement in the context of Central America: 'I find that the protest movements with a global reach, and the presence of leadership of young people in them, bring to mind the emergence of a new political cosmopolitanism among youth. Its native land is the world, and its strength lies in its (seeming) absence of structure, its intermittence and the multiple nodes in which its utopia is anchored' (Reguilo, 2009: 34). In her analysis the young generation in Central America is on the one hand 'disconnected and unequal', on the other, mainly in urban areas of these nations, 'well situated, connected and globalized', has access to education and technology (Reguilo, 2009: 23) and is increasingly engaged in national and transnational youth publics. Other authors seem to support these emerging youth publics in other developing regions: Arvizu suggests we identify 'mediated' youth agency around conceptual forms of local youth publics as 'networks of publicity' in Cairo (Arvizu, 2009: 387); Tufte et al. discuss forms of 'communicative' youth activism in Tanzania (Tufte et al., 2009); and Munoz-Navarro (2009) addresses social engagement in Chile (Munoz-Navarro, 2009).

From this transnational viewpoint, 'diasporic' communities are seen as supranational public spheres. For example as Lius argues, 'the Chinese Ethnic Internet has developed as an ideal channel for Chinese immigrants to unite themselves in order to protect the Chinese community in their host countries', which relates to protests about the media image of China in the USA, to influencing immigration policies (Liu, 1999:197).

Reflective inbetween-ness in contexts of 'diaspora' – the case of Arab communities in Europe

It might be useful to discuss the sphere of reflective inbetween-ness in some more detail in the context of 'diaspora' communication. 'Diaspora' communication is articulated as a dialectical space of 'subnational', 'displaced' minority cultures and hegemonic national identity. Diaspora debates have been associated with nostalgic 'imagined communities' (Anderson, 1983) or powerless 'sphericules' (Gitlin, 1998) but, viewed through the lens of public interdependence, constitute an active trans-national public terrain, seamlessly engaging on supranational levels. Although the term 'diaspora' – in itself a paradigmatic relict of the modern mass media culture of the nation-state – highlights important spheres of socio-cultural identity politics of mobile and migrant com-munities, it seems to overshadow the emerging complexity of transna-tional migrant publics as highly politicized and contested new terrains of public deliberation and legitimacy. Diaspora or 'migration' is often addressed through methodological nationalism, which does not allow us to assess the scope and structure of transnational relations. Glick Schiller has recently suggested entirely abandoning the approach of methodological nationalism in this context. She suggests 'rejecting methodological nationalism' as it would allow migration scholars 'to recover an approach to migration that does not use nation-states as units of analysis but rather studies the movement of people across space in relationship to forces that structure political economy' (Glick Schiller, 2010: 35).

As Kivisto and Faist note, minority cultures are 'engaged in activi-ties designed to define and enhance their position in the receiving nation, while simultaneously seeking to remain embedded in a par-ticipatory way in the everyday affairs of the homeland community' (Kivisto and Faist, 2010: 143). It is a particular 'embedded' 'social space' a nexus of supranational community and subnational spaces. However, it seems that many migrant studies, as Glick Schiller argues, do not address 'these contradictions' in the framework of social theory, 'especially those concerned with public policy, respond to contem-porary attacks on migrants and migration by adopting the perspective of their respective nation-states . . .' through a 'methodological nation-alist' approach (Wimmer and Glick Schiller, 2002). Other debates argue that it is important to 'bring agency back into the picture' (Faist, 2010: 18). In particular, digital connections, between country of residence and country of birth enable the a new cultural and social 'inbetween-ness' and address implications on identity and 'cultural particularity in the national context where they live, in relation to their homeland and within a broader diaspora of people claiming a space in a transnational decentralized community' (Georgiou, 2006: 142). Today, these debates either merge as varied forms of cosmopolitanization' (Beck, 2006: 4) and 'banal transnationalization' or – in the narrow context of diasporic debates – shift towards being a transnationally compressed almost post-global but rarely address dense and highly specific 'resonance' on subjective networked communication. In recent sociological debates, the reflective dichotomy of migrant cultures is constructed through ontologies of transboundedness: 'double consciousness' and 'bifocality'.

Through globalization and the positioning of diaspora as spheres of resistance between the 'local' within the 'global', the spheres of public interdependence of intersubjective loyalties and political agency, dynamically fluctuating within *and* beyond the boundedness of nation-states, have created new forms of deliberative migrant communities. Transnational 'migrant' publics constantly engage with ranges of transnational and national publics. These are emerging public formations that are no longer romanticized expatriate communities but highly dynamic transnational networks of loyalties that not only constantly communicate across national boundaries of 'home' and 'host' country, but, in a micro-perspective communicatively situated in the reflective space of inbetween-ness, continuously 'intertwine' the political agenda of dual national public spheres. This 'reflective' dichotomy of transnational public formations as a form of deliberation has been addressed, for example, in social sciences for some time: for example, the German sociologist Ferdinand Toennies famously identified forms of a deliberative dialectic between 'Gemeinschaft' (boundedness of kinship/community) and 'Gesellschaft' (boundedness of a rational/ moral society) in modern societies. However, in the context of the study on media and citizenship conducted among Arab communities in six European countries, such a 'reflective dichotomy' of linking two public spheres reveals not so much a double contingency of 'being here and being there' but rather a particular form of subjective 'reflection' of the engagement with multiple publics. This process of 'being here' and 'being there' is expressed in the following citation by a respondent:[3]

'Before we received Arab channels, it was for me a must to watch the *Tagessschau* (the prime time German news programme, I.V.) every day. Now, since we have Arab channels, I watch less and less German media.

> Now I hardly watch German TV anymore. Only *Jazeera, Jazeera, Jazeera, Jazeera!* Sometimes when I am fed up with *Al Jazeera* news, when they continue repeating it all over again, I try another TV station, like for example, Mustaqbal, only as a variation' (FG6: 3).

These are phenomena that overcome the traditional sphere of 'diasporic' communication through the density of compressed communicative spaces situated in trans-border societies or what Kvisito and Faist describe as 'living with one foot in two places' (Kivisto and Faist, 2010: 142). Such a communicative density could be described as 'public trajectories' which link national public spheres structurally and thematically and reveal very fine lines of reflective public engagement spaces. The following citation reflects new forms of deliberative practices:

> I installed the satellite in the room next to the window behind the curtain. They have to know that we are very much connected. We have an issue of a nation, a territory and rights. Not only our land is lost, but also our rights are lost . . . It is not permitted that we protest . . . Because of that we must be connected all the time to our countries, citizenship or belonging is not only a piece of paper that makes me become German. It is in the heart, feelings. People have to give you the feeling that you are welcome and part of it. (FG2, 25-45 years: 7)

As this citation of a respondent who is Palestinian illustrates, a public 'trajectory' or intersection relating to a 'horizontal' component of a constant link to 'our countries' also reveals a 'vertical' component reflecting what Roger Silverstone might have called 'symbolic power of connectivity'. The unpacking of such a 'communicative density' reveals an interesting framework of 'public trajectories' for the repositioning not only of the political but of public 'connectivity' as public deliberation. In our study, specific forms of public trajectories as reflective space of reterritorialized proximity emerged in a generational specific way.

> The German media tries to present conflicts in a short way. You get the feeling that they are not telling the real story. There is some kind of bias against you. Or you think that they are in a way against you, when you see that they are ignoring various issues. (FG3: 7)

The process of 'reciprocal filtering' is slightly different in the middle generation; whereas the members of the 45+ claim to watch entirely Arab channels, members of this cohort tend to watch German channels;

however they reflect German channels through the agenda setting of Arab television:

> Frankly, I watch two channels, *Al Jazeera* and *Iqraa*. . . . The German channels do not see us as a victim, they see only the other side, Israel, as a victim . . . The German TV shows only a false story' (FG2: 7); or concluding: 'German TV does not present a lot of news from Arab countries. It is only a short and incomplete coverage.

In the middle generation, respondents are much more critical of German media. The criticism is always linked to the fact that German television does not sufficiently cover conflicts in Arab countries and the way German media constructs and frames these conflicts. 'For example at the time of the incidents in Lebanon . . . they [German news] did not show the other side of the conflict . . . the news were skipping something' (FG5: 6).

For the young group (18–24), Arabic channels do not have the same meaning as for their parents' generation. Having been raised in Germany, they are not fluent in Arabic and watch mainly German channels, for example, news.

> Of course because I live in Germany, I hear first the German news. But they don't cover issues in detail . . . After that I move directly to Arab news, trying to find out through *Al Jazeera* online on the Internet, or try to read the Arab newspapers as well on the web. TV and Internet are very important to me. (FG1: 1)

However, although they might not be fluent in Arabic and just watch 'images', respondents agree that it is important to have access to Arab TV channels. Whereas the older group simply 'scans' German channels but heavily relies on Arab television for news and information, this young group due to their language competence but also their socialization in Germany seems to be actively engaged with both media cultures: 'Political news in the first place, but also social news. For social news, however, I do not watch channels like *Al-Arabiya* or *Al Jazeera*, but the homepage of 'Syrian news' . . . On the international level, I feel that the news of *Al Jazeera* and *Al Arabiya* are better than the German news. The German channels report more on local issues, mostly not political but German economic issues.' In this sense, 'trajectories' constitute not only a subjective sphere of linking national public communication but allow to reposition diasporic communities as active and deliberative publics in a transnational context.

These forms of a space of inbetween-ness are not only related to transnational diasporic 'localities' in the state-minority nexus and to larger contexts of 'reflexive unbundling' of the centrality and decentrality of the state. Globalized public communication emerges not only through network structures but rather more specifically through micro-structural 'reflexive' transnationalization, that is, as epistemological and ontological spheres of complex overlapping communicative 'layers' of, indeed, public spaces. These – through quite different forms of dialectics – shape world 'consciousness' and transnational normative constructions of legitimacy. In the advanced globalization process, it is not just about 'subjects' but about 'public subjects' within public 'assemblage' formations.

The term 'reflective' incorporates the (non-normative) 'space' of transnational public communication in a general way. In this sense 'reflective' globalization includes publics operating in the networked structure of dialectical political reflexivity. The term also allows us to include specific terrains of deliberation *within* globalization. Many of these new forms of public life cannot be captured by other globalization paradigms, since public communication is a complex structure, incorporating not only 'mediated' but communicative forms. Only very recently has, for example 'diaspora' been more deeply integrated into a transnationalized form of 'locality'.[4] However, what is often overlooked is the transnational public space where local media from countries 'of origin' create a particular 'transnational' public sphere among diasporic communities. I describe this process as 're-territorialization', which creates a new form of transnational public space. Other debates reposition the communicative sphere of a nation, for example, Knudsen (2010: 42), who argues that 'the reinventions of homelands are important cultural re-embedding strategies' are the core areas of advanced globalization. It is in these debates where not only 'inbetween-ness' has been defined as a particular 'public space' and where these particular public spaces are becoming increasingly transnationalized.

These are the new spaces of 'interpenetration' emerging in transnational communication where the national public is framed through a transnational understanding. These are the overlaps of 'publicity' and 'publicness' which merge in the Habermasian context but which need to be detached in a globalized public space. It seems that globalization is not only a new horizontal accumulation of various globalizations, but in addition a 'vertical' structure where constructions of globalizations (and the plural is deliberate here) influence local public discourse. In this sense, it is not only relevant to understand the new diverse forms of globalization being articulated by economists, political science, cultural contexts, along gender lines and technologies, and, as I have argued elsewhere, that 'interpenetration' is no longer a deterritorialized, 'negative space' but constitutes a new sphere of discursive reflexivity in the global public domain (Volkmer, 2007: 58). Modernity relates to nations and states and globalization to communities of an extra-societal kind (Volkmer, 1999: 55). This is an important distinction which is represented in the dual approach to globalization.

Deliberative democracy has established a 'normative model of self governance' and 'deliberation offers the conditions whereby citizens can widen their limited and fallible perspectives by drawing on each other's knowledge and experience' (D'Entreves, 2002, 2006: 25) *vis-à-vis* representative institutions. Furthermore, deliberative democracy is 'an association whose affairs are governed by the public deliberation of its members', and in consequence, public deliberation is viewed as shaping the identity and interests of citizens in ways that contribute to the formation of public conception of common good' (Cohen, 1988: 19). The dialectic between deliberative democracy and deliberative discourse has been further refined around issues of, for example 'civic obligations' *vis-à-vis* the 'public good' (Festenstein, 2002, 2006) or 'dialogue' as a means of deliberation and in the Habermasian model to normative consent and legitimacy.

In conceptions of media and globalization, it is argued that in neo-liberal globalization the local represents a site of resistance and 'renegotiation' of globalized media content (see, for example, Sparks, 2000; Lie and Servaes, 2000). In this sense the globalized media sphere is mainly perceived as a corporate single world-flow structure. Hafez (2007) notes that media research has 'allowed itself to be infected by the new euphoria of globalization', for example, 'naive concepts such as the "global village", the "network society", or the "globalization of culture"'(Hafez, 2007: 5). However, Hafez asserts that a 'synthesis' of local cultures emerges, for example in local contexts of 'migration' and as an example for 'localized' network spaces. Hassan argues for a more diverse perception of networks in order to identify the emerging power structures. He notes that 'the networked society is . . . at the same time an integrated and *global political society* – but one where the locus of political power has shifted decisively from relatively stable institutional forums to the rather more volatile settings for corporate boardrooms' (Hassan, 2007: 54). In his view, localities are created through 'connected asynchrony' with own 'temporal contexts' (Hassan, 2007: 51). And a more recent debate identifies forms of 'net locality' (Gordon and de Souza e Silva, 2011) across network spheres.

What these approaches seem to overlook, however, is the formation of new public territory where public discourse emerges through 'public assemblage' on the lifeworld level. It is about a 'mosaic' structure of new deliberative public territories within a globalized public sphere. Reflective globalization could be understood as globalization beyond globalization, post globalization, to capture the new notion of 'contraction' via spaces and networks. The transnational networked locality positions the subject in a dialectical process where de- and re-embedding become forms of deliberative communication. These are the consequences of relational 'spaces' between 'deterritorialized' forms of 'proximity' and 'distance' in the sphere of public communication.

4

Public Interdependence, Interlocutors and the 'Matrix' of Influence

It is worth assessing the specific configuration of media influence and power within a transnational field. Although discursive power is at the core of social philosophy and social sciences, it is the specific structure of media and communicative power in the sphere of public interdependence that is explored in this chapter. The conceptual framework of power in the context of media theory is traditionally situated in a complex space between media and society in the linearity of a 'bounded' sphere. Dimensions of media power are for example articulated as 'symbolic', the power of representation as 'mediatization' (Thompson, 1995) as a process of imposing a media-related logic on communication. Silverstone understands this space as 'mediation', a dialectical sphere in which communication and the social and cultural environments are negotiated (Silverstone, 2007). Furthermore, the term 'mediatization' identifies spaces in which there is a powerful appropriation of meaning of communicative structures.

When reviewing debates in international communication, the sphere of power is related to the outlined spaces of communicative structures, as addressed in the context of larger fields of mediation which take place in democratic nations and other society types. International communication is traditionally concerned with national 'boundedness'. Such a boundedness is caused by the traditional role of communication in the context of international relations and the distinction between domestic and foreign politics, which are guided by the centrality of the nation-states and governments as the key actors setting the framework of international relations. National media are embedded in these larger political structures of international relations. Such a nationally bounded conception of international communication and – in consequence – the assessment of media power in foreign affairs, has been increasingly critically reviewed over recent years. Rantanen deeply questions the approach of such a methodological 'internationalism' (Rantanen, 2010) as a useful concept for assessing transnational communicative processes. From a different angle, Thussu also argues that nationality might no longer be an important aspect of distinction as globalized media flows are undergoing a 'gradual commercialization' process. Corporate media structures their 'markets and advertising revenues' where nationality 'scarcely matters', since media view the audience as 'consumers' and not as 'citizens' (Thussu, 2007: 11).

The boundedness of media power is articulated, for example, in the dimension of geopolitical influence. During the time of the Cold War, media power was labelled 'communicative intervention' and related mainly to propaganda as a sphere of influence between national publics in the USA and the Soviet Union, and also across Europe, Asia, African regions and Australia (see McKnight, 2008). In the context of international communication, these spheres of powerful interference with national public spheres emerged early on as an important research area – one that explored 'communicative intervention' in two contexts: investigating the strategic influence of the manipulation of public opinion in international contexts, and the critical analysis of these forms of intervention. These particular spheres of influence have re-emerged as 'soft' or 'smart' power and 'public' diplomacy (see Hayden, 2012) through the narrative framework of the 'war on terror' (see Dimaggio, 2008), constituting a new strategic discourse tool of soft power. This tool of external international relations in times of military conflicts and wars was also a form of national internal communicative frame for creating a national public 'coherent' narrative, for example in China (Cao, 2011). Price suggests an integrative approach to 'foreign policy of information space' (Price, 2010) as 'countries are increasingly frustrated at the task of controlling the flow of information into their own boundaries; they try, unilaterally or multilaterally, to affect the mix of information that streams around the world through satellite and the Internet' (Price, 2010: 364). Although these spheres of influence are today on the periphery of media and communication research, it should not be overlooked that communicative intervention and soft power is also a phenomenon in networked public spaces. The context of politically extremist websites, delivered through thematic bundling of web communication across search and social network sites as well as hyperlinked platforms is rarely addressed when discussing spatial publics.

Beyond these forms of more traditional strategic geopolitical communicative power, spheres of influence over public communication in the context of transnational communication mainly relate to broader discursive spheres in the paradigms of structuralism and critical theory. These have helped to assess critically the emerging transnational public structures and the increasing implications of transnational communication as a 'fourth estate' in national contexts. In his book *Mass Media and Modernity*, Thompson defines formations of mediated 'symbolic' power as influencing the 'course of events' as well as 'the actions of others' and as being able to 'create events' by 'means of the production and transmission of symbolic forms' (Thompson 1995: 17). Thompson's definition has helped further to map influences of mass media on the discursive sphere within a (Western) society. The discursive spheres of mediated symbolic power as communicative intervention have been further explored through insights into the reflective 'articulation' of public discursive practices (Lundby, 2009; Chouliaraki and Fairclough, 1999). In particular the cultures of 'articulation', 'rituals' and 'events' (Dayan and Katz, 1994; Volkmer and Deffner, 2010; Couldry and Hepp, 2012) establish social (transnational) relations through dense discursive practices, and also new spheres of symbolic power. These articulations extend Thompson's notion of 'symbolic power' as discursive processes, since these practices are powerful rituals, operating alongside 'network practices' and often illuminating 'shifting articulations of practices, within and across networks' (Chouliaraki and Fairclough, 1999: 24). In addition, structural spheres of rituals and articulations highlighting the traditions of hegemonic mediated spaces become visible through the interpretive practices of multi-cultural 'belongings'.

Conceptions of discursive power have been further broadened as transnational communication appears on the one hand as a sphere of spatial practice of intended/unintended flows of for example satellite footprint overlap, and on the other as a bounded sphere of transnational circuits of policy structures as a new powerful control mechanism. Global policy imperatives regulating copyright, antitrust and the multidimensional sphere of security policies seem to lead to new forms of control mechanism in the communicative space and the privatization of public spaces (Sarikakis, 2012). Braman has suggested identifying these new spheres of power as 'informational' and 'virtual' power. Informational power relates, so Braman argues, to 'manipulating' earlier forms of power, such as 'instrumental', 'structural' and 'symbolic'. 'The ability to monitor compliance with intellectual property rights law through surveillance of Internet use is an example of the influence of informational power on the exercise of structural power' (Braman, 2006: 29). In consequence, Braman claims that the state has been transformed into an 'informational state' and the 'development of meta-technologies, and the increasing information intensity of society have magnified the value of policy techniques for manipulating informational power' (Braman, 2006: 2). Besides these 'policy techniques', communicative power is also incorporated into larger conceptions of 'digital capitalism' which are addressed through a neocritical analysis of network structures as a new key component of the neoliberal paradigms of global capitalism. New complexities regarding spheres of influence are more deeply entangled across large-scale sectors of digital corporate structures, from search sites to social network sites to personalized digital forms, through mechanisms of digital surveillance in order to control subjective digital space as a commodity and a sphere of distribution for digital corporations (see Fuchs, 2012).

Castells' approach has finally shifted the understanding of communicative power. Communicative power is no longer a state-related sphere of policies and softer power techniques; rather it is to be understood as a geographically dispersed, but horizontally linked, sphere of influence across large geographical sectors of public interdependencies through various connecting nodes of what Castells understands as power 'relations'. It is the moving of the power centre from the state to the network that is illuminated in this approach and it is one of the few conceptions that help further to assess communicative power structures in multiple horizons of horizontal transnational spheres. Castells suggests evaluating these interrelated power 'strata' along three types of dialectic which emerge across network flows. The first interrelated mechanism is situated in the dialectic of 'global and the local', which reveals the interrelation of globalized and localized forms of resistance. This nexus of global/local is differently configured for 'each network' (Castells, 2009: 50). The 'networks of power are usually global, while the resistance of counterpower is usually local' (Castells, 2009: 52). A second form of power dialectic is the inclusion/exclusion nexus: exclude 'a group', a person or a territory from 'one network', but 'include in others'. Castells argues that as space in the network society is 'configured' around the opposition between the space of flows (global) and the space of places (local), the 'spatial structure of our society' is a major source of the structuration of 'power relationships' (Castells, 2009: 50). The third power mechanism is the 'connecting/disconnecting' nexus. This nexus relates to the ability to 'constitute networks' and 'to programme', and, to 'the ability to connect and ensure the cooperation of different networks' (Castells, 2009: 45). Furthermore, power spheres emerge through 'programming' as a 'discursive capacity' (Castells, 2009: 53) and 'switching and programming the global networks are the forms of exercising power in our global network society' (Castells, 2009: 53).

We might add a fourth strata, which includes 'temporality' or 'simultaneousness' as another mechanism of power relations through the role of speed: instantaneous information as a power 'commodity' in transnational public interdependence. A fifth mechanism could also be added, which constitutes 'looping', the self-referential 'filtering' of information 'personalizing' the scope of information resources along individual 'patterns'; this process, in consequence, creates highly selected information 'bubbles' (Pariser, 2011) that emerge as another mechanism of power relationships through the code-related selection of information and communication.

These strata of dialectical relationships relate to macro-spaces of networks, which, no doubt, have implications on public communication and shaping spheres of influence through network relations.

Spheres of influence as the 'meta game'

From a quite different perspective, spheres of influence, also in a horizontal scope of transnational publics, are the process-oriented power 'relations' that Beck calls the 'meta' game of the public sphere. The 'meta' game is the 'enabler' of the 'visibility' of risk through – in Beck's context – mass-media, which is a sphere of influence of 'legitimation'. Despite Beck's conception of public discourse occurring in the sphere of traditional national mass media and less in network structures, Beck's main argument is interesting in our context as he identifies power and spheres of influence through the 'elevation' of 'thematic' publics, which, through such a globalized powerful 'magnification' (Volkmer, 2006), automatically become signifiers of symbolic legitimation. 'Risk publics' constitute in this sense realms of an intense 'meta game' of 'legitimation power' (Beck, 2005). In Beck's view, it 'becomes clear that distinguishing the national outlook from the cosmopolitan outlook and juxtaposing the two not only reveals new arenas for action and resources of power but also explains what is ultimately at stake in the meta game, namely the foundations of the legitimation of politics *per se*'. He continues, 'it is only in the narrow perspective of methodological nationalism, where the supranational order of actors and power is seen as the international order of power, that the transformation of the rules of the power game has to take place in the context of the old national draughts order. In actual, fact, however, the meta game entails the possibility of a *paradigm change in legitimacy'* (emphasis in original, Beck, 2005: 17).

The conception of 'legitimacy power' has shifted, in the context of risk societies, from a bounded national perception of risk to a 'magnified risk in a globalized society', and in the particular way that these risks are produced and mediated, which is at the core of new forms of public interdependent communication. Although I agree with Beck in his notion that 'reflexive cosmopolitanism' needs to address such a meta game, it is obvious that Beck's understanding of communicative spheres is mainly related to national (mass) media and does not address the specifics of meta game relations and interdependencies of transnational spheres, of public interdependence that communicatively adopts such a risk perception and continuously negotiates diverse perceptions of risk, for example, across various local sites and spheres of connectivity. In this view, Beck is right when suggesting that 'the theory of the meta-game needs to be developed in terms of a specific game logic, that is, as a strategic constellation of interacting, more or less collective, rule-abiding and rule-changing actors, whose positions, resources, and shares of power are determined and changed reciprocally' (Beck, 2005: 19). However, the particular 'game logic' and in particular the 'strategic constellation of interacting' shapes a new meta game in the context of reflective densities of public interdependence.

This model departs from Beck's approach, as it understands 'spheres of influence' as being constituted not only between 'media' and 'society', or transnational media and societies, but, taking Castells' power dimension further, *across* the horizontal space of public interdependence, across communicative relations between what might be called reflective nodes of public discourse. The 'magnification' of reflective nodes is engaged with a new type of meta game as a legitimizing force. Such a legitimizing force in a transnational meta game agenda could lead to resistance, for example in societies where the state controls national media forms and transnational resources are considered to be trusted information sources and influence civil society systems in other societies. For example, the magnification of environmental risks established not only social movements but also the Green Party and Greenpeace in a transnational public field. Beck's term 'meta game' could also be used to understand the increased 'sphere of influence' as viral forms of public communication, channelled through quite diverse formations of public interdependence, fluctuating across spaces and emerging as a new form of power mechanism.

These complex spaces of networked power flows revolve around communicative nodes and 'tags' and semantic webs of dominant terminologies. Numerous examples illustrate particular nodes or sites of emerging horizontal spheres of influence, in particular in contexts of political crisis. Transnational spheres of influence have, for example in recent political conflicts or uprisings, emerged through communication platform 'rerouting'; for example, the rerouting of *Twitter* postings about the uprising in North Africa through *Google* servers that transformed voice messages into *Twitter* postings, which could, again, be picked up anywhere in the world with Internet access. In the context of the Iranian demonstration about the last election, the Internet and mobile services and text messaging were cut off by the Iranian government; however, Iranian protesters rerouted web platforms to send political messages of protest as tweets. This process of utilizing transnational space as a sphere of communicative power revealed a new sphere of influence challenging state control, and, internally, a powerful challenge to state-sponsored media messages (see Snow, 2010: 100). This case also reveals a new sphere of powerful influence *vis-à-vis* the state-run Iranian television and established news media organizations, in this case satellite broadcasters such as CNN. Snow argues that the transnational coverage of CNN was, compared to the pace of discourse platforms, 'slow in its coverage' and, in addition, failed to pursue 'a sceptical line with its initial coverage' (Fisher, 2010: 106). As a consequence, protesters directly targeted through postings the 'attention of international broadcasters' and a 'loosely defined Western audience' (Fisher, 2010:108). This example shows the increasing link between network platforms and the increase of the influence of what used to be called 'citizen reporting' on transnational crisis coverage. These are interesting new dialogical power domains linking social media platforms and established media organizations across distance. These processes become particularly visible in times of crisis; however, they seem to remain invisible in the day-to-day process of public discourse. What seems to become apparent in this example is the shifting power angle of social media forms and the changing role of media forms in public discourse, where, through network communication, everyone can be a sender and receiver; but media forms take on diverse roles within such conflict discourse and communicative power is not merely decentred but constantly shifting in a dynamic dialogical relation of media forms, nodes and platforms.

A study of the public protest space in Egypt during the 'Arab Spring' has also shown a particular dialogical interplay across transnationally dispersed media forms, which is described as 'amplification'. It is this amplification that is seen as an interlinked conflict sphere, a 'media spectacular' (Nanabhay and Farmanfarmaian, 2011: 574). A 'media spectacular' where the 'mainstream media amplified the space defined by social media and turned it into an internationalized space of rolling new coverage, where audiences throughout the world were just a click away from 24/7 broadcasts'. It is this entangled linking of public nodes (of social network sites, national and international media) which intensifies the relationship between protesters, social media and national mainstream media, a public domain of the 'spectacular' as the outcome of these interlinked spheres.

The powerful influence of interlinked, amplified transnational spheres surfaces also in crisis communication where blogs and social media are incorporated into the crisis coverage of a news outlet. Networked journalism (see Gillmor, 2006), citizen journalism (Allan, 2009) or network journalism (Heinrich, 2011) have become established terms for the phenomenon of powerful dialogical relations in the news space. Early debates addressed the role of these dialogical relations as user generated content (UGC) on news production and in news organizations and newsroom studies. For example Wardle and Williams investigate the role of UGC at the BBC, and one outcome of this study is that journalists perceive UGC as a side-by-side source, in addition to other news sources. The authors observe that 'the dominant way of understanding UGC among BBC journalists involves seeing it as little more than another news source' (Wardle and Williams, 2010: 790). Although these are important insights in the debate about journalism in the context of a particular transnational news organization, it seems that most studies relate to mainly national 'audience content' (Wardle and Williams, 2010) within a national news outlet. As a side note it should be mentioned here that only a few debates even address UGC and citizen journalism in non-Western societies where citizen journalism is a more recent phenomenon. A recent study in Pakistan where media are government controlled and citizen journalists are registered before content can be posted (Riaz and Pasha, 2011) reveals that despite the fact that citizen journalism is in its initial stage in Pakistan, it has already taken on an important role in 'promoting and conveying the problems of society to the government' (Riaz and Pasha, 2011: 100). The sphere of UGC is considered as 'changing connectivity modes' (Heinrich, 2012) of the journalistic sphere and reconstitutes the traditional configurations of journalism. Connectivity nodes, so Heinrich argues, are constituted by journalistic organizations such as the BBC, the *New York Times* or Associated Press, and also 'Tweeters', Bloggers or 'the independent journalist freelancing on international territory'. It is an interactive networked sphere 'where "hierarchies" – at least in theory – do not exist' (Heinrich, 2012: 64). Another recent debate takes this approach even further and notes that a 'spatial turn' is required in journalism studies. Peters argues that a 'lack of spatial awareness in journalism scholarship is somewhat problematic, as the dramatic rise of alternative platforms to deliver journalism over the last two decades – the iPad, smartphones, *Twitter*, podcasts, video-on-demand online news, 24-hour news, commuter papers and so on – must be seen as doing something more than just multiplying the number of journalistic channels' (Peters, 2012: 700). Although I agree with Peters that a spatial turn in journalism studies is needed, it is important to consider journalism as a model existing alongside public communication. The spatial is required in order to consider journalism as only one constituency in the symbolic landscapes of public interdependence, and embedded in the mechanism of a new powerful dialogical relation of media and communicative forms. In this context a conceptualization of public interdependence across organizational, institutional, actor-related 'intersections' across the scope of public interdependence and its relationships is needed which would allow us to consider media organizations not as static statist or corporate structures but as sites and platforms of transnational dialogical relations establishing new forms of agency.

In this context network power is an intersection of 'switchers' and 'programmers', and in terms of public communication as a larger dimension of dialogical influence, situated *across* often geographically and/or spatially dispersed nodes. An example of such a dialogical influence is *Wikileaks*, which is often discussed as a linear media form where the centrality of the platform is mainly understood in its role of uncovering otherwise confidential resources. However, the particular 'dynamic' and dialogical strategy in which *Wikileaks* builds and maintains networked structures across geographical distance creates and sustains *Wikileaks*; its specific sphere of influence could be understood as the role of a 'connector'. Such a role underlies what Beckett describes as *Wikileaks*' particular power sphere of 'con-textualizing' or 'mirroring'; for example, when thousands of confidential US diplomatic cables were posted on *Wikileaks*. *Wikileaks*' connector role consisted of the strategy of mirroring selected documents through dialogical relations to print media. Collaborating news outlets were, in December 2010, *Le Monde* (France), *El Pais* (Spain), *Der Spiegel* (Germany), the *Guardian* (UK), all sharing material with the *New York Times*, but also with blogs and websites' news outlets, which in this case are no longer traditional journalistic institutions but became platforms for the *Wikilieaks* content. Such a thematic 'contextualization' and 'mirroring' is a new role for media organizations. A spatial turn in journalism studies should acknowledge these new forms of journalism spaces that are not only digital and networked but rather emerge as powerful dialogical spheres across geographically dispersed news organizations in a transnational interdependent context.

Thematically specific and 'authentic' websites, platforms or channels – and the new structure of a coordinated amalgamation of geographically stretched, highly specific, virally networked communication of 'hash tags' in dialogical relation to the 'geopolitics' of satellite footprints (Parks, 2012) – take on the role of discursive nodes within such new spheres of influence. Kai Hafez suggested some time ago that we should think about satellite television in Arab public cultures 'almost as a replacement for political parties' (Hafez, 2008). This remark reveals the geopolitical role of satellite television in subnational and even local public discourse in Arab regions and, overall, a new dimension of satellite television linked to other communicative and discursive forms. Hafez understands this role of public discourse in three dimensions. The first dimension is that in Arab regions satellite television intersects with public discourse; for example, satellite communicating is 'expressing what people think especially about politics'; a second dimension is that satellite channels take on the role of 'moulding' public opinion on 'urgent questions of modernization'; and a third is that these channels sometimes activate the 'Arab Street' for political demonstrations; and a fourth that they influence the behaviour of Arab regimes (Hafez, 2008: 2). Hafez's observation is related to the Arab region at a time of government controlled media but it is an important observation as it highlights the role of media platforms as authentic intersections in public discourse, a role which is mainly associated with web-based platforms such as social media. Hafez's observation also points to the different dimension of 'agency', of media forms such as satellite channels as 'equal' agents in communicative practices through 'linking', 'bundling' and, principally, continuously 'absorbing' and 'mirroring' local public discourse in the model of Arab countries within a wider global public space.

Spheres of influence through a mirroring role or through intersections with public spheres are no longer tied to particular regional media or network spheres, but should be considered a dialogical space of various actor-sites across geographically dispersed sites within the sphere of dense public interdependence. Such a structure of influence is often articulated in network debates and it is argued that networks break down previous forms of mediated linearity and particular platforms constitute new forms of communicative power (see Beckett and Ball, 2013). Whereas these larger formations of new connected forms of civic communication constitute the macro-structure, in the advanced sphere of globalization and, indeed, network society, the micro-structures of dialogical communicative power are constituted by diverse state formations and societies across dialogical partners. In addition, an awareness of the fine lines of these processes is relevant as power structures emerge across this new broadened scope of public space through a particularly dense territorial and 'aterritorial' dialogical relation (see Gripsrud and Moe, 2010: 11), which is rarely addressed in research. In particular, when it comes to 'spheres of influence' and new powerful communicative intervention in a globalized public space, public interdependence is situated across geographical distance and diverse societies. It is widely overlooked that so-called developing regions are also entangled in spheres of influence (through Internet hubs, mobile smart phones and social media); however, they are rarely integrated into conceptual models. The paradigm of 'compressed' modernity is mostly used in contexts of economic and societal transformation in developing regions due to neoliberal globalization, but rarely in contexts of powerful links within a transnational sphere of public interdependence. What is rarely addressed are the emerging transnationally linked spheres of public communication along the various networks of compressed modernities between territorial and aterritorial communication; the specific new forms of public communication in spheres of reflexive cosmopolitanism in developing or transitional regions. Whereas spheres of communicative power are often conceptualized as linear processes, either between media and society within a nation, or between the national and the transnational, it is necessary to reflect upon powerful influences in the densities of transnational public interdependence across larger communicative sectors, situated in geographically dispersed places and across diverse societies. There are at least three terrains of communicative power in the context of discourse across the sphere transnational communication. The first terrain is of state censorship, from denying access to websites to jamming of satellite channels. A second terrain is the policy terrain, from copyright issues to demands for open access code – in national and also in interregional and transnational contexts (for example, WIPO). Public interdependence as a networked structure, incorporating communicators from diverse society types and stretching across layers of networked communication, is objected to by new power figurations. A third terrain is surveillance. Over the last few years, surveillance platforms have almost become public assets. *Google Earth* was one of the first widely known mapping platforms which is time lagged and not 'live'. Other recent sites allow us to read live tweets and even view the tweeter's profile, both in the public terrain of a globalized context (www.onemilliontweets.com).

It is misleading to uncouple Castells' model (see above) completely from traditional paradigms of power figurations in the context of transnationalization of media, since imbalances of 'centre' and 'periphery' appear in new ways in the networked structure, where, for example, it might be argued that digital platforms, owned by corporations situated in Western regions dominate mass self-communication. In this sense, it might be interesting to revise the traditional arguments and identify new centre-periphery communication (see Schiller, 1976; Boyd-Barrett, 1977; Boyd-Barrett, 2006). In addition, as Nederveen notes, Western media forms traditionally shape narratives through the continuous reproduction of inequalities. Nederveen's argument is built upon the notion that Western media through these powerful narrative representations have 'celebrated the rise of the West for some two hundred years'. In consequence of such a self-referential paradigm, the 'main trends are that the rise of the rest is *ignored* because it doesn't fit national narratives in the West, or is represented as a *threat* because it fits or extends existing enemy images, or is *celebrated* in business media as triumphs of the marketplace (emphasis in original, Nederveen, 2012: 57). Nederveen concludes that the mainstream media 'ignore the rise of the rest; in effect they reinforce the relations between the rest and the rest rather than between the rest and the West and may thus contribute to the creeping irrelevance of the West'(Nederveen, 2012: 58). A third approach of network power is Sassen's concept of socio-digital networks and the phenomenon of 're-negotiating' digital knowledge. She argues that 'the greater velocities that digitization makes possible further drive the informalizing of whole bodies of knowledge, or some of their components. Velocity also makes legible, or helps us realize, the fact that a given knowledge might be in a trajectory that can include the use of that knowledge in political practices that in turn can generate emergent types of knowledge' (Sassen, 2012: 57). Sassen relates these socio-digital processes to national or subnational levels and even to the 'actor' sphere in a more general sense: 'As even small, resource-poor organizations and individuals can become participants in electronic networks, it signals the possibility of a sharp growth in cross-border politics by actors other than states . . . What is of interest here is that while these are poor and localized actors, in some ways they can partly bypass territorial state jurisdiction and, though local, they can begin to articulate with others worldwide and thereby constitute an incipient global common'(Sassen, 2012: 78). In addition, Sassen argues that 'key among these current conditions are globalization and/or globality, as constituting not only cross-border institutional spaces but also powerful imaginaries enabling aspirations to transboundary political practice even when the actors involved are basically localized and not mobile' (Sassen, 2012: 83). It is the socio-digital formation which transforms the 'local' into a 'symbolic' space.

In terms of public interdependence and public density, other mechanisms besides the socio-digital – in Sassen's work understood as a supra- and subnational transformative agent of the nation or the 'local' – should be considered. Public interdependence is driven by communicative processes that shape public density as a sphere of influence.

In the early phase of networked power it was assumed that 'the net' does not have a centre (compared to other media organizations at the time) and it was assumed that it would provide a new sphere for the unlimited exchange of dialogue and information between individuals. It was assumed that even critical information could be relatively easily exchanged (again, compared to other communication options at the time) nationally and simultaneously transborder. The second phase of conceptions of networked power relates to Castells' conceptions of the power of networks: 'networking power' as the inclusion of 'actors' and 'organizations' constituting the 'core of the global network society', of 'network power'; the 'rules of inclusion', for example following communication protocols, and 'networked power' as the sphere of 'power relationships of networks' (Castells, 2009). Castells' approach illuminates the power of connectivity as an organizational technology-centred form. In order to move away from technology or platform-centred approaches, I suggest the consideration of 'spheres of influence' as a dialogical relation of three processes: intensification, acceleration and dialogical connectedness.

'Connecting' agents: actor, connector and interlocutor

In the following, I propose such a process-oriented model of dialogical media formations. This model might serve as an approach for identifying 'spheres of influence' incorporating the dense spaces of public interdependence: intensification, acceleration and dialogical connectedness. This model allows us to consider the process-oriented 'spatial turn' of public communication and situates media forms within this sphere of dialogical relations, linking public discourse through a 'matrix of influence' where not so much the node and the space create diverse networked forms of power but rather the 'momentum' of linking which renegotiates spheres of influence in a process of reflection.

Such an enlarged sphere of influence, incorporating process-oriented discursive flows emerges across spatial communicative forms, including networked media forms which are often labelled digital media – a term which does not constitute a particular media form but rather an amalgamation of process-oriented media flows. This distinction is important as spatial media incorporate increasingly traditional media forms: newspapers are delivered as e-paper but also on platforms delivering audiovisual content, and thematically distinct television content is delivered through new streaming delivery forms. The BBC's 'iPlayer' streams BBC content accessible nationally and, since 2011, also internationally. Furthermore, traditional media forms reappear in social media contexts as news feeds on *Facebook*, as retweets on *Twitter* and on dedicated channel sites of *YouTube* and other video platforms. In this sense, traditional media forms are not only undergoing a deterritorialization where content can be accessed digitally anywhere in the world with Internet access but also a radical erosion of media forms where a media organization dissolves into content flows, packaged and fractured as spatial flows. Traditional media forms transform into flows which, in a transnational perspective, create a new equality of access for world regions which, in the past due to expensive satellite leasing fees, were unable to make content available internationally. The sphere of influence of traditional media organizations suddenly competes with new 'stream aggregators' such as *Ghana live TV*, a platform registered in California which streams live television content from television channels (among these *Al Jazeera* and *Euronews*) in addition to live *Facebook* debates targeting the African diaspora which are accessible anywhere in the world. A similar platform, called *livestream* provides live access to *Somali National Television*, and the Coptic channel *Africa TV1* (incorporating about forty television stations from thirty African countries), just to name some examples of the spatial spheres of traditional media forms which are incorporated into placeless digital space.

Furthermore, so-called 'apps' constitute new micro sites of thematically specific political information providing specific thematic information, such as the *UN News Reader* providing UN news, or an integrative app-platform, called *Newsstand*, which incorporates about 9,000 news outlets from different world regions accessible anywhere with a mobile smart phone. The app 'bundles' highly specific forms of political communication from diverse regions, from Brazil, Ecuador, Egypt, India, Japan, Jamaica, local community news, for example, *Tamil Daily News*.

These examples are used here mainly to show that the centrality of place-based media forms delivering packaged content internationally is radically transformed by the centrality of particular process-oriented flows. The place-based media influence of the national mass-media age is decreasing and the prime time news which was a collective experience is, in particular among young generations, increasingly replaced by media flows where the subjective linking of communicative forms constitutes the sphere of influence. This sphere of influence across interdependent publics is not linear, not national or transnational, but constitutes a reflective sphere across a transnational interdependent public that opens up a new form of discursive power which may include media as a reflective site. Power configurations within such a public density consist of the understanding of media as nodes and of the reflective connection of three processes: the processes of intensification, acceleration and dialogical connectedness, which are no longer embedded in a media form but dispersed across media and communicative platforms and linked in a subjectively chosen reflective space.

The process of 'intensification' could be understood as the 'actor' dimension. This is the dimension of the resource of information, of

Graphic 4.1   Process-oriented 'flows': intensification, acceleration, dialogical connectedness.

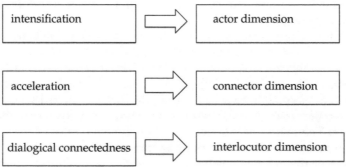

authentic content, which can be retrieved on media sites but also on social media, *Google* or from NGO websites. Acceleration is the dimension of the uploader of content, the students in Tunisia who saw the images of protests in the small Tunisian villages and made these 'go viral' on *Facebook*, to be subsequently picked up by news media organizations and citizens in Tunis – a process which, in consequence of such an acceleration, led to Arab Spring protests. Acceleration as the 'connector' dimension is also the sphere of the retweeting of content, creating appropriation in a transnational context. The dimension of dialogical connectedness is the dynamic process of rapid responsiveness, the interlocutor dimension. In addition, an 'interlocutor' re-negotiates through contextualizing and provides access to a wider interdependent public. The interlocutor renegotiates this discourse, which is often related back to the sphere of intensification and acceleration. This process-oriented flow scheme as a sphere of influence allows us to map the sphere of influence across geographically diverse regions as well as society types, and across media and communicative forms. The BBC, and also Ghana TV, could take on the role of the actor but also of the connector and interlocutor. A *Facebook* site could be considered actor, connector or interlocutor. This model might serve as a way to make these diverse roles within the communicative sphere of public interdependence visible, and allows us to integrate the emerging connecting relations of public discourse across world regions. This model could in this sense be understood as an inclusive approach for mapping the spheres of influence in the density of transnational fractured communication. The subjectively chosen reflective linking between actor, connector and interlocutor is understood here as a 'matrix of influence', stretching across networks of public interdependence as a new, powerful symbolic terrain, a new fluid field of public discourse across different society types. Across the matrix, spheres of power emerge as interrelated, intertwined spheres stretching across developed and developing regions.

The flow chart visualized as a matrix helps us to understand further that it is not just the Internet or websites themselves that have implications for public agenda, but the way in which diverse media and communicative forms are dialogically related and are integrated as a reflective space. We have discussed the public space as emerging between the network of centrality and centrality of networks in the first chapter. The matrix of influence and the dynamic roles of media and communicative platforms in public communication – across the three spheres of the actor intensifying the density of discourse; connector broadening the discourse; interlocutor targeting a larger space – might

Graphic 4.2   Matrix of influence as flow chart.

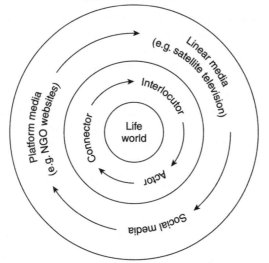

help to understand further the power structure of public interdependence across geographically dispersed regions. It also helps to unbundle the one-dimensional notion of networks that are divided into nodes and space and also, in terms of public interdependence, into discursive roles. For example, an NGO posting is picked up by a social network site and connected to a larger audience by a satellite channel. The flow chart of the matrix of influence reveals the different reflective roles of media and communicative sites as lifeworld spheres. These are the transnational communicative spheres influencing public communication. Spheres of influence are in this context related through established powerful discourse rituals and articulations, and also through structures of transnationally dispersed connectors of public interdependence, which constitute a new, powerful sphere. Authentic material produced by actors, connected by local agencies, establishes through the interlocutor a powerful sphere of influence by creating agency in a transnational context. The model of the matrix of influence identifies the different roles of agency in the transnational public space in specific flows of public discourse.

An example that might illustrate some aspects of such process-oriented matrices of influence across various and shifting media sites are the networks of political information practices of migrant communities. The dynamic and focused, simultaneous engagement with several communicative sites, of the country of origin and of the country of residence, has been revealed in several studies addressing the media use of so-called diasporas in national contexts (see the discussion in Chapter 3). A study identifying the role of satellite television in contexts of civic spaces of belonging among Arabic speakers in Stockholm, Berlin, Amsterdam, London, Paris and Madrid has revealed a particular way of forming reflective spaces in specific contexts of news and information (see Slade and Volkmer, 2012; Slade, 2010). Graphic 4.3 shows the diverse layers of this enlarged sphere of news consumption. It also shows the practice of selecting and ordering diverse resources across the multi-dimensional web of layers of news channels. Respondents utilize these sources for different purposes and critically compare political frames and agendas.

However, within this network of layers of diverse television channels, *Al Jazeera* (Arabic) takes on a significant role – referring to the matrix model as interlocutor – in Madrid, London, Amsterdam, Stockholm and Berlin. Across these six cities, *Al Jazeera* is used as the core information platform. The role of *Al Jazeera* has been reflected in the diary survey that captured actual television consumption over a one week period and is used by a majority within diverse, subjectively chosen and reflectively arranged nodes of national news channels; for example, Dutch, German, French public service and commercial channels as well as other Arabic channels, such as *2MTMaroc, Al-Maghrabiyya, Arrydia, Al-Assadissa, Iqraa, BBC Arabic, Alsharqiya, MBC, Al Arabyia, Nile TV, Dubai TV* and *Al Manar*. As the study shows, these diverse Arabic channels are networked in a particular way, depending on the region of origin of respondents. Satellite channels are deliberatively chosen as geographically dispersed media forms and these nodes constitute subjectively chosen networks of trust.

Spheres of influence: Satellite channels as supra- and sub-national 'interlocutors'

In the following section, I will provide examples for this model and will explore the role of 'dialogical interlocutor' in the context of three satellite channels, *Al Jazeera*, BBC World and *Deutsche Welle*.

These three channels, chosen as satellite channels, take on the important role of 'interlocutor', as outlined in the study mentioned above but also in contexts of public crises where, despite the increasing relevance of social media as actor or connector space, satellite channels provide a narrative and responsiveness in public communication. Despite the growth of satellite television channels over recent years, it is surprising,

Graphic 4.3   *Al Jazeera* web. Results from a one-week diary survey (October, 2008) among Arabic speakers (n = 709) in six European cities. Results show that public proximity of media forms and practices are no longer a linear 'flow' but communicative 'webs'. Graph shows the most watched Arabic channels.
Source: Media and Citizenship, Framework 7 project, funded by the European Union, Consortium Leader Christina Slade, University of Utrecht, Netherlands. Results from Workpackage 2, Media Survey, led by Ingrid Volkmer and Renate Moeller.

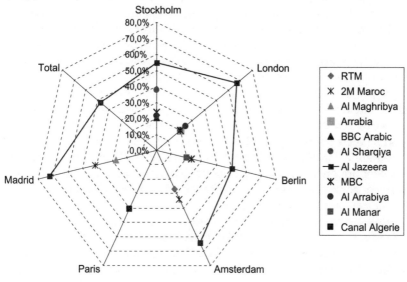

as I have mentioned earlier, that satellite communication is rarely addressed in media research and in the context of a transnational dis-cursive space. This is surprising, since satellites constitute one of the technological backbones of network structures. In addition (as outlined in Chapter 2), particular satellite television channels create a transna-tional universe and, over recent years, the increase of satellite television channels goes hand in hand with a 'fracturing' of content from a national perspective and the increased density of content from a tran-snational angle. However, recent developments in satellite communica-tion are rarely articulated in the context of the larger scope of transnational public communication. As Lisa Parks argues, 'Satellite footprints are much more than static maps – they are politically charged documents that showcase previous, existing, or desired political alli-ances, trade relations and/or intercultural campaigns' (Parks, 2012:

125); they are, however, often overlooked in the geopolitics of media policy. Some recent studies reveal the particular role not only of digital platforms but of particular satellite channels as powerful large-scale links in the complexity delivering political information and targeting particular micro-publics worldwide, especially in the context of political conflicts (Ray, 2011; Schaar, 2011). Parks suggests considering satellite 'footprints' as a 'territorializing gesture' (Parks, 2012). This observation helps to describe the way in which transnationally delivered content targets not a particular territorial public but a symbolic national territory, in particular public discourse spaces. Although it might be argued that satellite communication even in the early days aimed to focus on particular territorial terrains, its reach relates today not only to territorial regions but more deeply into particular densities of public discourse. Transnational satellite channels traditionally influence public cultures of various world regions. As has been argued in the context of the Arab Spring, it is the negotiation of the common narrative of a conflict which, in the account provided by *Al Jazeera*, bundled and shaped the narrative of the event (Ray, 2011: 191).

Satellite communication is mainly discussed in the context of political economy and the mainly unrestricted transnationalization of satellite corporations, and the centrality of geographical regions and platforms, but less in the particular context of the ways in which satellite television engages with transnationally dispersed publics. However, 'fractured' satellite channels take on the role of interlocutor as an active sphere of influence. As outlined earlier, it is interesting to assess the quite different supra- and subnational spheres of satellite communication as a stretching of the horizons of globalized public discourse. The satellite provider EUTELSAT is an example of such a new fractured universe, providing thousands of satellite television channels for the larger territory of geographical Europe, and also what is called MENA, the Middle East and North Africa. Among channels of the wider European footprints are those such as *Rossiya24* – a Russian news channel targeting the Russian communities and those interested in Russian political information across Europe and North Africa – *One Sri Lanka Channel*, the Malaysian channel of *Asianet*, and *CCCTV*, Chinese Central Television with a European angle.

Eickelman and Anderson argue that: 'Minor and emergent channels of communication that have proliferated are not mass in the same sense as conventional print and broadcasting. They are composed and consumed within more specialized, often voluntarily entered fields, where producers and consumers, senders and receivers, are far less distinguishable than broadcasters or the press and their audiences. Instead,

Graphic 4.4   Dialogical interlocutor: dimensions.

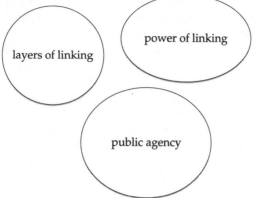

they merge in a kind of transnational community that moves the centre of discussion and its impetus off-shore or overseas because their technology is mobile or was first available there. At times these contributions are anonymous, as is the case with some internet postings, a tactic that transforms the notion of the public towards participation, as might illicit leaflets' (Eickelman and Anderson, 2003: 8).

The following case study addresses the diverse roles of interlocutor, creating a dialogical connectedness of three satellite channels: *Al Jazeera* (Arabic), BBC and *Deutsche Welle*. Interviews have been conducted at *Al Jazeera*, London, BBC World, London and *Deutsche Welle* in Berlin and Bonn, Germany. Respondents are leading executives in each of the media organizations. The case study shows the diversity of the roles played by dialogical connectedness and identifies the way in which each organization situates itself in the space of dialogical supra- and subnational public communication. Although these three satellite channels represent a fracture of the transnational satellite sphere, they also serve as case studies here and reveal interesting particular approaches when addressing the interdependent transnational public.

Al Jazeera: *dialogical interlocutor in the sphere of linking connectedness*

As mentioned earlier, one of the increasingly densely developed supra- and subnational network spheres is the Arab sphere. Only some decades ago, this sphere was mainly connected through the production and exchange of audio and audiovisual tapes, which, in consequence, led to an 'Arab postal union ban' on the delivery of this material (Eickelman and Anderson, 2003: 9). However, despite this ban, local and neighbourhood television and radio stations in Turkey as well as 'narrowcasting' sites emerged, and as Eickelman and Anderson note, 'from pamphlets to the telephone and internet discussion groups link religious identity and civic action to activities in daily life, family, neighbourhood, education, dress, jurisprudence, and patterns of consumption' (Eickelman and Anderson, 2003: 9).

Today, however, the Arabic satellite domain is one of the most developed worldwide, emerging at a time when television and radio were state institutions. Furthermore, as Anderson has argued, the characteristic of satellite communication is that it occupies an interesting space between 'the super-literacy of traditional religious specialists and mass sub-literacy or illiteracy' (Anderson, 1995). These emerging transnational media forms are targeting 'emerging middle, bourgeois classes of the Muslim World. They draw . . . on the techniques of multiple media domains, producing a creolized discourse that is not authorized anywhere, but instead links others in an intermediate discourse' (Eickelman and Anderson, 2003: 10). In consequence, the authors note that 'the publics emerging around these forms of communication create a globalization from below that complements and draws on techniques of globalization known in finance and mass marketing. While globalization from above is driven by multinational corporations, globalization from below is traditionally associated with labour movements' (Eickelman and Anderson, 2003: 10). The role of satellite communication in Arab regions has emerged in particular with pan-Arabic satellite platforms as a counterbalance to otherwise government controlled publics across the Arab region. Today, *Al Jazeera* is no longer a channel but rather a transnational network of diverse news channels (in Arabic and English), of nine sport channels, live political interest, a children's channel, in addition to a documentary channel, a channel targeting Egypt and a channel for Bosnia, Croatia and Serbia.[1] However, on a different level, *Al Jazeera* also constitutes a particular form of 'dialogical interlocutor' relating to the following levels.

Layers of linking

This first dimension reveals the way in which *Al Jazeera* is positioned within the specific transnational public space. The original aim of *Al Jazeera* is broadly described across levels. The main aim was 'to launch a satellite television channel which would go out in Arabic for whoever can understand Arabic'. This was crucial at the time when satellite television mainly addressed Western world regions. In this context, *Al Jazeera* aimed to adopt a geographical scope and to target specifically 'people who . . . live in such a volatile part of the world, Middle East and Northern Africa' but not exclusively. *Al Jazeera*'s aim from its beginning was also to target audiences beyond the traditional geography of the Arab region and include 'those who live elsewhere . . . in America or Australia or Asia or Africa or migrated there or are second or third generation'. A third approach was to address those individuals who 'are interested in the Arab culture or in Islam or the rest of it'. Despite these different target audience 'layers', situated in diverse societal contexts, the news channel delivers the same programmes transnationally. One interview respondent from *Al Jazeera* remarked that 'you get CNN International, CNN domestic, BBC World, BBC Prime, BBC Select, BBC 24 – *Al Jazeera* is the same anywhere in the world'.

The reason for this decision, is related to the state-owned national television structure in Arab countries but also to satellite technology. It is noted that this strategy also goes back to the early days of *Al Jazeera* where the main aim was linking to Arabic speakers. In addition, the aim was to link the Arab region as well as the diaspora through the delivery of the same content: 'In the beginning when, thanks to technology, when satellite was invented, they wanted to reach out primarily to their own people in the diaspora or those who migrated or whatever, again from the same philosophy. And the output did not actually change. It was a matter of switching the plug from terrestrial broadcast to satellite broadcast.' This approach has established consistent and continuous links between the diasporic community and the Arab region: 'For an Arab who would be living in America, for instance, he gets the chance to get the same TV channel that he used to watch back at home on satellite. Such a simultaneous delivery of content has not only shifted the approach of "foreignness" but also the notion of "connectedness"; I don't think he would look at it as a "foreign" broadcast, he would probably look at it as "home" being presented to him wherever he happens to live.' *Al Jazeera* seems to consider itself deeply integrated into this public interdependence, as a part of this interdependent community of 'our people'. It is an interdependent sphere stretching across geographical distance but also being situated in diverse societies. As the respondent notes: 'And that is what *Al Jazeera* has provided our people. Our people were and still are our men wherever they happen to be within the Arab world or on the stretches of the Arab world, perhaps Moslems or Arabs who live in Asia or Africa.

I have people calling me from Africa, from Asia, Europe.' This terrain is the specific, connected 'layering' of interdependence in *Al Jazeera*: communication; not so much pre-produced content, but the ability to 'speak up'. It is perceived as platform for the connection of opinions and debate within one nation and in a transnational context, creating a dialogical node between the Arab region and the Arab diaspora elsewhere in the world:

> 'The easiest way professionally speaking from an industry point of view is to get a couple of people in a studio and film it. It is cheap, it is direct. The Arab world is so thirsty to talk about things. The form didn't matter. Just to get someone to talk about things. And to open the lines for people to phone in – that in itself was a revolution. In Syria, Egypt actually being able to pick up the phone, speak their minds up so that millions of people outside of their country would be able to listen to them live. That in itself was a revolution . . . People just wanted to talk about things. They wanted to give things out of their chests in the open.'

The power of linking

The overall strategy of connectedness has gained geopolitical relevance, in particular across Arab states and between different Arab governments. It is argued that: 'With the introduction of satellite the reality of journalism especially in our part of the world has changed tremendously. I mean thanks to technology. The Saudis, for instance, with all the money they have got, they cannot jam the signal; I know that they would love to be able to jam *Al Jazeera* for instance. But it is just too costly, in every sense, financially, politically and in every sense.'

The implication of such a 'linking' sphere on powerful regimes underwent three phases. The first phase is described by an interviewee as an 'utter shock on the part of Arab governments', which had immediate political implications on governments in the Arab region and led to the withdrawal of ambassadors from Doha, some 'sending their own ministers of information to try to persuade the Emir of Qatar'. When this did not work, as the respondent notes, other implications were 'smear campaigns' in the national press in Egypt and Saudi Arabia. In addition, *Al Jazeera* offices were closed down and Arab journalists were arrested. Since these attempts were unsuccessful, new initiatives were launched and other satellite news channels established, based on the view that 'we can't beat them' but 'we can't actually join them either'. The outcome was 'something that looks from the outside . . . that looks like *Al Jazeera*, but not really seriously'. Respondents note that new satellite channels were launched, for example 'by Dubai, Abu Dhabi, *Al Arabya* and the rest of it. I cannot even begin to count them all now.' The respondent states that the number of these channels is not important, rather the implications, and states, 'that's one very important thing. Because I do not really measure the "success" of *Al Jazeera* by what you see on *Al Jazeera*'s screen. I measure the success of *Al Jazeera* by what *Al Jazeera* has forced others to have on their own screens. That in my opinion really epitomizes the whole situation and the Arab media scene. So this is the third phase we are in.' It is this implication for governments to copy *Al Jazeera* and the influence within this sphere of linking Arab communities in the region and worldwide which, in the view of the respondent, constitutes *Al Jazeera*'s influence, and it is assumed that *Al Jazeera* will maintain its role.

> But after a while, the mud will go away and you start to see clear water. And that will happen in time. And from that point of view, I am not too bothered about discrediting Al Arabya or Abu Dhabi. Actually . . . *Al Jazeera* has to be even better and to look better and to take up certain things. Still *Al Jazeera* has the initiative in its hand simply because anything could be discussed. On *Al Arabya* or Abu Dhabi, I don't blame them. I know that they have got a hold of a lot of very good journalists and they tried to do something.

This is an example for communication through a communicative node and the demand for public 'agency': 'in time people tried to abandon this kind of naive way of dealing with the issues and started to demand some more of a sophisticated way of looking into the world. They demanded more programmes based on research, facts and stuff like this. They demanded a quieter voice discussing things and not just screaming for the sake of screaming'.

Public agency

Al Jazeera considers itself a public agency, a dialogical interlocutor delivering information sources and discursive forms of debates. As the interviewee notes, 'It is impossible to imagine somebody who cannot read or write would be able to be part of any kind of political process. I mean you go and vote somebody and you do not know who the candidates are, you can't read the ballots. How could you be part of any political process? And you are talking about this part of the world where *more than half* the people cannot read or write. Full stop. Where do you go from here? In my opinion, *Al Jazeera* has helped a lot in this direction.' He argues that for the first time in history, 'Yemen tribesmen, who live in remote areas in a tent, you find satellite dishes like this by their tents.' In the respondent's view, this is one of the important functions of *Al Jazeera* – to deliver concepts like political participation, voting, democracy, human rights, women's rights. This is the sphere where *Al Jazeera* seems to operate as an interlocutor on the one hand and an agent on the other. As the respondent argues, 'This in my opinion is the kind of thing that opposition parties usually do . . . try to arm the people with facts and information so that they can hold their own governments accountable'. This sphere emerged as a by-product, since nobody from *Al Jazeera*, or any other media outlet, has ever established or launched their project or has said 'this is one of my aims to do this'. However, *Al Jazeera* considers this element of providing crucial information, allowing agency building, to be as important 'as the product itself'. The respondent notes, 'if you do not know, you won't even begin to feel that you miss something. You miss something, because you have tried it. If you don't try it, you won't even begin to feel that you miss it. And that is what happened in the case of *Al Jazeera*. When *Al Jazeera* came to being. People did not know what they were missing until *Al Jazeera* came and then they suddenly realized that they were missing something and they did not know what it was.'

This particular role is important in the Arab region as one respondent notes: 'The ruler' in the Arab region has always been willing 'to give a little bit of freedom' or 'space' to writers, authors, the book industry. However, such a space is restricted in the sphere of electronic media, given the high illiteracy rates. 'They can just about read or write but they do not have the time or the capacity to buy certain books or orient themselves to the outside world.' In addition, it is emphasized that 'we are talking about a tiny portion of people that the regime would actually be concerned about when it comes to books and print journalism. But when you talk about electronic media, it has never happened before that the government of that part of the world started to compromise, started to give the private sector a chance, started to inject their own TV channels with a lot of programmes that *Al Jazeera* presents, started to launch new channels. This is a huge leap forward. So this in my opinion is the measure of "success" so to speak of *Al Jazeera*. *Al Jazeera* is far from perfect. Professionally speaking, there is a lot for all of us *Al Jazeera* people to learn on a professional level and the rest of it.'

In this sense, the 'by product' of *Al Jazeera*'s being an information source allows agency building to be considered as one of the most important roles 'because people start to see light for themselves' and they start to compare. They start to criticize: 'Why is it that we are not seeing this on our channels?' In this sense, the government 'just has to respond'. This role of agency is difficult in the context of the large number of satellite channels available in the Arab region today, as 'some people estimate them, 700; some people even say they exceed 1,000 channels available from the days not very far away when we only had one or two channels, state-owned of course'. Despite this enlarged number of other satellite channels, the role of agency remains an important link, but with an enlarged geographical scope. 'And when I think of my audience, I think of anybody who can speak Arabic.' Such an agency role also seems to include non-Arabic speakers: 'I mean I have been recognized in countries that don't speak Arabic. Because they like what *Al Jazeera* does, they can pick a word or two. I am talking here about the millions of Moslems in Asia. When I was in Pakistan for instance people would stop me: "Ah, *Al Jazeera*, how are you doing guys? We like you a lot. Are you launching a channel in English and when would that be?" So I would think of those people and in consequence . . . would consider them as part of my target audience.' Such a transnationally interdependent public agency is difficult, as it includes quite diverse political constituencies. 'In Africa I get also correspondence from African people even suggesting ideas for doing research for me and sending them to me. And of course, there are those in Europe and America; that also poses another set of questions about you as a programme maker.'

To identify the roles of linking spheres and of agency, which could be assigned to the role of a dialogical interlocutor, becomes increasingly difficult in the transnational sphere in which *Al Jazeera* operates today. The respondent sees the main problem as the great diversity of the audience:

'Because we are talking about, first of all, people who are very different in their degree of education, degree of awareness, and the rest of it. From another dimension, those who live in different parts of the world have different interests that they would like to focus on, rather than others. It is not as though if I were working for BBC 1. I would know very well. I would go out terrestrial for people who only live here within Britain. But a Yemenese tribesman who does not read or write. . . or am I talking to the Professor of Chemistry who lives in Los Angeles who migrated from Syria or Egypt? This process has consequences for the programme production: I do a programme every three months; it takes me three months to put the investigation together and you can't imagine if I would feel, it happened several times, that I would be walking down the street either here in Edgeware Road, in a remote area in Jordan or in Yemen or in

Egypt and somebody who cannot even read or write stops me to say "thank you", you have told me a lot about this subject or that idea three or four years ago.'

It is argued that *Al Jazeera* is perceived as leading other Arab media organizations who would like 'to be part of that caravan.' In addition, the respondent claims that at 'the same time, we should keep the Arab governments on their toes. *Al Jazeera* gets tired that would be very good news as far as many Arab governments are concerned.'

BBC World: dialogical interlocutor in the sphere of interregional connectedness

BBC World constitutes a quite different type of interlocutor. The BBC, as one of the most trusted news organizations worldwide, situates itself in a much broader public horizon and could be described as an interlocutor positioned in a dynamically chosen interregional connectedness.[2]

Layers of linking

The BBC's aim is to increase the visibility of BBC World as a brand through its 'reputation in a fast changing market'. This brand is entirely built around content as the key domain for BBC World. One respondent notes that 'content is crucial', particularly as 'access to multiple sources of information requires a particular focus on content quality' as 'people gaze out there on the Internet, on radio, on television, their newspapers, their magazines. They move around, they shift away, they come back.' It is noted that 'mobile phone with digital camera . . . you can upload and download in a matter of seconds on a platform which is linked to Wi-Fi . . . Distance is no object anymore . . . is it local, is it national, is it international? It is everything.' This is the sphere in which the BBC World operates as an interlocutor transnationally and, according to one respondent, aims to position itself within this enlarged network of information resources through high-quality content. However, journalism in the global public space is operating in a new domain, since there are no distances: 'Distance is eliminated in certain world regions'; distance is negotiated. These are the perceived 'challenges of real time'. It seems that BBC World has defined 'key audiences' in different geographical areas. As one respondent notes, 'We are looking at the world at the moment where clearly the Middle East

is critical.' BBC World has both a broad and dense transnational perspective, as BBC World competes with regional news outlets in various
world regions. As one respondent argues: 'You have to look to the news
stations cropping up in the region to realize there is really a battle for
information and for a commitment from that audience.' Besides the
Middle East, other regions are increasingly in focus on BBC World for
different reasons: 'Look at south Asia, look at China, here are huge,
vast audiences, we have to tap into . . . the United States certainly,
Middle East certainly, Asia, we have a growing success in Europe as
well. Ultimately, you pull all these regions together and what do you
get? You get the whole world.' It is interesting that respondents state
that BBC World positions itself as an 'open space' where the traditional
constructions of international, national and foreign news no longer
have relevance for transnational news platforms. Instead, journalism is
perceived as supranational: 'We are all supranational if you have the
platform to broadcast.' In addition the space is enlarged through multiple information sources. It is argued that 'the Internet is already
changing that because people are now accessing and using the Internet
as a platform for video-on-demand news without even being streamed'.
It seems that the BBC actively engages in this new transnational sphere
of dialogical relations. The particular sphere for BBC World, and the
particular challenge, consists in the aim to provide information that
relates to these diverse forms of spatial information flows and, at the
same time, to be aware of diverse perspectives. It is argued that it
is the role of journalism 'to bring information to someone's doorstep
even though they may be not thinking about it. So, for someone in Iraq
or someone in the Gulf Region, it is local and regional, but if you are
in Brazil, you are in Chile or you are in Washington and you are watching about Faluja, it is national.' Furthermore, as one respondent notes,
interaction with audiences is relevant as the 'corrector' of content in
such an enlarged network sphere: 'People . . . email us, they send pic-
tures, they correct the record in a way in which we could not, sitting
in an office.'

Power of linking

This sphere of power is perceived as challenging in a new way. As
one respondent states: 'Do we have power over governments? I am
not sure I would use that word, I would say "influence on the process"
but I am certainly of the view that what this is doing (showing a
mobile phone), is creating a new brittleness of power in governments
and institutions . . . a lot of governments find themselves on the "back

foot" and vulnerable to accusations that they did not know what was going on. Is that power? I think it leaves us in a situation where this asymmetrical smart card in there can often have more power than the institutions of governments.' Furthermore, the BBC is also aware of this new power sphere: 'not just policymakers, but NGOs, participants in international political processes, are sensitive as they are portrayed as organizations by the BBC'. The role of BBC World as a dialogical interlocutor seems to be addressed when one respondent notes: 'If you want people in Delhi to be watching you really should be looking to recognize that they have an interest in stories which affect them. Even international stories which affect them.' Although BBC World's attempt is 'to make things as neutral as possible' and although targeting a 'wider world', it is unknown 'who is viewing it at any moment in time'. However, world regions are addressed through time zones: 'We are aware that at certain times of the day perhaps we are targeting certain parts of the world . . . there is a recognition that regions count and at certain times we target those.' Furthermore, it is claimed, that 'If there is anything that is very close to hearts they will be there and they will be able to watch us 24 hours'; according to one respondent, 'this is achieved through "trust"' and he notes that 'the core value is to be able to convince people that they can trust what you are telling them'.

Public agency

Within such an open space, the traditional values of journalism seem to be refined *vis-à-vis* diverse information resources. Both authenticity and objectivity are news values to strive for; however, these are perceived as relativistic values within such an enlarged transnational public space. A respondent remarks: 'we are trying to be "authentic". Of course we try to be objective. The question is what "objectivity" is by our standards, sitting in London as a national or global news broadcaster. The trouble is, our standards of objectivity and our view of objectivity may be not the same as a radical Palestinian's, sitting in Gaza or a member of Al Qaeda sitting in Iraq or Afghanistan . . . They have a very different view of objectivity.' The aim of objectivity has always been a challenge in an international context. One interviewee remarks, 'If you think back to the cameraman and my former colleagues who used to go to difficult spots with a video camera or a film camera and then ship the tape back and it might have been a day or two before that was transmitted, often there were few journalists if any there. How objective were they? They gave a personal view of what was happening. Now if anything with the multiple matrix coming from any location, any location now, sometimes it is two or three dimensions, sometimes it is so multiple you cannot keep up with it.' It could be argued that this one challenge of the new process-oriented dimension of news flows – where there is a dialogical connectedness to audiences who have access to numerous authentic sites and information resources – establishes a new form of journalism.

It is argued that 'the definitions of "objectivity" and "authenticity" are really up for grabs'. This is particularly the case in today's multinational pluralistic digital environment where platforms are being compared to each other. An example mentioned is the platform *Allmynews* in South Korea: 'They got a citizen journalist on location who is maybe not a trained journalist but is providing another view which is thereby possibly underpinning or also throwing doubt upon our version.' This challenge creates, what one respondent perceives as 'a new brittleness for us as broadcasters' where organizations, such as *BBC World* are 'even more accountable for accuracy'. He notes, that this situation is 'even creating a greater brittleness for governments and for institutions of power'.

Deutsche Welle: dialogical interlocutor in thematic connectedness

The third example of a sphere of a dialogical interlocutor is *Deutsche Welle*. Compared to the sphere of *Al Jazeera* as an interlocutor, linking the connectedness of Arab communities in a transnational context and BBC World as an interlocutor of interregional connectedness, *Deutsche Welle* is situated as a dialogical interlocutor in a sphere of thematic connectedness.[3]

Layers of linking

Deutsche Welle has gone through various phases and has addressed different transnational audiences. Today, *Deutsche Welle* is, as one executive remarks, 'no longer a programme for expatriates'. It is argued that news organizations are more connected 'than before' which results in a 'boom' of news channels. Examples are those channels which also broadcast in different languages, such as *Russia Today, France 2*. *Deutsche Welle* positions itself in such a sphere of national satellite channels, which are often only small outlets, but operating globally. It is mentioned that 'not many people know that South Korea also runs a global programme, called *Ariana TV*, which airs in Arabic'. *Deutsche Welle* promotes itself not so much as a state broadcaster but as providing 'public service . . . to be fit for the *YouTube* and post-*YouTube* age.'

Deutsche Welle considers itself to be a supranational platform delivered via a global satellite network. Based on this global reach, *Deutsche Welle* is defined as a supra-national platform, as is claimed:, 'we are supra-national in our angle, also in our news angle'. Despite this overall 'supra-national' angle, *Deutsche Welle* targets particular regions which are not national regions but which relate to larger regional or 'transboundary' terrains: 'Regionalization means "continentalization"; for us a region is a continent with sometimes, sub regions.' The aim is to be aware of these subregions; overall 'we cover large territories without looking at each aspect which might play a role in that region'.

Power of linking

Despite this overall aim to operate as a supra-national platform, the fact that *Deutsche Welle* is identified as a German news provider seems to be perceived as a burden; it might be perceived as a national frame contradicting the particular role of a supra-national broadcaster. As one executive notes: 'It is supra-national what we do, however, we are perceived not only by our name as something national – this particular "G" for German sticks on our brand.' *Deutsche Welle* aims to situate itself in the larger scope of Europe: 'Our tagline is "from the Heart of Europe" and we are taking on a European perspective in the way we cover news very seriously and we try to clearly reflect this angle.' The interviewees are considerate about the value of transnational news versus national news. 'In each country, the largest segment of the society is interested in national affairs . . . based on this, we will never be anything more than a niche programme in the region where we can be received. It is impossible for us to provide a programme for large national audiences, we aim to be interactive across all media platforms.'

The German angle of *Deutsche Welle* is critically reflected and an overly German frame is widely rejected: 'I can show Germany only in the way it is, if things turn worse here, I need to cover that – that is our duty.

Relating to authenticity it is argued that proximity is not always geographical. Authenticity becomes increasingly important; however, objectivity also needs to be preserved. Despite the European perspective, *Deutsche Welle* is widely available transnationally and, is stated, 'It must feel strange . . . you are sitting somewhere in south India and you set your news agenda along news from Berlin.' The executives claim that *Deutsche Welle* does not consider itself to be a top news provider. It is assumed, however, that *Deutsche Welle* has an influence in various world regions. Given the role as a niche broadcaster, this influence is not so much on larger audience segments but on specific audiences: 'In the various countries and cultures where our programme can be received, there are also subnational "mini" audiences that can be tremendously different and diverse, for example in India, or in Africa, the so-called "info elites", the "multipliers" are quite diverse'.

Despite considering itself as a supranational broadcaster *Deutsche Welle* practises subnational journalism: 'We have journalists from more than 50 nations who are able to provide specific news angles and perspectives and a particular "weighting" of events, in addition to more analytical way of news reporting. This means that *Deutsche Welle* is very strong in the in-depth analysis of events in the perspective of quite different cultural communities. This is where we increasingly see our role. To carefully analyse political developments and particular values.'

In this sense, and on a subnational level *Deutsche Welle* is, so to speak, the 'corrector' of BBC and CNN. 'This is often stated among our audience. This means that people of course watch BBC and CNN, as these are global brands . . . but they also watch *Deutsche Welle*, just to be able to check for confirmation of what the others have covered.' It seems that through being a supra-national broadcaster practising subnational journalism, the role of *Deutsche Welle* as 'public agency' emerges.

Public agency

Deutsche Welle takes on 'agency' in three ways. The first type of agency is among the 'mini' audiences, such as the 'info elites' described above, but also in providing an information resource for regions which are censored by government. 'We provide our service in 30 different languages.' The second type relates to delivering information to regions which are government censored: 'We also target people in unfree media regions, in those countries we want to deliver trustworthy and reliable information.' The third type reflects agency in a domestic context, where *Deutsche Welle* delivers 'information from their own regions, which often they would not get through their own government censored media'. A fourth type of agency relates to crisis regions 'where the media infrastructure has been destroyed'. It should be noted that at the time of the interviews, this remark related to shortwave radio, which has recently been closed down in developing regions. However, a new service, delivering *Deutsche Welle* news via mobile phones, has been established in these regions.

These three case studies serve here as examples of quite diverse dialogical interlocutors. However, they not only reveal their different 'situatedness' within horizons of transnational public interdependence but also the active roles in generating such a public interdependence. The three types of connectedness reveal models of the bracketing of public interdependence in a supra-and subnational context. The examples also show how media organizations begin to dissolve into new forms of content provider in a dialogical public space. Whereas in the case of *Al Jazeera*, this dialogical relation has been addressed in the context of cultural proximity, in the BBC World case the active engagement with audiences and interactive platforms reveals a different approach to connectedness. In the case of *Deutsche Welle* this connectedness is established through thematic links and the engagement with selected subnational spheres.

This chapter has identified the new spheres of influence in a context of transnational reflective public interdependence that is no longer situated within media organizations but rather in the dialogical relations arising across emerging process-oriented, subjectively chosen reflective public spaces. The next chapter will take this discussion further and will identify the notion of public consciousness within a transnational context.

5

From the Public Sphere to Public 'Horizons'

In previous chapters we have discussed deliberation in larger terrains of 'reflective inbetween-ness'. As suggested earlier (see Chapter 3), the 'axis' of transnational 'spatial' public communication is no longer situated in the nation but in the 'lifeworld'. The lifeworld constitutes the space of interdependent 'public' reflection, enabled and sustained by subjectively selected 'reflective' networks. The formation of the 'matrix' of influence in relational spheres of media and communicative platforms has been developed in Chapter 4. Taking these discussions further allows us now to conceptualize the 'space' of deliberative discourse within these enlarged spheres of public communication.

It is often assumed that the 'world' society is linked to a global public sphere, enabling new forms of democratic participation between 'the nation' and globalized governance polity. Despite quite distinct debates within globalized or transnational communication over the last years, it is somewhat surprising that the specific fine-lined consequences of these severe transformations for the traditional model of deliberative discourse *vis-à-vis* such a spatial, 'non-national', 'non-territorial' sphere have not been fully addressed. Strictly speaking, we could argue that debates in areas such as political economy, post-colonialism and 'media scapes' or approaches to cultural and mediated trans-locality (see Appadurai, 1996; Tomlinson, 1999) have mapped out at least some conceptual frameworks which demarcate the larger terrain of transnational deliberative discourse in new communicative spaces. For example, approaches of political economy identify the 'disentangling' of the situated-ness of the civic 'individual' from a normative national (territorial) context through engagement with spheres of neoliberal network structures. Conceptions of 'post colonialism', 'hybridity' (Kraidy, 2005) and 'mediation' (see Silverstone, 1999; Lundby, 2009) assess communicative spaces which make other forms of deliberative discourse 'visible', such as those which we might call 'deliberative negotiations': the 'deterritorialization' of civic identity through trans-'local' mechanisms within media spheres. Post colonialism addresses these forms of deliberative negotiation *vis-à-vis* hegemonic structures and debates of 'hybridity' and 'mediation' remap the deliberative discursive space of 'identity' in a transnational field of communicative cultures. These conceptions are relevant for understanding the complexities of the emerging globalized form of public communication and, viewed from the angle of 'deliberative' communicative practices, address particular stages in which the traditional ideal of deliberative discourse has begun to shift in the dynamics of new communicative practices.

However, we should not overlook the fact that deliberative discourse is also tied to the enlarged dynamic communicative space of technology-centred interaction and – due to this lens – is sometimes understood as a somewhat one-dimensional sphere of specific 'digital' or 'online' deliberation. Quite often the 'ideal' of traditions of rational deliberative discourse is broadly adopted in these one-dimensional network contexts and in consequence it is assumed that deliberative network engagement is either an 'alternative' sphere of deliberation or due to the boundedness of this ideal model is restricted to a territorially (often nationally) shared space. The dialectic between the 'national' and the 'spatial' of the traditional model of deliberative discourse has been problematized already in the early days of the 'Internet' and it has been argued that 'the utopian vision' of the 'Internet' as a worldwide agora' has a great potential to reshape democracy which, however, is undermined by the 'harsh reality' of 'lawsuits' and 'regulations', commercial interests and 'entertainment', political parties, organized interest groups, political activists, and 'masses of bored indifferent citizens' (Margolis and Resnick, 2000: 14). More recently, conceptual approaches assessing 'online' deliberation are more critical and it has been argued that the 'revolution/normalization' frame of 'online deliberation' is too narrow and one-dimensional (Wright, 2012). Wright argues that the deliberative potential of the Internet has not been fully explored as online research, often related to 'traditional definitions of politics' with 'normative underpinnings that may not hold in the context of new media' (Wright, 2012: 245). In addition, deliberative discourse is, very recently, explored in transnationally focused, thematic areas of climate change in the paradigm 'risk' communication that indicates a shift away form the 'modern' (by this term I mean modern deliberative discourse paradigm by Rawls and Habermas) notion of deliberative discourse towards a 'reflexive' form of deliberative discourse in contexts of globalized 'risks' (see Johnson, 2012), which seems to begin to dislocate deliberative practices in a larger, unbounded, communicative space and to articulate a different, i.e. 'reflexive' understanding of the dialectic between the 'national' and the 'spatial'.

Given the advanced stage not only of globalization but also of the complexity of networked 'public' communication in such an enlarged terrain, a conceptualization of the dimensions of spatial, transnational 'principles' of deliberative discourse in today's advanced phase of globalization can no longer be addressed through an adoption of the 'modern' ideal of deliberative discourse, a technology-centred focus on the lens of thematic threads of 'risk' communication. Instead, the debate of deliberative discourse should be positioned, and here I am taking Beck's term further, in an understanding of 'reflexive' processes as a 'reflective' communicative space which would allow us to identify the fine-lined implications of transnational communicative' flows' on local, 'vertical' democratic formations. It is only through this angle that the axis of deliberative discourse can be relocated in communicative trajectories, situated in chosen interdependent spatial 'flows' where, for example, selected 'actors', 'connectors' and 'interlocutors' (see Chapter 4) interact, not being situated within a shared polity and engaged in deliberation about a 'common good' but – physically and eventually virtually dispersed – engaged in deliberative discourse in the context of a globalized 'common good'.

Despite these emerging 'reflexive' structures not only of 'networked' but 'reflective' communicative dimensions in contexts of larger scopes of globalized 'issues' which situate deliberative discourse in interactive 'public' interdependence, it is mainly the Habermasian conception of rational discourse among consensus-oriented interlocutors which serves as the core paradigm of deliberative discourse in transnational communicative structures, even beyond the Western nation-states. It is a liberal-democratic model which, as Mouffe has noted, 'very few dare to challenge openly' (Mouffe, 2000: 80).

The ideal conditions of deliberative discourse or 'argumentation' require a set of at least six conditions (Habermas, 2001b). The first condition relates to 'equality' and the requirement that nobody is 'excluded', in the 'equal' opportunity to make contributions. The second requirement is 'truthfulness', that participants 'mean what they say' and the third suggests that communication 'must be freed from external and internal coercion'. The fourth relates to the 'public character of practised discourse', the fifth condition demands 'equal communicative rights' for all participants as it is assumed that only reasons giving 'equal weight to the interests and evaluative orientations of everybody can influence the outcome of practical discourses'. The sixth condition required is consent-oriented and requires that 'participants reciprocally impute an orientation to communicative agreement on one another, this . . . acceptance can only occur jointly or collectively' (Habermas, 2001b: 44). As Habermas notes 'the discursive level of opinion formation and the 'quality' of the outcome vary with this 'more or less' in the 'national' processing of 'exhaustive proposals, information, and reason' (Habermas, 1999) and the 'public' is made up of citizens who see acceptable interpretation for their social interests and experiences and who want to have an influence on institutional opinion- and will-formation' (Habermas, 1999). These are the conditions of rationalized discourse reached through what Habermas describes as a 'higher-level intersubjectivity of communication processes' which 'flow through both the parliamentary bodies and the informal networks of the public sphere'. Such a discourse practice constitutes deliberation 'within' and 'outside' of the 'parliamentary complex'. It is only through such a formal process or, as Habermas notes, 'subjectless' forms of communication that 'a more or less rational opinion- and will-formation take place' (Habermas, 1996: 28) as a theoretically and conceptually universal validity; however, within the collective moral and interest related civic boundedness in modern societies and through this model, nation-states.

Conceptions of global and networked communication have not yet produced alternative models which would allow us to capture the particular spaces of deliberative discourse across new spheres that are no longer 'national' but rather incorporated into the deliberative force of 'reflective' engagement through dynamically shifting densities of public interdependence. Densities of public interdependence where it is not that rational discourse procedures are the aim of the 'ideal' speech situation but, given the interactive nature of the networked environment, there is continuous civic engagement in discursive practices across multi-layered 'dialogical relations'. Habermas' distinction between public 'opinion' and the 'thick contexts of simple interactions' (Habermas, 1999: 361), between the 'ideal speech situation' and more 'generalized' forms of public opinion, reveals the dilemma of identifying public communication 'as such' but also the dilemma of identifying an ideal discourse, taking into account the influences of public opinion formations on such an 'ideal' discourse. As an outcome, the ideal of rational discourse can only be considered as an abstract form of 'subjectless-ness' communicative action. However, communicative space of deliberative discourse is no longer shared along the boundedness of moral values and the shared understanding of the 'common good' but is the discursive engagement of 'actors' who are situated in a communicative terrain that is not a subjectless sphere but rather a subjectively chosen dimension and who engage in 'reflective' communicative action. This reflective communicative space is no longer tied to and bounded by the parameter of strategic consent-oriented discourse principles of 'utterances' and the larger scope of 'public opinion' as a general form of 'legitimate influence' (Habermas, 1999: 363), closely related to (national) institutional forms. 'Reflective' communicative action across densities of public interdependence is no longer a 'hierarchical' process between (equal) citizens and (national) 'institutions'. It is rather a de-hierarchical process, which, for example, through interactive social media, engages a diversity of 'citizens' (not only from one nation) as well as diverse 'institutional nodes' (see Chapter 4) within the scope of spatial networked structures. Habermas suggests that 'processes of opinion-formation, especially when they have to do with political questions, certainly cannot be separated from the transformation of the participants' preferences and attitudes, but they can be separated from putting these dispositions into action and he argues that to this extent, 'the communication structures of the public sphere relieve the public of the burden of decision making: the postponed decisions are reserved for the institutionalized, political process' (Habermas, 1999: 362). In this sense, public opinion is a sphere of political influence on 'institutionalized procedures' (Habermas, 1999: 363).

The ideal speech situation as deliberative discourse is centred upon reaching consensus among (morally bounded) equals. This is the process which, as a consequence, produces a bounded model of deliberative discourse. This particular angle is shifting in contexts of reflective public interdependence and it is such a boundedness that is no longer related to discourse partners exposed and engaged with rational discourse principles. This model of an ideal speech situation has greatly influenced the particular conception of 'discourse-orientation' of a public, geared towards the formation of influence on political institutions. Such an approach, however, hides not only alternative formations of deliberative discourse but the strict procedural principles of the rational discourse model leave little room for the processes of, for example, non-rational discourse traditions in an enlarged not always consensus-oriented public environment of deliberative discourse.

The use of the model of an ideal speech situation with the outcome of identifying consensus through discursive principles and interest-related consent-orientation of (for example, national) equals also seems to serve as a 'normative' model in debates of transnational publics. Deliberative discourse, for example in thematic 'risk' communication of climate change, is either conceptualized through the lens of an 'extension' of consensus orientation of (national) publics or in separate spheres of 'national' and 'transnational' or 'international' deliberation. Such a notion of consensus-oriented deliberative discourse in the modern tradition has been useful for a long time in the age of 'linear' communication of the (national and limited international) mass-media age and has helped us to understand not only the public debate but also transnational media formations and the extended domain of deliberative discourse. The debate about international media operating as a 'fifth' estate in national public spheres, that is, transnational media creating public opinion and influencing national governance, reflects such a nationally bounded approach, even in larger contexts of networked transnationalization. Such a bounded 'fifth' estate approach is, for example, also used to 'frame' the influence of networked communication on national publics, for example, when assessing the role of the Internet on national news media. Newman et al. (2012) argue that content produced by 'networked individuals' form a 'fifth estate' and the mechanism of such a spatial 'flow' is interpreted by following a mass-media model. It is suggested that 'content can bypass or be amplified by the traditional media of the fourth estate' and conclude that 'thus a Fifth estate is also a potentially potent political force, but without the centralized institutional foundations of the Fourth Estate' (Newman et al., 2012: 7). The authors argue that 'networked citizens' influence not only the 'fourth' estate but rather engage directly with fourth estate 'institutions', such as 'media' and government institutions for example through 'direct' democracy spheres but also e-government discourse. This approach shows that 'deliberative discourse' takes on new practices and is no longer consensus-oriented but rather a 'dialogical' space, which not only influences the 'fourth estate', that is, as a space of media influence and 'public opinion' but surpasses these institutional mediated forms through direct discourse bearing the potential for a deliberative process. In this sense, it would be misleading to assume deliberative discourse with an outcome of consensus as the result of rational discourse but rather, as I argue, a deliberative discourse as 'reflective' process with the outcome of a repositioning of the perception of the civic 'self' within a transnational sphere. It is *this* perception of the civic 'self' that shapes deliberative engagement.

As modern societies are increasingly fractured and public debate is 'decoupled' from discourse among equal partners we simply can no longer assume that deliberative discourse relates to interlocutors whose discursive 'action' targets consensus through the assumption that they share a common understanding of civic identity and a perception of moral values and, thus a common understanding of the 'common good' for example, within a nation. It is the consensus orientation based on the perception of common public 'good' which shifts towards consensus orientation in the perception of shared public 'dimensions' in the time of public interdependence. As Spichal has recently argued, a 'normative condition of an equal treatment of alternatives presupposes the possibility of an unhindered deliberation that could eventually bring about consensus, which would only be possible if irreducibly different 'alternatives' never existed. Unfortunately, this is not commonly the case' (Spichal, 2012: 61). Spichal's argument is important here as it addresses the fact that 'interests' range not only along different social groups but across larger transnationally shared communities, for example, often overlooked, not only different societal strata but also generations in particular in contexts of networked communication. Despite the fact that Habermas' model of the ideal speech situation seems to constitute the blueprint for an understanding of deliberative discourse, it is now important to broaden the narrow scope of the normative discourse practice towards a more inclusive sphere of communicative ethics of an 'ideal speech' situation within the spheres of public interdependence.

A broadening of the communicative space of 'consensus-orientation' of modern deliberative discourse through an emphasis on a 'subject' orientation within the scope of pluralist societies has been proposed – mainly in political science – in at least four dimensions.

Dimension 1: 'Agonistic pluralism'

The first dimension is the critique of the consensus-orientation based on the principle of 'inclusion' and 'exclusion' which is one of the main 'narratives' of critique of the liberal and democratic models. This lens has been addressed in contexts of 'gender' (Fraser, 1996) and 'identity politics' (Cohen, 1996). However, I will follow Mouffe's argumentation here, who understands the liberal (Rawls, 1999) and democratic (Habermas, 1999) model as a 'democratic paradox' (Mouffe, 2000). Mouffe argues that the aim, to establish 'communicative power', requires establishing 'the conditions for a freely given assent of all concerned' (Mouffe, 2000: 87) which should have a 'universal' reach (Mouffe, 2000: 89). She argues that it should be accepted that 'consensus' as a deliberative form can only exist 'temporarily' as a 'result of a provisional hegemony', which, in her view, serves as a 'stabilization of power'. On the other hand, this process simultaneously entails forms of exclusion. It is only through such an acknowledgement that 'we can begin to envisage the nature of a democratic public sphere in a different way' (Mouffe, 1999: 756). In Mouffe's view, deliberative discourse cannot be reached by 'rational justification' as a somewhat principle-oriented subjectless form but rather through the 'availability of democratic forms of individuality and subjectivity'. 'Individuality' and 'subjectivity' are related to central argument of the democratic paradox by what she describes as 'privileging rationality' of the modern model, relating to both the 'deliberative' and the 'aggregative' perspectives. Both leave aside a 'central element' which is the crucial role 'played by passions and affects in securing allegiance and democratic values'. In Mouffe's view, the central issue of democratic theory is to 'tackle the question of citizenship' as an 'abstract' form. In this sense deliberative discourse as a consensus-oriented process has to build upon a specific subject construction. This involves a construction of subjectivity that understands 'individuals as prior to society' and as 'bearers of national rights' and 'either utility maximizing agents or rational subjects'. Mouffe suggests that 'in all cases they are abstracted from social and power relations, language, culture and the whole set of practices that make agency possible. What is precluded in these rationalistic approaches is the very question of what are the conditions of existence of the democratic subject (Mouffe, 2000: 95/6). She suggests focusing less on the forms of rational argumentation than on the 'types of practices' (Mouffe, 2000: 96). Futhermore, Mouffe's approach aims to address deliberative discourse not as a consensus-oriented 'principle' but rather as a practice, that is, the 'agreement on the definition of a term is not enough and we need agreement in the way we use it'. This means, so Mouffe argues, that discourse 'principles' should rather be understood as 'procedures' and be envisaged as a complex set of ensembles of practices. 'It is because they are inscribed in shared forms of life and agreements in judgements that procedures can be accepted and followed. They cannot be seen as rules that are created on the basis of principles and then applied to specific cases' (Mouffe, 2000: 97). In consequence, Mouffe suggests a model of 'agonistic pluralism' and constructs the 'other' (meaning the formal 'non citizen') no longer as being 'perceived as an enemy . . . but as an 'adversary', that is, somebody whose ideas we combat but whose right to defend those ideas we do not put into question, where discourse is not consensus or resolution-orientated but an 'ongoing confrontation' (Mouffe, 2000: 102). Mouffe also argues for a model of agonistic pluralism 'the prime task of democratic politics is not to eliminate passions from the sphere of the public, in order to render a rational consensus possible, but to mobilize those passions towards democratic designs' (Mouffe, 2000: 103). It is such an approach of 'agonistic pluralism' which 'reveals the impossibility of establishing a consensus without exclusion' (Mouffe, 2000: 105).

Dimension 2: 'Identity as agency'

A second dimension, however, closely relating to Mouffe's work, addresses the broadening of communicative space of deliberative discourse in a more radical approach of 'agonistic' discourse through an 'identity' dimension as a deliberative practice. Dryzek's point of departure from the Habermasian model is the argument that 'agonistic' discourse – taking Mouffe's model further – is related to a conception for deliberative practice within 'divided' societies due to diverse forms of 'identities'. In this sense, Dyzek's model considers the fracturing of modern nation-states and seeks to construct an inclusive model which would allow us to acknowledge diverse identities, however, within the boundedness of a multi-cultural society. Dryzek's conception opens up the 'consensus'-model through a communicative space of deliberative discourse which allows the engagement of diverse identities within 'divided societies'. Dryzek's model proposes a 'decoupling' of deliberation and 'decision aspects of democracy' and locates 'deliberation in engagement of discourses in the public sphere at a distance from any contest of sovereign authority'. In consequence. he argues that 'the public spheres in question can transcend national boundaries, and their transnational aspects can have an important moderating influence on the clash of identities'(Dryzek, 2006: 47). Dryzek's notion of 'agonistic' discourse understands deliberation as a 'robust and passionate exchange across identities' (Dryzek, 2006: 48). Furthermore, he argues that 'acceptance of the legitimacy of the positions of others comes not through being persuaded by argument, but through openness to conversion as a result of a particular kind of democratic attitude (Dryzek, 2006). His model is based on the assumption that 'identity' is an important aspect of deliberation. In his view, it is important to understand 'discursive democracy' as a process which 'can handle deep differences'. In addition, Dryzek also positions this model in a transnational context which does not understand the national and the transnational as two separate discourse entitites but rather as a common sphere, however, a sphere of conflict. In his view, the public sphere in question can transcend national boundaries, and their transnational aspects can have an important moderating influence on the clash of identities' (Dryzek, 2006: 47). Agnostic deliberation, in Dryzek's model, incorporates diverse forms of communication, 'rhetoric, testimony, performance,' however, communication requires 'reflection,' has to be 'non-coercive' and 'capable of linking the particular interest of the group with some more general point of principle' (Dryzek, 2006: 52).

Dimension 3: 'Resituating the self'

It is Seyla Benhabib's work which is relevant here as a third dimension of critique of the modern deliberative principle of the ideal speech situation. Benhabib's critique focuses on the 'self' within the scope of deliberative discourse. She proposes that participation in deliberative discourse is 'governed' not by a civic 'contract' but rather by 'norms of equality and symmetry'. It is equality and symmetry as 'all have the same chances to initiative speech acts, to question, to investigate, and to open debate'. Furthermore, 'all' have the rights to initiate reflexive arguments about the very rules of the discourse procedure and the way in which they are applied and carried out' (Benhabib, 1996: 70). She argues that which norms and normative institutional arrangements are made should be only justified as valid by 'those who would be affected if they were participants in special moral argumentations called discourse' which is based on the ethics of a mutual respect of capacity to 'agree' or 'disagree on the basis of reasons which equally apply to us both' (Benhabib, 2004: 131/2). Benhabib claims that discourse ethics should incorporate the 'situating of the self', the individual within deliberative discourse. It is not 'the people' but rather the 'self' and 'peoplehood is an aspiration not a fact' (Benhabib, 2004: 82). Furthermore, the self is positioned between the 'vision of the universal' and the 'attachment of the particular' (Benhabib, 1996:16) and she argues that the 'unit of the demos ought not to be understood as if it were a harmonious given, but rather a process of self-constitution, through more or less conscious struggles of inclusion and exclusion (Benhabib, 2004: 216).

Dimension 4: 'Communicative democracy'

A fourth dimension suggests extensions of the traditional model of deliberation not only through a reconception of the 'self', of 'agonistic' discourse but of 'communicative' democracy as such (Young, 1996). This model suggests that the notion of 'equal' speakers in the modern deliberative model are not 'culturally inclusive' and 'neutral' and 'dispassionate' and 'disembodied' (Young, 1996: 124). Young argues that 'the norms of "articulateness", however, must be learned; they are culturally specific and in actual speaking situations in our society exhibiting such speaking styles is a sign of social privilege' (Young, 1996: 124). Young's model of communicative democracy might be useful and in her argumentation she situated this model in an approach to address the 'equal privileging of any forms of communicative inter-action where people aim to reach understanding' (Young, 1996: 125). Communicative means here to articulate 'difference' and to transcend difference and only through this process is it possible to address the 'common good'. This also includes the understanding of another social location. However, Young's model although aiming to be inclusive, seems less centred upon the notion of communication and the par-ticular spheres of communication individuals relate to when they enter a discourse.

Although these conceptions attempt to identify communicative spaces of deliberative discourse models mainly in contexts of pluralist societies, it seems that deliberative discourse is no longer 'rooted' within one society but rather engages in interdependent communica-tive intersections as practices within globalized deliberative discourse spheres. Although Mouffe's argumentation opens up the space of deliberative discourse to not just 'the other' but also other forms of 'utterances' and Dryzek's model conceptualizes identity as an impor-tant aspect of passionate discursive engagement, his notion of 'divided societies' and conflict discourses are mainly still geared towards modern societies. Globalization constitutes a new complexity and sphere incorporating not only 'divided' societies but incorporating dif-ferent society types (as I have outlined in previous chapters). Benha-bib's approach acknowledges not only identity but the 'self' and argues for a discourse ethic constructed around issues of 'equality' and 'liberty'; however, this should also be addressed in the larger scope of a transnational sphere of inclusion. Reviewing these four dimensions reveals that the space of deliberative discourse might call for new 'principles' not just of deliberative discourse but of communicative space, enabling deliberative discourse, for example, principles of 'authenticity' incorporating different 'selves' in deliberation across a multi-cultural spectrum of modern societies, principles of conflict inter-action and, overall, of 'communicative democracy'.

It is not so much the re-introduction of the 'subject' within delib-erative discourse of a pluralist society but the *situating* of the subject not only within a pluralist public sphere of one society type but within the lifeworld scope of strategically chosen trajectories of net-worked communication. In this sense, the subject could be understood as a 'civic self', situated in a transnational public sphere terrain. In this context it is important to identify the communicative space of such a subjectively centred deliberative discourse in broader terms and incorporate new forms of political communication that not only apply to regions in the tradition of modernity. It is such a subjective communicative space which posits deliberation in an increasingly 'interdependent' but also 'inclusive' (incorporating a number of civic agencies from various state formations) and 'interactive' (directly responding and providing access) sphere, incorporating various forms of public cultures. Such a conceptual mapping is needed for a deeper understanding of new communicative sphere of a global civil society.

Towards reflective discourse

Beck's notion of 'reflexive' cosmopolitanism could be used here as a starting point for identifying reflective communicative space in the larger terrain of different forms of societies. The perception of reflexive cosmopolitanism allows us to open up the horizontal scope of intersec-tions of epistemological connectedness. Beck suggests that the process of reflexive cosmopolitanism not only overcomes methodological nationalism but also internationalization. Although Beck mainly situ-ates reflexive cosmopolitanism in the agenda of contexts of 'risk', the concept of 'reflexivity' in the enlarged non-national sphere allows us to understand reflective communicative action as a deliberative dis-course in the transnational dimension, which in Beck's work relates to 'risk communication'. It provides a framework for identifying the communicative space for discursive deliberation in such a 'horizontal' epistemologically connected dimension.

Building on Benhabib's argumentation and her conceptual notion of a space of the 'self' within deliberative discourse practice, I extend this further, as I have argued in earlier chapters, and suggest consider-ing deliberative discourse as repositioned from the national to the lifeworld 'axis'. This means not only a 'reflexive' process (see Beck) but also a 'reflective' practice, that is reflectively 'relating' discourse within larger networks of 'dialogue'. In our discussion, the sphere of deliberative discourse is engaged in contexts of interdependence and engaged with subjectively chosen transnationally positioned 'actors', 'reflectors' and 'interlocutors'. It is a discursive practice of interdependent networked discourse situated within the 'lifeworld' and, for example, reflected 'vertically' in the prism of local, national or other forms of thematically specific deliberative discourse.

The 'equal' citizen might be understood as civic 'self', relating to chosen discourses. The lifeworld territory emerges as a centre not only of 'networked' communication 'as such' but within discursive networks of choice. Deliberative discourse is situated within such a larger 'field' (which I have pointed out in Chapter 3). Furthermore, the civic 'self' engages not so much with the 'other' (which suggests an exclusion of public communication) but rather with other 'civic' selves in such a transnational space in the aim to debate a 'common good' which is no longer exclusively related to national contexts but, for example, related to a strategic common interest in a 'global' civil society agenda (for example, human rights, climate change, multi-culturalism, pacifism). It has been argued that transnational publics are geared towards globalized institutions; however, deliberative discourse is increasingly geared towards a new form of global 'common good'. The engagement in discursive fields of interdependent publics requires 'dialogue' as a continuous public form of 'interaction' and engagement. What is often overlooked in conceptions of public discourse is the way in which discursive relationships are established among partners, which are not physically present, and how these discursive relationships are maintained in order to establish deliberative practices and, for example, identify a 'common good'. As deliberative discourse in networked contexts of public interdependence is situated in the virtual 'assembly' of dialogical relation is Watzlawick's model of communicative axioms comes to mind here as an example of the strategic aspect of communicative spheres that are particularly relevant as the 'civic' self engaging in deliberation in a networked context and needs to build and maintain relations in order to engage in deliberative practice (Watzlawick, 1967). Watzlawick has defined a set of communicative 'axioms', for example, the axiom of 'content and relationship', which is relevant for the building and maintenance of dialogical relations and might be useful here. The 'axiom' defines the process in which 'every communication has a content and relationship aspect such that the latter classifies the former and is therefore a meta-communication'. Another example is, of course, Wittgenstein, who noted that before having agreement in opinion there must first be agreement in 'forms of life'. In his view, to agree on the definition of a term is not enough as we need an agreement in the way we use it. Symbolic interactionism might be a third example here which suggests another form of relational understanding through a 'reciprocity' of interactional relations and Schuetz and Luckmann (1973) identify the need for taking on the perspective of the other. Mouffe has argued that 'procedures should be envisaged as a complex ensemble of practices' (Mouffe, 2000: 97); however, I would argue that dialogical relations form 'trust' and 'trusted' public networks and constitute the subjectively chosen communicative space, which, in consequence, sets the stage for deliberative discourse.

This discourse practice is, however, a dialectical process reaching not consensus but dialogue. In the Habermasian model the 'lifeworld' and the public are related through two different dimensions. Habermas argues that 'we have become acquainted with the "lifeworld" as a reservoir for simple interactions, specialized systems of action and knowledge' on the one hand and public speech on the other. 'These public spheres cling to the concrete locales where an audience is physically gathered. The more they detach themselves from the public's physical presence and extend to the virtual presence of scattered readers, listeners, or viewers linked by public media, the clearer becomes the abstraction that enters when the spatial structure of simple interactions is expanded into a public sphere' (Habermas 1999: 361). The structures of networked communication, such as the various 'self-referential' social platforms, satellite television landscapes, take on subjectively chosen roles as networks of centrality (the monitoring sphere) and centrality of networks (the engagement sphere). Deliberative discourse is related to this dialectic within the lifeworld, directly embedded in a 'virtual presence' not so much of 'scattered readers, listeners, or viewers linked by public media' as in the Habermasian model, but of simultaneous dialogical 'networked' relations with 'actors', 'connectors' and 'interlocutors'. The lifeworld constitutes a 'node' of such a dialogical network. It is not a 'higher level of intersubjectivity' (Habermas, 1996) but rather a new deliberative discourse 'order' with the subject at the centre of networks of public interdependence, choosing – in an interesting twist of the term – a quite different, virtual form of 'subjectless' discourse. In this sense, 'subjectless' discourse takes place not only 'virtually' but is discursively chosen from a globalized 'horizon' of dialogical relations. The lifeworld gains a new relevance as larger contexts of these networks are coordinated here, shaping new relations to civic 'others'. These are not necessarily 'civic' others in the same nation but are related to multiple other forms of 'identity'. In this sense, it is not about public connections but the imaginations of the civic self and the multiple imaginations of public 'horizons'. 'Vertical' public discourses, between the lifeworld and 'spatial' public interdependence are reflectively engaged across dense contexts of 'spatial' (often 'transnational') spheres which are 'related', for example to the nation and/or other forms of public community. Such a process of vertical 'reflection' relates to specific forms of deliberative discourse between the 'self' and 'the world'. Deliberative discourse is situated in the sphere of the reflexive disentangling of the civic self through a reflective discourse practice.

From intersubjectivity to discursive consciousness

Conceptual approaches of deliberative discourse relate mainly through Rawls and Habermas to the Kantian theme of rational discourse and, through this contexualization, a specific scope of public space in a communicative sphere closely related to the specific understanding of public reasoning as it unfolds in the enlightenment tradition. Kant's notion of public discourse as a process of 'enlightenment' under the condition that the 'freedom to use reason publicly in all matters is possible' and, furthermore, linked to the claim that the 'public use of one's reason must always be free' (Kant, 1983: 42) is the core principle of public deliberation as the means to enlightenment. Kant's understanding of discourse believes that 'the public should enlighten itself' with the consequence that, 'if it is only allowed freedom, enlightenment is almost inevitable' (Kant, 1983). Kant emphasized that 'nothing is required for this enlightenment, however, except, freedom; and the freedom in question is the least harmful of all, namely the freedom to use reason publicly in all matters' (Kant, 1983: 42). Beyond the notion of a public process of 'enlightenment', Kant is also very distinct about 'public' and 'private' use of reason and notes that 'the public use of one's reason must always be free, and it alone can bring about enlightenment among mankind; the private use of reason may, however, often be very narrowly restricted' (Kant, 1983: 42). Whereas Kant means by the 'public use of reason', that 'anyone as a scholar makes of reason' and the 'private' use of reason which a person may make in a 'civic post' (Kant, 1983: 42). Kant's ideal of public reason is a universal conception. Kant's understanding of reason is closely related to a particular engaged 'public' performance and is the core of the understanding of public deliberation in modern societies, in the way in which public debate is 'kept from deformation' (Habermas, 1999).

This idea of public reason, although claiming a universal validity, has implications for the understanding and further conceptualization of deliberative (communicative) practices. However, despite Kant's assumption of a universal claim of such a model of public reason, for example further developed in his conception of cosmopolitanism, excludes not only traditions and societal cultures of public reason processes of diverse world regions but does not provide sufficient conceptual 'space' for inclusive models of deliberative discourse across a transnational communicative space where individuals are no longer discursively 'co-located' within a shared 'value' territory. Although public interdependence in today's advanced network structures, which incorporates engaged actors of multiple societies, the model of modern deliberative discourse represents only one model which, however, could be understood as excluding not only societal actors within the modern pluralist society but rather the specifics of dialogical relations as a communicative space of diverse societal actors, coming together to deliberate on themes of a globalized 'common good'. These mechanisms of inclusion of diverse societal actors has been on the periphery of debates of deliberative discourse. As discussed above, 'inclusion' and 'exclusion' are addressed, however, in contexts of pluralist societies and less in contexts of deliberative discursive practices of, for example, non-modern societies.

This model as the paradigm of deliberative discourse has focused on conceptual debates on this particular dimension of public deliberation. With transnational interlocutors and networks of communication, this dimension of deliberation is still important; however, the deliberative 'axis' of the lifeworld as a subjective node of discourse trajectories might require a shift away from the specific principles of rational orientation towards a larger 'reflective' scope of discursive 'consciousness', in order to 'connect' and deliberatively 'engage' with thematically similar discourses in the scope of networked communication. This is a shift from 'rationality' to a softer sphere of 'experience'. In this sense, not only social theory but also public-sphere debates cannot mainly be centred upon the rationalism of 'classical' social theory but need to incorporate the world of interrelatedness of experience. This is in particular the case in contexts of deliberative discourse in a transnational scope. In addition, it might also be useful to consider a broadening of the deliberative discourse from the 'ideal' of specific principles to a broader sphere of deliberation that acknowledges not only the enlarged transnational but rather trans-societal communicative territory of public communication and, from this angle, the subjective practices of networked discourse *across* these new spheres of public interdependence.

In order to comprehend this emerging sphere as a communicative space of deliberative discourse, I suggest considering Hegel's understanding of 'reasoning' in this context, which is quite different to Kant's understanding of public reason. Hegel's conception of 'reflection' of the world as a dialectical form helps to disentangle deliberative discourse from the 'normative model' of the ideal speech situation and to understand deliberative discourse embedded in contexts of reflective 'horizons' not so much of rationality but rather of 'world consciousness'. A world 'consciousness', constituted through a discursive 'reality' across spheres of public interdependence of not only 'national' but rather across the larger scope of transnational discursive deliberation. It is Hegel who considers 'reason' not as 'subjectless' but, quite the opposite, rather suggests a 'subjective being' and 'identity' and 'self consciousness' as reason (Hegel, 1995: 139). Hegel identifies three levels of reasoning: (a) the abstract side or that of understanding, (b) the dialectical, that of negative reason, (c) the speculative, positive reason (see Stern, 2002: 15).

It seems that Hegel's understanding of 'reason' which is of relevance in contexts of discursive deliberation in an enlarged 'spatial' and transnational communicative space is tied to a 'reflective' dialectic of what he understands as 'scientific reason': 'to him who looks at the world rationally the world looks rationally back: the two exist in a reciprocal relationship' (Hegel, 1985) and, as a consequence, the aim is to 'bring rationality to consciousness' (Stern, 2002: 11). Even though this dialectic is related to scientific 'reason' the process could serve as a framework in contexts of discursive engagement in a transnational context where deliberative discourses are 'reflective' in such a way that 'the world' is related to the 'vertical' 'connection' to the 'locality', which could be the national sphere but also a thematically 'fractured' transnational sphere of deliberation.

Hegel defines reason furthermore 'as the unity of thought and reality' (Gadamer, 1976: 56) and 'reason' is linked to a larger community of a civil society. Recently, Ferguson and Mansbach (2012) have noted the particular way in which Hegel understands the subject within a sphere of experience. Ferguson and Mansbach note that 'well over a century ago', Hegel had given 'civil society' including private corporations and associations, 'a pivotal sociological and normative role in linking the individual to the wider community realized in the state' (Ferguson and Mansbach, 2012: 85). However, in terms of public communication linked through networked communication, it is the 'wider community' not so much of a 'state' but of the world and the way in which spatial communicative experience relates to discourse practices: '. . . we should rather step back and apply ourselves 'reflectively' and ask how it is the problem has arisen in the first place; once we see that the problem has its source . . . if we overcome that onesidedness, then the problem will simply dissolve and we can escape the 'oscillation' between one unsatisfactory stance and its equally unsatisfactory opposite' (Stern, 2002: 17). In Hegel's understanding such a process of reasoning involves a process of reflective manoeuvring: 'Thus, after we have been forced to re-think our concepts in such a way as to break down the 'abstract either-or' of the understanding, we will then arrive at a new conceptual standpoint, from which it can be seen that these concepts can be brought together, thereby overcoming the sceptical aporia of the dialectical stage' (Stern, 2002: 16).

Furthermore, as Stern argues, 'Hegel can point to whole divisions in our view of the world, between abstract and concrete, ideal and real, one and many, necessity and freedom, state and citizen, moral law and self-interest, general will and particular will, reason and tradition. Hegel believed that the division between universal and individual lies behind all these dichotomies: but at the same time, he believes that we do no have to set these categories apart, but can see things as combining individuality with universality' (Stern, 2002: 20).

The dialectic unfolds between 'universality 'and 'individuality' and discourse means that 'conceptual assumptions that must be made dialectical if the damaging one-sidedness in our thinking is to be avoided' (Stern, 2002: 21). Hegel argues that 'every cultured consciousness has its . . . instinctive way of thinking. This is the absolute power within us, and we shall only master it if we make it the object of our knowledge . . . All revolutions, whether in the sciences or world history, occur merely because spirit has changed its categories in order to understand and examine what belongs to it, in order to possess and grasp itself in a truer, deeper, more intimate and unified manner' (Stern, 2002: 21). This conceptual notion of 'cultured consciousness' might relate to what Delanty and Rumford understand as 'post-national' self-understanding that 'expresses itself within, as much as beyond, national identities' (Delanty and Rumford, 2005: 23). It is the integration of the levels of local, national and global publics, and, as Krossa has argued 'the view of cosmopolitanism draws attention to dynamics of becoming that arise when the national and the global interconnect' (Krossa, 2006).

In Hegel's view, the world is rational and the goal 'of human enquiry is to bring this rationality to consciousness' (Stern, 2002: 11). As the world appears through media and communication, it is Hegel's 'inverted world' model that has also consequences for the formation (and deliberation) of publics. In a way it is the dialectic between the '"real"' ('"supersensible"') world that determines the structure of the '"sensible"' world (Krasnoff, 2008: 89). Hegel suggests, that we see that the warrant for this distinction comes not from the truth of the real or supersensible world – which we have no real access to – but rather from the nature of the apparent or sensible world, which is understood as defective in some ways' (Krasnoff, 2008: 89).

When taking these conceptions of reason as 'consciousness' further and back into our discussion, this concept might help to identify formations of what might be called 'discursive consciousness', which are no longer situated in a national public sphere, but are subjectively constructed 'self-contained' perceptions of public 'horizons'. It is through such an approach that not only subjective 'worldliness' is expressed and also the way in which the subject 'selects' dialogical relations in lifeworld networks. It is no longer the 'network' but rather in advanced globalization, public horizons which determine not only the way in which the subject 'looks into the world' and 'how the world looks back rationally', that is, how this perception is related to 'vertical', local, national or otherwise thematic discourse structures. This space is both subjective but also a shared reality which goes beyond traditional modern deliberative discourse as it enables the vertical discourse through public horizons and not only through national public spheres.

In this sense, we might argue that public horizons create new forms of 'discursive consciousness', shared not because of similar notions of public good but of similar understanding of the world of citizenship in contexts of particular notions 'worldliness'. In this context, not the 'self' and 'identity' (see Benhabib, Dryzek) but a 'civic self' relates no longer to a public sphere but to public horizons or, as Latour has noted, in contexts of assumptions of cosmopolitanism relating to a single form, 'the one cosmos has disappeared' (Latour, 2004).

Within such a dimension, the notion of public horizons could be understood through the formation of 'discursive' consciousness as a 'reflective' vertical engagement within a particular transnational public space and the 'local', for example, thematic and/or national lifeworld context.

Linking spheres of consciousness

The formation of 'consciousness' is often related to particular 'globalized' themes, such as risk communication, which, through a 'reflexive' mechanism connect to a larger transnational, cosmopolitan sphere. Robertson understands this phenomenon as a 'contraction' of the world through a common epistemological 'positioning' (Robertson, 1992). This is particularly important because networked communication is interactively subject related. For this reason, the subject is positioned not only as a 'civic' self in these new forms of public communication but also the public self is no longer necessarily assumed to be publicly situated and engaged in the territory of a nation. These new issues are important as the civic 'self' could be understood as renegotiating identity through engagement in selected densities of public interdependence. Spheres of connected discursive consciousness of 'public horizons' are increasingly relevant as communicative forms and communicative engagement and are no longer necessarily related to national cultures.

It is interesting to explore such a sphere of 'discursive consciousness' not only in the content of 'risk' communication but in the broader context of generations as an example of a new form of common 'connected' public consciousness beyond the nation-state. Karl Mannheim, in his work on the sociology of knowledge has addressed the ways in which generations develop a common 'entelechy' a generational specific 'common location' (Mannheim, 1952). Mannheim has argued that 'the fact that people are born at the same time, or that their youth, adulthood and old age coincide, does not in itself involve a similarity of location: what does create a similar location is the that they are in a position to experience the same events and data, etc. and especially that these experiences impinge upon a similarity of 'stratified' consciousness' (Mannheim, 1952: 291). Mannheim notes that 'no one would assert that there was community of location between the young people of China and Germany about 1800. Only where contemporaries definitely are in a position to participate as an integrated group in certain common experiences can we rightly speak of a community of location of a generation' (Mannheim, 1952: 298). Different generational media and communicative cultures manifest in public engagement. Mannheim's understanding of generations allows us also to conceptualize public consciousness beyond the nation in a larger understanding of similar public 'horizons' in a collectively shared notion of a transnational sphere. A study on media memories of youth years of three generations, using the Mannheim approach, has revealed a similar 'location' of consciousness of three generations in nine countries. This study has identified particular spheres of generational consciousness through the dialectic of 'distance' and 'proximity' *vis-à-vis* specific international political events (Volkmer, 2006). Countries involved were Austria, Australia, Germany, India, Japan, Mexico, South Africa and the USA and the three generations involved were between 70 and 75 years, 40 and 45 and 18 and 25 years when interviewed. The study has identified the way in which a generational world consciousness through the construction of 'distance' and 'proximity' *vis-à-vis* political events, is perceived through mediated spheres. 'Globalized' events, delivered by national media in a first phase of mass-media internationalization in the 1960s such as the Kennedy assassination, the Vietnam War, the Moon Landing, the OPEC crisis and Woodstock seemed to constitute generational specific positioning in memory of the youth generation of the time which, overall, seemed to form a generational consciousness or, in Mannheim's term, 'generational location' in the dialectic of the 'global' and the 'local' (Mannheim, 1952).

However, with advanced forms of densities of networked communication, a generational consciousness becomes more 'concrete' and the situating of the 'location' is no longer positioned between 'distance' and 'proximity' but between 'the world' and 'me'. Such a positioning may be understood as 'discursive consciousness', relating to transnational discourses of chosen densities and 'reflecting' these in a vertical' local' context. Results from a recent international comparative study[1] might illustrate this practice and identify the specifics of such a 'discursive consciousness' relating to the understanding of cosmopolitanism among 14–17-year-olds in nine countries which – despite severe societal differences between these nine countries – constitute the first generation, socialized in the sphere of the 'network society'. The study has addressed high-school youth in mid-sized cities in Malaysia, South Africa, Kenya, Trinidad and Tobago, Japan, Australia, Germany, New Zealand and Mexico. Despite these societal differences and the difference in the development status of these diverse societies, results show that 14 to 17-year-old youth collectively shares the engagement in social media (*Facebook*), participates through a transnational angle in transnational events and engages collectively in concerns of a globalized nature, human rights, the environment, a concern about military conflicts and wars. Results reveal layers of a discursive consciousness between the 'lifeworld' and the 'world' as a space of negotiation of the civic self and through this, engages in a particular form of deliberation. The study has been carried out mainly in countries rarely included in transnational media research. This is the generation, positioned between the lifeworld 'locality' and the globalized public in both the developed and the so-called 'low-income' regions. Given the emerging debates of youth engagement in developing countries, it is important to gain a deeper understanding not only of forms of communicative practices but to highlight cartographies of public epistemology across different societies in a transnational perspective in order to investigate the cultural specific fine-grained role of transnational networked communicative practice. Such an approach allows us not only to identify diverse parameters of national transformation *within* a transnational context but to juxtapose 'public' implications of the communicative 'crisscrossing' of societies. This is an important aspect, particularly when attempting to investigate the role of communicative networks in these transformation processes, which operate beyond the mechanisms of the paradigmatic 'boundedness' of methodological nationalism in larger contexts of globalized 'risk' communication (Beck, 2007) and overcome traditional globalization approaches which posit the modern nation-state *vis-à-vis* globalized structures. The study helps to identify generational specific public horizons. This change not only relates to new areas of sovereignty across communicative spaces (Volkmer, 2007) but in particular to a 'relativistic' civic epistemology that not only situates western European nations in different ways within new forms of communicative flows but rather creates a 'reflexive' sphere of civic identity (through communicative networks) across all societies through particular public cartographies, or, in other words, conceptualizing the national 're-embedding' not as a 'consequence' of 'reflexive modernity' (Beck, Giddens and Lash, 1994) but rather of 'reflective' public horizons.

The survey has included a sample of n = 6240 of 14 to 17-year-old youth in high schools in nine diverse countries. The results reveal very particular 'generational specific' public horizons, grounded on active engagement with a similar dialectic of 'spatial' communicative forms, common transnational networked sites, in a particular combination with national media. Whereas national television seems to provide an important individual news source and is the only national medium ranked within the scale of 'linear' information sources, interactive forms, such as social media (in particular *Facebook*) and mobile communication are used to 'verify' information as subjective networks of 'trust' and seem to establish a parallel information 'universe'. Social and mobile media are used in a communicative space of 'verification' as an often overlooked type of discursive engagement. This verifying space creates a trusted 'link' to a shared collective (such as a *Facebook* community), which is no longer situated within a nation. In addition, *Google* is used as an additional 'verifying' source. When asked for the top websites for gaining news and information, *Google*, *MSN* and *Yahoo* are the main sites (in different degrees across countries) for assessing 'news' and 'information' on the web. This communicative pattern is similar across all nine countries.

Communicative practices in contexts of political engagement which was the main aim of the study, reveal a particular generational specific 'relation' to the world which is no longer country specific. We might argue that this generation is, despite national differences, situated within a generational specific 'discursive consciousness': a discursive consciousness that could be demarcated by four 'reflective' layers: a feeling of insecurity, the distrust in government, a concern for human rights, the environment and an interest in other cultures and the perception of world citizenship.

One layer of discursive consciousness is the overall feeling of insecurity. The responses to the question 'Do you feel the world today is more or less secure than it was when your parents were young?' reveals an overall sense of a heightened feeling of 'insecurity'. The feeling of 'insecurity' peaks in countries such as Kenya, Mexico, Trinidad and Tobago but also shows high levels in Malaysia, South Africa, Australia, New Zealand and Germany. This is an important layer and identifies the ways in which respondents are consistently concerned about 'the world' and about local or national insecurities, such as corruption and violence. It is notable that the feeling of heightened insecurity is not only characteristic of those who are politically interested but seems widespread, despite different degrees of political interest.

Although survey respondents are a young age group, it is surprising how intensely they localize themselves in 'the world'. Responding to the question if they perceive themselves as citizens of a country or citizen of the world, across all nine countries, respondents feel about half as citizens of the world and half as citizens of their country and a majority is interested in 'information about the world'.

In addition to the sense of 'insecurity', across all nine countries a deep distrust of 'politicians' is evinced. However, respondents 'trust'

Table 5.1 Degree of feeling secure by country. Question: Do you feel that the world today is more or less secure than it was when your parents were young?

			Countries/percentage									
		Trinidad & Tobago (n = 618)	Japan (n = 593)	South Africa (n = 760)	New Zealand (n = 638)	Germany (n = 557)	Kenya (n = 668)	Australia (n = 583)	Malaysia (n = 833)	Mexico (n = 886)	Total (n = 6,136)
World security	More secure	7.9	19.9	22.5	17.4	23.4	10.6	19.9	16.2	10.3	16.2
	Less secure	75.8	35.4	53.3	46.4	40.0	80.5	48.5	65.5	79.5	59.9
	Don't know	16.3	44.7	24.2	36.2	36.6	8.9	31.6	18.3	10.2	24.0

Results from the international project Global Youth and Media, led by Ingrid Volkmer, funded by the Australian Research Council.

Table 5.2 Degree of world citizenship. Question: In terms of how you see yourself in the world, do you feel more like a citizen of your own country or more a citizen 'of the world'?

		Trinidad & Tobago (n = 604)	Japan (n = 578)	South Africa (n = 605)	New Zealand (n = 600)	Germany (n = 535)	Kenya (n = 646)	Australia (n = 550)	Malaysia (n = 820)	Mexico (n = 860)	Total (n = 5,798)
						Countries/percentage					
Citizen	... of my own country	61.3	78.0	58.5	64.8	61.1	45.8	72.0	54.1	60.6	61.2
...	... of the world	38.7	22.0	41.5	35.2	38.9	54.2	28.0	45.9	39.4	38.8

Results from the international project Global Youth and Media, led by Ingrid Volkmer, funded by the Australian Research Council.

Table 5.3 Trust in institutions overview. Question: Which institutions do you trust in today's world?

		United Nations (UN) (n = 6,000)	News/Media/ Outlets (n = 5,952)	National Military Forces (n = 5,946)	Schools (n = 6,003)	Police (n = 6,028)	Politicians (n = 5,999)	Church and Religion (n = 6,015)
					Values/percentage			
World security	Trust very much	16.2	8.4	11.5	21.8	11.2	2.5	30.8
	Trust	48.3	49.8	44.5	58.2	41.5	18.9	30.5
	Do not trust	11.7	25.9	21.6	13.1	37.6	60.0	24.0
	Don't know	23.8	15.9	22.4	6.9	9.6	18.6	14.7

Results from the international project Global Youth and Media, led by Ingrid Volkmer, funded by the Australian Research Council.

news media outlets and they trust the United Nations. This particular 'constellation' also relates to the feeling of insecurity and, as we might argue, the particular 'discursive consciousness' of this youth generation.

Political interest is related to policy spheres. Results reveal an overall interest in 'economy, wealth and poverty', in 'human rights', the concern about terrorism, the understanding of other cultures and a concern about wars and military conflicts. The interest in human rights is greatest in South Africa, Trinidad and Tobago, Kenya and Malaysia. However, an interest in politics 'as such', however, is comparatively low. Results also reveal that 'international issues' are broadly considered in all nine countries 'as important as national issues' and 'more important than national issues', only a minority considers international issues 'less important than national issues'. These results are related to the particular sense of concrete 'globalization', which is not considered as a neoliberal sphere but in concrete subjective political terms, is arising from a sense of public 'connectedness'. For example a respondent from Kenya states that globalization means 'when other parts of the world are affected by what is going on in a smaller region, for example pollution from Western nations is destroying African nations'.

Based on these results, it could be argued that in the advanced stage of networked 'spatial' publics, civic identity is constantly being discursively re-negotiated and re-conceptualized, not so much with regard to a national or even a 'global' public but rather across sets of 'publics of belonging', a 'discursive consciousness' overarching multiple subjectively constructed public spaces, accessible, in the case of this study, through 'linear', social and mobile media forms which (ideally) intersect but which also have the potential to create large-scale ambiguities in the construction of normative legitimacy. In this sense, the term 'publics of belonging' represents not a static construction of civic identity but allows for a constant renegotiation across trans-local spaces, framed through the 'fluidity' of communicative spheres.

Deliberative discourse in public horizons

The suggested shift from the Kantian sphere of reasoned discourse and deliberation to the Hegelian sphere of 'reflection' in the context of scientific reason where 'to him who looks at the world rationally the world looks rationally back: the two exist in a reciprocal relationship' (Hegel, 1985) allows, in our context, to identify the space of 'reflective' deliberation in the larger scope of transnational public horizons. Public horizons are no longer situated in a national boundedness but emerge through the engagement with subjectively chosen scopes of spatial networked spheres which not only constitute sites of 'information' but also of 'trust', interactive 'verification' and 'worldliness' as an overall concern about larger issues of globalized political spheres. These are the notions of 'looking into the world', which are, in consequence, related to local and national, 'vertical' contexts, not only 'frame' but shape deliberation through such an angle. The concern for human rights on a global scale, assessed through networked communicative spaces, results, for example, in engaged deliberative practice on the local level through such a 'globalized' lens.

The 'cosmopolitan moment' (Beck, 2007) has been identified as a new angle attempting to define the dialectic between 'difference' and 'unity'; however, in contexts of existential world perceptions of 'risk'. Essentially, 'we are all trapped in a shared global space of threats – without exit' (Beck, 2007: 57) and in Beck's view this shared global space calls for 'normative cosmopolitanism'. Beck notes that 'world risk society forces us to recognize the plurality of the world which the national outlook could ignore' (Beck, 2007: 57).

Individuals, civic selves, no longer remain 'static' in one 'place' such as a nation and are 'naturally' exposed to the same information and information resources. They are mobile subjects moving physically between different nations and, across communicative spaces, generating knowledge and 'perception' of 'the world' from a variety of communicative angles. These inform the 'location' of the civic self and the notion of the world and, in this sense, a new form of cosmopolitanism that is 'reflective' in the sense of outward- and inward-looking at the same time. It is this space where public deliberation is positioned and, engages through spheres of discourse consciousness. This is particularly important as networked communication is interactively subject related. For this reason, the subject is positioned not only as a 'civic' self in these new forms of public communication but also the public self is no longer assumed to be publicly situated and engaged in the territory of a nation. These two issues are important as the civic 'self' renegotiates 'identity' through engagement in selected densities of public interdependence.

In contexts of public communication characterized by advanced glo-balization processes and networked communication such a 'normative cosmopolitanism' is absorbed by deliberation engaged in 'reflective' discourse as dialogue in a spatial context. As Benhabib has argued 'discourse theory has the success of deliberative politics depending not on a collectively acting citizenry but on the institutionalization of the corresponding procedures and conditions of communication' (Benha-bib, 1996: 27). Although it has been claimed, for example by Sassen (2006) that the nation is a site of globalization, this new sphere of glo-balized national space has not been incorporated into debates of public spheres and discursive spaces of deliberation. Rawls and Habermas are vaguely addressing this sphere through a claim of 'universalism' of deliberative discourse practice and the normative relation to demo-cratic institutions and government structures, which are not necessarily placed within a nation but also as intergovernmental institutions on the global level. What seems to be overlooked is that in the advanced phase of globalization, global governance structures and global civil society spheres are deeply embedded within nations through new forms of intergovernmental polity, through globalized NGOs operating across national 'sites', and through an increasing role of global govern-ance in national affairs.

In this sense, the discursive form of consensus-oriented debate, as suggested by Rawls and Habermas, has to be positioned *across* these national scales of globalization. It is only through *this* lens that public agency can be refined in contexts of a 'compression' of shared glo-balized interests within and beyond national contexts.

Notes

1 Public Territories and the Imagining of Political Community

1 In Habermas' work, the Kantian dialectic of 'public' and 'private' discourse constitutes the core ideal model for public discourse. It was Kant who conceptualized public 'reasoning' as being deeply intertwined with private spheres of civic life, i.e. not morally secluded from public debate but rather as a particular civil sphere of reasoning. He understands as 'public use of one's own reason' the use 'that anyone as a scholar makes of reason before the entire literate world' whereas the 'private use of reason' is that which 'a person may make in a civic post or office that has been entrusted to him'(Kant, 1983: 42). This dialectical relation between 'public' and 'private' reason is reflected in Dewey's, Habermas' and Chomsky's work.

2 The terms 'low' income', 'lower middle income','upper middle income' and 'high income' countries are defined through the GNI per capita, the terms 'developing' and 'developed'countries are used by the UN. The UN states that 'the assignment of countries or areas to specific groupings is for statistical convenience and does not imply any assumptions regarding political or other affiliation of countries and territories by the United Nations' (www.unstats.un.org).

3 So-called 'failed' states are characterized by a loss of territorial control and governance legitimacy, ranked by the US think tank Fund for Peace.

4 Both cities are located in Germany.

5 See for debates in political science about International Society, Cosmopolitanism, and 'Weltstaatlichkeit' Ruggie, John Gerard 'Territoriality and Beyond. Problematising Modernity in International Relations, International Organization, (47: 1 winter, 1993.)

6 See also Wolin, Sheldon (1960: 16) Politics and Vision: Continuity and innovation in Western Political thought, Boston), see for detailed debates in international relations and sociology, for example, Ferguson, Y.H., Mansbach,, R.W. *Remapping Global Politics*, 2004, Ferguson and Mansbach

define political space 'Political space refers to the ways in which identities and loyalties among adherents to various polities are distributed and related, and territorial space is only one of the possibilities (Ferguson and Mansbach, 2004: 67), see also Kaelble, H. et al. (eds) *Transnationale, Oeffentlichkeiten und Identitaeten im 20. Jahrhundert.*

7   See Brunkhorst (2007) in original: 'Durch ihr globales Zusammenspiel wird es den Exekutivgewalten immer leichter, sich . . . demokratischer und rechtsstaatlicher Bindung und Verantwortlichkeit zu entziehen. Die Emanzipation der Exekutivgewalten aus dem demokratischen Rechtsstaat aber beschleunigt . . . ihre globale Vernetzung zu neuen Zentren imperialer und hegemonialer Macht.' (Brunkhorst, 2007: 75). He also argues 'Eine nur noch schwer adressierbare, flexible und dynamische Hegemonialmacht loest staatliche Souveraenitaet ab und erbt von ihr die demokratieferne Herrschaftsfunktion, in deren Schatten die scharf geschnittenen rechtsstaatlichen Konturen undeutlich warden, die den Norm- vom Massnahmestaat trennen' (Brunkhorst, 2007: 74).

8   See also Scholte, 2000 and Held, 2010:18 who argues that the 'liberal model' to be replaced by a 'cosmopolitan model of sovereignty' as ' the networked realms of public authority shaped and delimited by an overarching cosmopolitan legal framework' (Held, 2010:19). In his view 'bounded political communities lose their role as the sole centre of legitimate political power' (Held, 2010:19) 'and legitimate decision-making is conducted in different loci of power within and outside the nation-state' (Held, 2010: 19). However, the nation-state itself is a site of these new power formations. See also Ferguson and Mansbach (2004: 84).

2   Post-Territoriality in Spheres of 'Public Assemblages'

1   Scholte argues that 'Something of a lull occurred in sociological investigation of the international during the 1940s and 1950s, when only an occasional general article appeared on this subject' (Scholte, 1993: 22). In his account, the World Congress of Sociology in 1966 included for the first time the 'sociology of international relations' and he quotes Moore, who has argued that 'society is coterminous with national states' and advocates 'freeing the concept of (social) system from the automatic limits at the "boundaries" of societies or cultures' (Moore, 1966: 481 in Scholte, 1993: 22).

2   Castells conceptualizes the network society as a spatial architecture which is 'global' and 'local' at the same time (Castells, 2008:14).

3   See for further details, Rantanen (1998), who describes the control of agencies of local markets.

3   From 'Reflexive' Modernity to 'Reflective' Globalization: The Public Space of 'Inbetween-ness'

1   See also for the debate of 'subjectivation' (Bayart, 2007).

2   Beck has raised this through his conceptualization of cosmopolitanism.

3 Focus group interviews, Berlin (led by Ingrid Volkmer), workpackage 3 of project 'Media and Citizenship: Transnational Television Cultures Reshaping Political Identities in the European Union', funded by the European Union from 2008–11. Project consortium led by Christina Slade, University of Utrecht, The Netherlands.
4 See for a paradigm shift in diaspora theory, Bruneau in Brauboeck/Faist and for models of diaspora between mobility and locality.

4 Public Interdependence, Interlocutors and the 'Matrix' of Influence

1 Interviews have been conducted in London with a programme presenter, the Acting Bureau chief (London office) and one of the founders of *Al Jazeera*.
2 Interviews have been conducted with three executives at BBC World, London, UK.
3 Interviews have been conducted with three executives at *Deutsche Welle* in Berlin and Bonn, Germany.

5 From the Public Sphere to Public 'Horizons'

1 The study is directed by the author and is still ongoing. The study has the title Global Youth and Media: Notions of Cosmopolitanism in the Global Public Space and is funded by the Australian Research Council. The study has been conducted in collaboration with UNESCO, Paris.

References

Abdelhay, Nawaf (2012) 'The Arab uprising 2011: New media in the hands of a new generation in North Africa', *ASLIB Proceedings* 64(5): 529–39.

Agnew, John (2009) *Globalization and Sovereignty*. Lanham, Boulder, New York, Toronto, Plymouth, UK: Rowman and Littlefield.

Albert, Mathias (2007) 'Weltstaat und Weltstaatlichkeit: Neubestimmungen des Politischen in der Weltgesellschaft', in Albert, Mathias and Stichweh, Rudolf (eds), *Weltstaat and Weltstaatlichkeit. Beobachtungen globaler politischer Strukturbildung*. Wiesbaden, Germany: VS, pp. 9–24.

Albert, Mathias; Bluhm, Gesa; Helmig, Jan; Leutzsch, Andreas; Walter, Jochen (2009) 'The Communicative Construction of Transnational Political Spaces', in Albert, Mathias; Bluhm, Gesa; Helmig, Jan; Leutzsch, Jochen Walter (eds), *Transnational Political Spaces*. Frankfurt, New York: Campus, pp. 7–34.

Albrecht, Steffen (2006) 'Whose voice is heard in online deliberation? A study of participation and representation in political debates on the internet', *Information, Communication and Society* 9(1): 62–82.

Albrow, Martin (1996) *The Global Age. State and Society beyond Modernity*. Palo Alto, CA: Stanford University Press.

Allan, Stuart (2009) 'Histories of citizen journalism', in Allan, Stuart and Thorsen, Einer (eds), *Citizen Journalism: Global Perspectives*. New York: Peter Lang, pp. 17–32.

Alqudsi-ghabra, Taghreed (2012) 'Creative use of social media in the revolutions of Tunisia, Egypt and Libya', *International Journal of Interdisciplinary Social Sciences* 6 (6): 147–58.

Anderson, Benedict (1983) *Imagined Communities: Reflections on the Origin and Spread of Nationalism*. London: Verso.

Appadurai, Arjun (1996) *Modernity at Large*. Minneapolis, London: University of Minnesota Press.

Arendt, Hannah (1982) *Lectures on Kant's Political Philosophy*. Chicago, Ill: University of Chicago Press.

Arvizu, Shannon (2009) 'Creating alternative visions of Arab society: Emerging youth publics in Cairo', *Media, Culture and Society* 31(3): 385–407.

Axtmann, Roland (2001) Society, globalization and the comparative method in Robertson, Roland and White, Kathleen E. (eds), *Globalization. Critical Concepts in Sociology*. London, New York; Routledge, pp. 328–49.

Avle, Seyram (2011) Global flows, media and developing democracies: The Ghanian case', *Journal of African Media Studies* 3(1): 7–23.

Bach, Jonathan and Stark, David (2005) 'Recombiant technology and new geographies of association', in Latham, Robert and Sassen, Saskia (eds), *Digital Formations*. Princeton: Princeton University Press, pp. 37–54.

Bakardjieva, Maria (2005) *Internet Society: The Internet in Everyday Life*. London Thousand Oaks: Sage.

Baker, Keith Michael (1992) 'Defining the public sphere in eighteenth-century France: Variations on a theme by Habermas', in Calhoun, Craig (ed.) *Habermas and the Public Sphere*. Cambridge, MA: MIT Press, pp. 181–211.

Banda, Fackson; Mudhai, Okoth Fred; Tettey, Wisdom J. (2009) 'Introduction: New media and democracy in Africa: A critical interjection' in Mudhai, Okoth Fred; Tettey, Wisdom J.; Banda, Fackson (eds), *African Media and the Digital Public Sphere*. New York: Palgrave Macmillan, pp. 1–20.

Bassett, James and Smith, William (2010) 'Deliberation and global civil society: Agency, arena, affect', *Review of International Studies* 36: 413–30.

Bayart, Jean-Francois (2007) *Global Subjects. A Political Critique of Globalization*. Cambridge, Polity.

Beck, Ulrich (1992) *Risk Society. Towards a New Modernity*. London: Sage.

Beck, Ulrich; Giddens, Anthony; Lash, Scott (1994) *Reflexive Modernization*. Stanford: Stanford University Press.

Beck, Ulrich (1994) 'The reinvention of politics' in Beck, Ulrich; Giddens, Anthony; Lash, Scott *Reflexive Modernization*. Stanford: Stanford University Press, pp. 1–55.

Beck, Ulrich (2000) *What is Globalization?* Cambridge: Polity.

Beck, Ulrich; Bonss, Wolfgang; Lau, Christoph (2003) 'The theory of reflexive modernization: Problematic, hypotheses and research programme', *Theory, Culture and Society* 20(2): 1–33.

Beck, Ulrich (2005) *Cosmopolitan Europe*. Cambridge, UK; Malden, MA: Polity

Beck, Ulrich (2006) *Cosmopolitan Vision*. Cambridge: Polity.

Beck, Ulrich (2007) *Power in the Global Age. A New Global Political Economy*. Cambridge: Polity.

Beck, Ulrich (2009) *World at Risk*. Cambridge: Polity.

Beck, Ulrich and Beck-Gernsheim, Elisabeth (2009) 'Global generations and the trap of methodological nationalism', *European Sociological Review* 25(1): 25–36.

Beck, Ulrich and Grande, Edgar (2010) 'Varieties of second modernity: The cosmopolitan turn in social and political theory and research', *British Journal of Sociology* 61(3): 409–43.

Beckett, Charlie and Ball, James (2013) *News in the Networked Era*. Cambridge: Polity.

Bendix, R (1977) *Nation-Building and Citizenship: Studies of our Changing Social Order*. Berkeley: University of California Press.

Benhabib, Seyla (1992) 'Models of Public Space', in Calhoun, Craig (ed.), *Habermas and the Public Sphere*. Cambridge, MA: MIT Press, pp. 73–98.

Benhabib, Seyla (1996) 'Toward a deliberative model of democractic legitimacy', in Benhabib, Seyla (ed.), *Democracy and Difference*. Princeton, NJ: Princeton University Press, pp. 67–94.

Benhabib, Seyla (2004) *The Rights of Others: Aliens, Residents, and Citizens*. Cambridge, NY: Cambridge University Press.

Benhabib, Seyla (2006) *Another Cosmopolitanism*. New York: Oxford University Press.

Benkler, Yochai (2006) *The Wealth of Networks: How Social Production Transforms Markets and Freedom*. Washington, DC: TechFreedom.

Bennett, Lance (2005) 'Social movements beyond borders: Understanding two eras of transnational activsim', in Della Porta, Donatella (ed.), *Transnational Protest and Global Activism*. Lanham, Boulder, New York, Toronto, Oxford: Rowman and Littlefield, pp. 203–26.

Bennett, Lance and Segerberg, Alexandra (2013) *The Logic of Connective Action: Digital Media and the Personalization of Contentious Politics*. Cambridge: Cambridge University Press.

Bell, Daniel (1973) *The Coming of Post-Industrial Society*. New York: Basic Books.

Bernal, Victoria (2006) 'Diaspora, cyberspace and political imagination: The Ertirean Diaspora online', *Global Networks* 6(2): 161–79.

Bodanksy, Daniel (1999) 'The legitimacy of international governance: A coming challenge for international environmental law', *American Journal of International Law* 93(3): 596–624.

Bohman, James and Rehg, William (1997) 'Introduction', in Bohman, James and Regh, William (eds), *Deliberative Democracy*. Cambridge, MA: MIT Press, pp. 9–30.

Bohman, James (2001) 'Cosmopolitan republicanism: citizenship, freedom and global political authority', *The Monist* 84(1) (January): 3–21.

Bohman, James (2007) *Democracy across Borders*. Cambridge, MA: MIT Press.

Bohman, James (2010) 'Expanding dialogue: The internet, the public sphere, and prospects for transnational democracy', in Griprud, Jostein et al. (eds), *The Idea of the Public Sphere*. Plymouth, UK: Lexington Books, pp. 247–69.

Boltanski, Luc (1993, 1999) *Distant Suffering: Morality, Media and Politics*. Cambridge: Cambridge University Press.

Boyd-Barrett, Oliver (1977) 'Media imperialism: Towards an international framework for the analysis of media systems', in Curran, James; Gurevitch, Michael and Woollacott, J. (eds), *Mass Communication and Society*. London: Edward Arnold, pp. 116–41.

Boyd-Barrett, Oliver (1980) *The International News Agencies*. London: Constable; Beverly Hills, CA: Sage.

Boyd-Barrett, Oliver (1998) 'Global news agencies', in Boyd-Barrett, Oliver and Rantanen, Terhi (eds), *The Globalization of News*. London, Thousand Oaks, New Delhi: Sage, pp. 19–34

Boyd-Barrett, Oliver and Rantanen, Terhi (2004) 'News agencies as news sources: A re-evaluation', in Paterson, Chris and Sreberny, Annabelle (eds), *International News in the Twenty-First Century*. Eastleigh, UK: John Libbey, pp. 31–46.

Boyd-Barrett, Oliver (2006) (ed.) *Communications, Media Globalization and Empire*. Eastleigh, UK: John Libbey.

Braman, Sandra (2006) *Change of State. Information, Policy, Power*. Cambridge, London: MIT Press.

Braune, Ines (2008) *Aneignungen des Globalen*. Bielefeld, Germany: Transcript.

Breitmeier, Helmut (2008) *The Legitimacy of International Regimes*. Farnham, UK: Ashgate.

Briggs, Asa and Burke, Peter (2010) *A Social History of the Media*. Cambridge: Polity.

Brunkhorst, Hauke (2007) 'Die Legitimationskrise der Weltgesellschaft. Global rule of law, global constitutionalism und Weltstaatlichkeit', in Albert, Mathias and Rudolf Stichweh (eds), *Weltstaat und Weltstaatlichkeit*. Wiesbaden: VS Verlag, pp. 63–108.

Bruns, Axel (2008) 'Life beyond the public sphere: Towards a networked model for political deliberation', *Information Polity* 13(1/2): 65–79.

Cabrera, Luis (2010) *The Practice of Global Citizenship*. Cambridge: Cambridge University Press.

Calhoun, Craig (1992) 'Habermas and the public sphere', in Calhoun, Craig (ed.), *Habermas and the Public Sphere*. Cambridge, MA: MIT Press, pp. 1–50.

Calhoun, Craig (2003) 'The democratic integration of Europe: Interests, identity and the public sphere', in Berezin, Mabel and Schain, Martin (eds), *Europe without Borders. Remapping Territory, Citizenship, and Identity in a Transnational Age*. Baltimore, London: Johns Hopkins University Press, pp. 243–74.

Calhoun, Craig (2010) 'Beck, Asia and second modernity', *British Journal of Sociology* 61 (3): 597–619.

Cao, Qing (2011) 'The language of soft-power: Mediating socio-political meanings in the Chinese media', *Critical Arts: A South–North Journal of Cultural and Media Studies* 25(1): 7–24.

Carey, James (1989) *Communication as Culture: Essays on Media and Society*. Boston: Unwin Hyman.

Castells, Manuel (1996) *The Information Age: Economy, Society and Culture*. Malden, MA, USA: Blackwell (3 vols).

Castells, Manuel (2006) 'The network society: From knowledge to policy', in Castells, Manuel and Gustavo Cardoso (eds), *The Network Society. From Knowledge to Polity*. Washington, DC: Center for Transatlantic Relations, pp. 3–22.

Castells, Manuel (2009) *Communication Power*. Oxford: Oxford University Press.

Castells, Manuel (2010) 'The new public sphere', in Thussu, Daya Kishan (ed.), *International Communication*. London: Routledge, pp. 36–47.

Castells, Manuel (2012) *Networks of Outrage and Hope: Social Movements in the Internet Age*. Cambridge: Polity.

Chase-Dunn, Christopher and Niemeyer, Richard (2009) 'The world revolution of 20xx', in Albert, Mathias; Bluhm, Gesa; Helmig, Jan; Leutzsch, Jochen Walter (eds), *Transnational Political Spaces*. Frankfurt, New York: Campus, pp. 35–58.

Chaudhuri, Brahma (1996) 'India', in Vann, Don J. and VanArsdel, Rosemary (eds) *Periodicals of Queen Victoria's Empire*. Toronto, Buffalo: University of Toronto Press.

Chernilo, Daniel (2007) *The Social Theory of the Nation-State: The Political Forms of Modernity Beyond Methodological Nationalism*. London, New York: Routledge.

Chomsky, Noam (2006) *Failed States: The Abuse of Power and the Assault on Democracy*. New York: Metropolitan Books.

Chouliaraki, Lilie and Fairclough, Norman (1999) *Discourse in Late Modernity*. Edinburgh: Edinburgh University Press.

Chouliaraki, Lilie (2006) *The Spectatorship of Suffering*. London: Sage.

Chow, Kai-Wing (2004) *Publishing Culture, and Power in Early Modern China*. Stanford, CA: Stanford University Press.

Clark, Ian (2005) *Legitimacy in International Society*. Oxford: Oxford University Press.

Cohen, Joshua (1988) 'Democracy and liberty', in Elster, J. (ed.) *Deliberative Democracy*. Cambridge: Cambridge University Press.

Cohen, Joshua (1996) 'Procedure and substance in deliberative democracy', in Benhabib, Seyla (ed.), *Democracy and Difference*. Princeton, New Jersey: Princeton University Press, pp. 187–217.

Coleman, Stephen and Ross, Karen (2010) *The Media and the Public*. Malden, USA: Wiley Blackwell.

Cooper, Stephen (2006) *Watching the Watchdog: Bloggers as a Fifth Estate*. Spokane, Wash.: Marquette.

Cottle, Simon (2006) *Mediatized Conflict: Developments in Media and Conflict Studies*. Maidenhead, England, New York: Open University Press.

Cottle, Simon (2009) *Global Crisis Reporting: Journalism in the Global Age*. Maidenhead, England, New York: Open University Press.

Couldry, Nick; Livingstone, Sonia; Markham, Tim (2007) *Media Consumption and Public Engagement. Beyond the Presumption of Attention*. New York: Palgrave Macmillan.

Couldry, Nick (2008) 'Mediatization or mediation? Alternative understandings of the emergent space of digital storytelling', *New Media and Society* (10)3: 373–93.

Couldry, Nick (2010) *Why Voice Matters: Culture and Politics after Neoliberalism*. London: Sage.

Couldry, Nick (2012) *Media, Society, World: Social Theory and Digital Media Practice*. Cambridge: Polity.

Couldry, Nick and Hepp, Andreas (2012) 'Media cultures in a global age: A transcultural approach to an expanded spectrum', in Volkmer, Ingrid (ed.), *Handbook of Global Media Research*. Malden, MA: Wiley-Blackwell, pp. 92–109.

Cox, Robert (2006, 2010) *Environment Communication and the Public Sphere*. London: Sage.

Curren, James (1991) 'Press history', in Curren, James and Seaton, Jean (ed.) *Power without Responsibility. The Press, Broadcasting, and New Media in Britain*. London, New York: Routledge, pp. 1–67.

Cushion, Stephen (2010) 'Three phases of 24-hour news television', Cushion, Stephen and Lewis, Justin (eds), *The Rise of 24-Hour News Television*. New York: Peter Lang, pp. 15–30.

Cusimano, Maryann K. (2000) 'Beyond sovereignty: The rise of transsovereign problems', in Cusimano, Maryann K. (ed.), *Beyond Sovereignty. Issues for a Global Agenda*. Boston, New York: Bedford/St Martin's, pp. 1–40.

Dahinden, Janine (2010) 'The dynamics of migrants' transnational formations: Between mobility and locality', in Braubock, Rainer and Faist, Thomas (eds),

Diaspora and Transnationalism. Amsterdam: Amsterdam University Press, pp. 51–71.

Dahlberg, Lincoln (2007) 'Rethinking the fragmentation of the cyberpublic: From consensus to contestation', *New Media and Society* 9(5): 827–42.

Dahlberg, Lincoln (2007) 'The internet, deliberative democracy, and power: Radicalizing the public sphere', *International Journal of Media and Cultural Politics* 3(1): 47–67.

Dahlgren, Peter (1995) *Television and the Public Sphere: Citizenship, Democracy and the Media.* London: Sage.

Dahlgren Peter (2001) 'The public sphere and the net: structure, space, and communication', in Bennett, Lance, Robert M. Entman (eds), *Mediated Politics. Communication in the Future of Democracy.* Cambridge: Cambridge University Press, pp. 33–55.

Dahlgren, Peter (ed.) (2007) *Young Citizens and New Media: Learning for Democratic Participation.* New York: Routledge.

Dahlgren, Peter (2009) *Media and Political Engagement: Citizens, Communication and Democracy.* Cambridge: Cambridge University Press.

Dallmayr, Fred (1999) 'Democracy and multiculturalism', in Benhabib, Seyla (ed.), *Democracy and Difference: Contesting the Boundaries of the Political.* Princeton: New Jersey: Princeton University Press, pp. 279–94.

Dayan, Daniel and Katz, Elihu (1994) *Media Events. The Life Broadcasting of History.* Cambridge, MA: Harvard University Press.

Deleuze, Gilles and Guattari, Felix (1987) *A Thousand Plateaus: Capitalism And Schizophrenia.* London: Athlone Press.

Delanty, Gerard and Rumford, Chris (2005) *Rethinking Europe: Social Theory and the Implications of Europeanization.* London, New York: Routledge.

Della Porta, Donatella and Kriesi, Hanspeter, (1999) 'Introduction', in Della Porta, Donatella; Kriesi, Hanspeter; Rucht, Dieter (eds), *Social Movements in a Globalizing World.* New York: St Martin's Press.

Della Porta, Donatella; Tarrow, Sidney (eds) (2005) *Transnational Protest and Global Activism.* Lanham, Boulder, New York, Toronto, Oxford: Rowman and Littlefield.

D'Entreves, Mauritzio Passerin (2002, 2006) 'Introduction: Democracy as public deliberation', in D'Entreves, Mauritzio Passerin (ed.), *Democracy as Public Deliberation.* New Brunswick and London: Transaction, pp. 1–20.

Deutsch, Karl (1953) *Nationalism and Social Communication: An Inquiry into the Foundations of Nationality.* Cambridge: Technology Press of MIT and New York: Wiley.

Dewey, John (1927, 1954) *The Public and its Problems.* Athens, Ohio, USA: Ohio University Press.

Diani, Mario and McAdam, Dough (2003) (eds), *Social Movements and Networks.* Oxford: Oxford University Press.

Dimaggio, Anthony (2008) *Mass Media, Mass Propaganda: Examining American News in the 'War on Terror'.* Lanham, MD: Lexington Books.

Distad, N. Merrill and Distad, Linda M. (1996) 'Canada', in Vann, Don J. and VanArsdel, Rosemary (eds), *Periodicals of Queen Victoria's Empire.* Toronto, Buffalo: University of Toronto Press, pp. 61–174.

Dryzek, John S. (1990) *Discursive Democracy.* Cambridge: Cambridge University Press.

Dryzek, John S (2006) *Deliberative Global Politics.* Cambridge: Polity.

Duara, Prasenjit (1996) 'Historising national identity, or who imagines what and when', in Eley, Geoff and Ronald Rigor Suny (eds), *Becoming National*. New York, Oxford: Oxford University Press, pp. 150–77.

Durkheim, Emile and Mauss, M. (1913) 'Note on the notion of civilization', *Social Research* (38) (Winter 1971): 808–13.

Eickelman, Dale F. and Salvatore, Armando (2002) 'The public sphere and muslim identities', *European Journal of Sociology* 43(1): 92–115.

Eickelman, Dale F. and Anderson, Jon W. (2003) 'Redefining muslim publics', in Eickelman, Dale F. and Anderson, Jon W. (eds), *New Media in the Muslim world: The Emerging Public Sphere*. Bloomington, IN: Indiana University Press, pp. 1–18.

Eisenstein, Elizabeth (1997) *Die Druckerpresse. Kulturrevolutionen im fruehen modernen Europa*. Wien, New York: Springer.

Ekecrantz, Jan (2009) 'Media studies going global', in Thussu, Daya Krishan (ed.), *Internationalizing Media Studies*. London: Routledge, pp. 75–90.

Eley, Geoff and Ronald Grigor Suny (1996) 'Introduction: From the moment of social history to the work of cultural representation', in Eley, Geoff and Suny, Ronald Grigor (eds), *Becoming National*. Oxford University Press, pp. 3–37.

Ernst, Dieter (2005) 'The new mobility of knowledge. Digital information systems and global flagship networks', in Latham, Robert and Sassen, Saskia (eds), *Digital Formations*. Princeton: Princeton University Press, pp. 89–114.

Faist, Thomas (2010) 'Diaspora and transnationalism: What kind of dance partners?', in Brauboeck, Rainer and Faist, Thomas (eds), *Diasproa and Transnationalism*. Amsterdam: Amsterdam University Press, pp. 9–34.

Farivar, Cyrus (2011) *The Internet of Elsewhere: The Emergent Effects of a Wired World*. New Brunswick, NJ: Rutgers University Press.

Fenster, Mark (2012) 'Disclosure's effects: Wikileaks and transparency. *Iowa Law Review* 97: 753–807.

Ferguson, Yale H. and Jones, Barry R.J. (2002) *Political Space. New Frontiers of Change and Governance in a Globalizing World*. Albany: State University Press.

Ferguson, Yale H. and Mansbach, Richard W. (2004) *Remapping Global Politics. History's Revenge and Future Shock*. Cambridge: Cambridge University Press.

Ferguson, Yale H. and Mansbach, Richard W. (2009) 'The sociology of the state: The state as a conceptual variable', conference paper, *International Studies Association*, January.

Ferguson, Yale H. and Mansbach, Richard W. (2012) *Globalization: The Return of Borders to a Borderless World*. Milton Park, UK; New York: Routledge.

Festenstein, Matthew (2002, 2006) 'Deliberation, citizenship and identity', Passerin D'Entreves, Maurizio (ed.), *Democracy as Public Deliberation*. New Brunswick, London: Transaction, pp. 88–111.

Firdaus, Amira (2012) ' "Network newswork" across "glocal" spaces: A study of the integration of user-driven networked sources among global and national news outlets in Malaysia'. Doctoral dissertation, University of Melbourne, Australia.

Fischer-Lescano, Andreas and Teubner, Guenther (2007) 'Fragmentierung des Weltrechts: Vernetzung globaler Regimes statt etatistischer Rechtseinheit', in

Albert, Mathias and Stichweh (eds), *Weltstaat und Weltstaatlichkeit. Beobachtungen globaler Strukturbildung.* Wiesbaden: VS, pp. 37–62.

Fisher, Ali (2010) 'Bullets and butterfly wings', in Kamalipour, Yahra R. (ed.), *Media, Power, and Politics in the Digital Age.* Lanham, Md, USA: Rowman and Littlefield, pp. 105–19.

Fishkin, James (1995) *The Voice of the People: Public Opinion and Democracy.* New Haven, CT: Yale University Press.

Forst, Rainer (2007) *The Right to Justification.* New York: Columbia University Press.

Friedland, Lewis A.; Hove, Thomas; Hernando, Rojas (2006) 'The networked public sphere', *Javnost-The Public*, 13(4): 5–26.

Fraser, Nancy (1999, 1992) 'Rethinking the public sphere', in Calhoun, Craig (ed.), *Habermas and the Public Sphere.* Cambridge, MA: MIT Press, pp. 109–42.

Fraser, Nancy (1996) 'Gender equity and the welfare state: A postindustrial thought experiment', Benhabib, Seyla (ed.), *Democracy and Difference.* Princeton, New Jersey: Princeton University Press, pp. 218–42.

Fraser, Nancy (2007) 'Transnationalizing the public sphere', *Theory, Culture and Society* 24(7): 7–30.

Frere, Marie-Soleil and Kiyindou, Alain (2009) 'Democractic process, civic consciousness, and the internet in francophone Africa', in Mudhai, Fred; Tettey, Wisdom; Branda, Fackson (eds), *African Media and the Digital Public Sphere.* New York: Palgrave Macmillan, pp. 73–88.

Frohock, Fred (1999) *Public Reason.* Ithaca, London: Cornell.

Fuchs, Christian (2012) 'Critique of the political economy of web 2.0 surveillance', in Fuchs, Christian; Boersma, Kees; Albrechtslund, Anders and Sandoval, Mariosol (eds), *Internet and Surveillance.* New York, London: Routledge, pp. 31–70.

Fugger Newsletters (1924, 1926, 1970) 'News and rumours in Renaissance Europe', New York: Capricorn (2 vols).

Gadamer, Hans-Georg (1976) *Hegel's Dialectic.* New Haven, London: Yale University Press.

Garnham, Nicholas (1992) 'The media and the public sphere', in Calhoun, Craig (ed.), *Habermas and the Public Sphere.* Cambridge, MA: MIT Press, pp. 359–76.

Gastin, John (2008) *Political Communication and Deliberation.* Thousand Oaks: Sage.

Georgiou, Myria (2006) 'Diasporic communities online: A bottom-up experience of transnationalism', in Katherine Sarikakis, and Daya, Thussu (eds), *Ideologies of the Internet.* Cresskill, New Jersey: Hampton Press, pp. 131–45.

Gerbaudo, Paolo (2012) *Tweets and the Streets. Social Media and Contemporary Activism.* London, UK: Pluto.

Gerbner, George and Marvanyi, George (1977) 'The many worlds of the world's press', *Journal of Communication* 27(1): 52–66.

Gibson, Rachel K. and McAllister, Ian (2011) 'Do online election campaigns win votes? The 2007 Australian "youtube" election', *Political Communication* 28: 227–44.

Giddens, Anthony (1990) *The Consequences of Modernity.* Cambridge: Polity.

Giddens, Anthony (1991) *Modernity and Self-Identity in the Late Modern Age.* Cambridge: Polity.

Giddens, Anthony (1994) 'Living in a post-traditional society', in Beck, Ulrich; Giddens, Anthony; Lash, Scott *Reflexive Modernity*. Cambridge: Polity, pp. 56–109.

Gilboa, Eytan (2002) 'The global news networks and U.S. policymaking in defense and foreign affairs', *The Joan Shorenstein Center on the Press, Politics and Public Policy*, Harvard University.

Gillmor, Dan (2006) *We the Media. Grassroots Journalism by the People, for the People*. Sebastopol, CA: O'Reilly.

Gilman-Opalsky, Richard (2006) 'Against the dichotomy of national and transnational: A case for transgressive public spheres', *American Political Science Association*, Philadelphia (conference paper).

Gitlin, Todd (1998) 'Public sphere or public sphericules?, in Liebes, Tamar and Curran, James (eds), *Media, Ritual and Identity*. London, New York: Routledge, pp. 168–74.

Glick Schiller, Nina (2010) 'A global perspective on transnational migration: Theorising migration without methodological nationalism', in Bauboeck, Rainer and Faist, Thomas (eds), *Diaspora and Transnationlism*. Amsterdam: Amsterdam University Press, pp. 109–30.

Goldstein, Joshua and Rotich, Juliana (2008) 'Digitally networked technology in Kenya's 2007–2008 post election crisis', *Internet and Democracy Case Study Series* 2008–9: 2–10 (Berkman Center Research Publication).

Gordon, Eric and de Souza e Silva, Adriana (2011) *Net Locality: Why Location Matters in a Networked World*. Chichester and Malden, USA: Wiley Blackwell.

Graber, Doris (ed.) (2011) *Media Power in Politics*. Washington, DC: CQ Press.

Graetz, Tilo (2011) 'Contemporary African mediascapes: New actors, genres and communication spaces', *Journal of African Media Studies*, 3(2): 151–260.

Gripsrud, Jostein and Moe, Hallvard (2010) 'Introduction' in Gripsrud, Jostein and Moe, Hallvard (eds), *The Digital Public Sphere*. Gothenburg: Nordicom, pp. 9–19

Guertin, Carolyn (2012) 'Mobile bodies. Zones of attention and tactical media interventions', in Suetzl, Wolfgang and Hug, Theo (eds), *Activist Media and Biopolitics*. Innsbruck, Austria: Innsbruck University Press, pp. 17–28.

Guidry, John A.; Kennedy, Michael D; Zald, Mayer N (2000) 'Globalization and social movements', in Guidry, John A; Kennedy, Michael D; Zald, Mayer N (eds), *Globalizations and Social Movements: Culture, Power, and the Transnational Public Sphere*. University of Michigan Press, pp. 1–34.

Gutman, Amy and Thompson, John (2004) *Why Deliberative Democracy?* Princeton, New Jersey: Princeton University Press.

Habermas, Jürgen (1964, 1991) *The Structural Transformation of the Public Sphere*. Cambridge, MA: MIT Press.

Habermas, Jürgen (1987, 1984) *The Theory of Communicative Action*. Boston: Beacon Press (2 vols).

Habermas, Jürgen (1996) *Between Facts and Norms*. Cambridge, MA: MIT Press.

Habermas, Jürgen (2001a) *Die postnationale Konstellation. Politische Essays*. Frankfurt, Main: Suhrkamp.

Habermas, Jürgen (2001b) *The Inclusion of the Other*. Cambridge, MA: MIT Press.

Habermas, Jürgen (2011) 'Europe's post-democratic era', *Guardian*, London (10 November).

Hafez, Kai (2007) *The Myth of Globalization*. Cambridge: Polity.

Hafez, Kai (2008) *Arab Media: Power and Weakness*. New York: Continuum.

Hamelink, Cees (2012) 'Global media research and global ambitions', in Volkmer, Ingrid (ed.), *Handbook of Global Media Research*. Wiley-Blackwell, pp. 28–39.

Hanitzsch, Thomas and Mellado, Claudia (2011) 'What shapes the news around the world? How journalists in eighteen countries perceive influences on their work', *The International Journal of Press/Politics* 16: 404–26.

Hanley, David (2007) *Beyond the Nation-State. Parties in the Era of European Integration*. Basinstoke: Palgrave Macmillan.

Harvey, D (1989) *The Condition of Postmodernity*. Oxford: Basil Blackwell.

Hasebrink, Uwe and Popp, Jutta (2006) 'Media repertoires as a result of selective media use', *Communications* 31: 369–87.

Hassan, Robert (2004) *Media, Politics and the Network Society*. Maidenhead, UK: Open University Press.

Hassan, Robert (2007) (ed.) *24/7: Time and Temporality in the Network Society*. Stanford, CA: Stanford Business.

Hassanpour, Amir (1998) 'Satellite footprints as national borders: MED-TV and the extraterritoriality of state sovereignty', *Journal of Muslim Minority Affairs* 18(1): 53–72.

Hayden, Craig (2012) *The Rhetoric of Soft Power: Public Diplomacy in Global Contexts*. Lanham, MD: Lexington Books.

Headrick, D. (1991) *The Invisible Weapon: Telecommunications and International Politics, 1851–1945*. New York: Oxford University Press.

Hegel, Georg Wilhelm Friedrich (1952) *Philosophy of Right* (trans. T. M. Knox). London, Oxford, New York: Oxford University Press.

Hegel, Georg Wilhelm Friedrich (1985) *Introduction to the Lectures on the History of Philosophy*. Oxford: Oxford University Press.

Hegel, Georg Wilhelm Friedrich (1995) *Phenomenology of Spirit*. University Park, PA: Pennsylvania State University Press.

Heikkilae, Heikki and Kunelius, Risto (2006) 'Journalists imagining the European public sphere', *Javnost – The Public* 13(4): 63–80.

Heinrich, Ansgard (2011) *Network Journalism: Journalism Practice in Interactive Spheres*. New York, London: Routledge.

Heinrich, Ansgard (2012) 'What is 'network journalism', *Media International Australia* 144 (August): 60–7.

Held, David (1996) 'The decline of the nation state', in Eley, Geoff and Suny, Rigor Grigor (eds), *Becoming National*. New York, Oxford: Oxford University Press, pp. 407–17.

Held, David and McGrew, Anthony (2000, 2006) 'The great globalization debate: An introduction', in Held, David and McGrew, Anthony (eds), *The Global Transformations Reader*. Cambridge: Polity, pp. 1–50.

Held, David (2005) 'Democratic accountability and political effectiveness', in Held, David and Koenig-Archibugi (eds), *Global Governance and Public Accountability*. Malden, MA and Oxford: Wiley Blackwell, pp. 240–67.

Held, David and Koenig-Archibugi (eds) (2005) *Global Governance and Public Accountability*. Malden, MA and Oxford: Wiley Blackwell.

Held, David (2010) *Cosmopolitanism*. Cambridge: Polity.

Hepp, Andreas (2009) 'Differentiation: Mediatizaton and cultural change', in Lundby, Knut (ed.) *Mediatization*. New York: Peter Lang, pp. 139–58.

Hopmann, David Nicolas; Vliegenthart, Rens; de Vreese, Claes; Albaek, Erik (2010) 'Effects of election news coverage: How visibility and tone influence party choice', *Political Communication*, 27, 389–405.

Ibrahim, Yasmin (2010) 'Distant suffering and postmodern subjectivity: The communal politics of Pity', *Nebula* 7(June): 122–35.

Innis, Herold Adam (1951) *The Bias of Communication*. Toronto: University of Toronto Press.

Jamal, Amal (2009) *The Arab Public Sphere in Israel*. Bloomington and Indianapolis: Indiana University Press.

Jenkins, Henry, Ford, Sam; Green, Joshua (2013) *Spreadable Media: Creating Value and Meaning in a Networked Culture*. New York: New York University.

Johnson, Branden (2012) 'Climate change communication: A provocative inquiry into motives, meanings, and means', *Risk Analysis: An International Journal* 32(6)(June): 973–91.

Kaelble, Hartmut (2002) *Transnationale Oeffentlichkeiten und Identitaeten im 20. Jahrhundert*. Frankfurt/Main: Campus.

Kaldor, Mary (2003) *Global Civil Society: An Answer to War*. Basingstoke: Palgrave Macmillan.

Kant, Immanuel (1983) *Perpetual Peace and other Essays*. Indianapolis, IN: Hackett.

Kassner, Joshua (2013) *Rwanda and the Moral Obligation for Intervention*. Edinburgh: Edinburgh University Press.

Kelly, John and Etling, Bruce (2008) 'Mapping Iran's online public: Politics and culture in the Persian blogosphere', *Berkman Center Research Publication* 2008 (April).

Koopmans, Ruud and Erbe, Jessica (2004) 'Toward a European public sphere? Vertical and horizontal dimensions of Europeanized political communication, *Innovation* 17 (2): 97–118.

Knight, Nick (2008) *Imagining Globalization in China. Debates on Ideology, Politics and Culture*. Cheltenham, UK: Edward Elgar.

Knudsen, Britta Timm (2010) 'The nation as media event', in Roosvall, Anna and Slovaara-Moring (eds), *Communicating the Nation*. Gothenborg, Sweden: Nordicom, pp. 41–58.

Kivisto, Peter and Faist, Thomas (2010) *Beyond a Border. The Causes and Consequences of Contemporary Immigration*. Los Angeles, London, New Delhi, Singapore, Washington: Pine Forge Press.

Kraidy, Marwan (2010) *Reality Television and Arab Politics: Contention in Public Life*. Cambridge, New York: Cambridge University Press.

Kraidy, Marwan (2005) *Hybridity, or the Cultural Logic of Globalization*. Philadelphia: Temple University Press.

Krasnoff, Larry (2008) *Hegel's Phenomenology of Spirit*. Cambridge: Cambridge University Press.

Kyung-Sup, Chang (2010) 'The second modern condition?', *British Journal of Sociology* 61(3): 445–63.

Lash, Scott and Urry, John (1994) *Economies of Signs and Spaces*. London, Thousand Oaks: Sage.

Latham, Robert and Sassen, Saskia (ed.), (2005) *Digital Formations*. Princeton and Oxford: Princeton University Press.

Latour, Bruno (2004) 'Whose cosmos, which cosmopolitics? Comments on the peace terms of Ulrich Beck', *Symposium: Talking Peace with God, Part 1*.

Latour, Bruno (2005) 'From realpolitik to dingpolitik or how to make things public', Latour, Bruno and Weibel, Peter (eds) *Making Things Public. Atmospheres of Democracy*. Cambridge, MA: MIT Press, pp. 14–42.

Li, Shubo (2010) 'The online public space and popular ethos in China', *Media, Culture and Society*, 32(1): 63–83.

Lie, Rico and Servaes, Jan (2000)'Globalization: Consumption and identity', in Wang, Georgette, Servaes, Jan and Goonasekera, Anura (eds), *The New Communications Landscape*. London, New York: Routledge, pp. 307–32.

Lim, Merlyna and Kann, Mark E. (2008) 'Politics: Deliberation, mobilization, and networked practices of agitation', in Varnelis, Kazys (ed.), *Networked Publics*. Cambridge, MA, MIT Press, pp. 77–108.

Liu, Dejun (1999) 'The internet as a mode of civic discourse: The Chinese virtual community in North America', in Kluver, Randy and Powers, John H. (eds) *Civic Discourse, Civil Society, and Chinese Communities*. Stamford, Connecticut: Ablex, pp. 195–208.

Livingston, Steven and Eachus, Todd (1995) 'Humanitarian crisis and US foreign policy', *Political Communication* 12: 413–29.

Livingstone, Sonia (2009) 'On the mediation of everything', *Journal of Communication* 59(1): 1–18.

Luhmann, Niklas (1984) *Soziale Systeme*. Franfurt, Main, Germany: Suhrkamp.

Lundby, Knut (ed.) (2009) *Mediatization*. New York: Peter Lang.

Lunt, Peter and Pantti, Mervi (2007) 'Popular culture and the public sphere: Currents of feeling and social control in talk shows and reality TV', in Butsch, Richard (ed.), *Media and Public Spheres*. New York: Palgrave Macmillan, pp. 162–74.

Lynch, Mark (2003) 'Beyond the Arab street: Iraq and the Arab public sphere', *Politics Society* 31(1): 55–91.

MacGregor, Brent Mac (1992) 'Peter Arnett, CNN, reporting live from Baghdad', *Film and History* 21 (February/March): 26–31.

McGrew, Anthony (1997) 'Globalization and territorial democracy: an introduction', in McGrew, Anthony, *The Transformation of Democracy? Globalization and Territorial Democracy*. Cambridge: Polity, pp. 1–24.

McGuigan, Jim (1998) 'What price the public sphere?' in Thussu, Daya (ed.), *Electronic Empires: Global Media and Local Resistance*. London, New York: Arnold, pp. 91–107.

McKnight, D. (2008) 'Not attributable to official sources': Counter–propaganda and the mass media', *Media International Australia* 128 (August): 5–17.

McLuhan, Marshall (1962, 1986) *The Gutenberg Galaxy: The Making of Typographic Man*. Toronto: University of Toronto Press.

McLuhan, Marshall and Powers, Bruce R. (1989) *The Global Village. Transformations in World Life and Media in the 21st Century*. New York, Oxford: Oxford University Press.

McNair, Brian (2006) *Cultural Chaos: Journalism, News, Power in a Globalised World*. London, New York: Routledge.

Mcquire, Scott (2008) *The Media City: Media, Architecture and Urban Space*. London: Sage.

Madianou, Mirca and Miller, Daniel (2012) *Migration and New Media: Transnational Families and Polymedia*. Oxon, UK; New York: Routledge.
Mannheim, Karl (1952) *Essays on the Sociology of Knowledge*. London: Routledge and Kegan Paul.
Mansbach, Richard, Ferguson, Yale H., Lampert, Donald E. (1975) *The Web of Politics. Nonstate Actors in the Global System*. New Jersey: Prentice-Hall.
Margolis, Michael and Resnick, David (2000) *Politics as Usual: The Cyberspace Revolution*. London: Sage.
Marjanen, Jani (2009) 'Undermining methodological nationalism', Albert, Mathias et al. (eds), *Transnational Political Spaces*. Frankfurt: Campus, pp. 239–63.
Matheson, Donald and Allan, Stuart (2009) *Digital War Reporting*. Cambridge, UK, Malden, MA: Polity.
Mattelart, Armand (2000) *Networking the World, 1794–2000*. Minneapolis, MN: University of Minnesota Press.
Mau, Stefffen *Transnationale Vergesellschaftung. Die Entgrenzung sozialer Lebenswelten*. Frankfurt/Main, New York: Campus.
Michalski, Milena and Gow, James (2007) *War, Image and Legitimacy: Viewing Contemporary Conflict*. London, New York.
Mill, John Stuart (1865) *Considerations on Representative Government*. London; Longman.
Mittelman, James H. (2004) *Whither Globalization? The Vortex of Knowledge and Ideology*. London: Routledge.
Miller, David (1999) 'Group identities, national identities, and democratic politics', in John Horton and Susan Mendus (eds), *Toleration, Identity and Difference*. Basingstoke: Macmillan.
Mody, Bella (ed.) (2004) *International and Development Communication. A 21st Century Perspective*. Thousand Oaks, London, New Delhi: Sage.
Moehler, Devra C. and Singh, Naunihal (2011) 'Whose news do you trust? Explaining trust in private versus public media in Africa', *Political Research Quarterly* 64(2): 276–92.
Moltchanova, Anna (2007) 'Nationhood and political culture', *Journal of Social Philosophy* 38(2): 255–73
Mossberger, Karen; Tolbert, Caroline; McNeal, Ramona (2008) *Digital Citizenship*. Cambridge, London: MIT Press.
Mouffe, Chantal (1999) 'Deliberative democracy or agonistic pluralism?, *Social Research* 66: 745–58.
Mouffe, Chantal (2000) *The Democratic Paradox*. London. New York: Verso.
Moy, Patricia and Gastil, John (2006) Predicting deliberative conversation: The impact of discussion networks, media use, and political cognitions', *Political Communication* 23: 443–60.
Munoz-Navarro, Antonieta (2009) 'Youth and human rights in Chile. Otherness, political identity and social change', in Tufte, Thomas and Enghel, Florenca (eds), *Youth Engaging with the World*. Gothenburg, Sweden: Nordicom, pp. 43–60.
Nanz, Patrizia and Steffek, Jens (2005) 'Global governance, participation and the public sphere', in Held, David and Koenig-Archibugi (eds), *Global Governance and Public Accountability*. Malden, MA and Oxford: Wiley Blackwell, pp. 190–211.

Natarajan, S. (1962) *The History of the Press in India*. London: Asian Publishing House.

Ndlela, Nkosi (2009) 'African media research in the era of globalization', *Journal of African Media Studies* 1(1): 55–68.

Nederveen Pieterse, Jan (2012) 'Media and hegemonic populism: Representing the rise of the rest', in Volkmer, Ingrid (ed.), *The Handbook of Global Media Research*. Malden, MA: Wiley Blackwell, pp. 57–73.

Newman, Nic; Dutton, William; Blank, Grant (2012) 'Social media in the changing ecology of news: The fourth and the fifth estate in Britain', *International Journal of Internet Science* 7(1): 6–22.

Nieminen, Hannu (2009) 'The European public sphere as a network?' in Salovaara-Moring, Inka (ed.), *Manufacturing Europe. Spaces of Democracy, Diversity and Communication*. Gothenburg, Sweden: Nordicom, pp. 19–34.

Nisbet, Erik C. and Myers, Teresa A. (2010) 'Challenging the state: Transnational TV and political identity in the Middle East', *Political Communication* 27(4): 347–66.

Nye, Joseph (2004) *Soft Power. The Means to Success in World Politics*. New York: Public Affairs.

Oleson, Thomas (2007) 'The porous public and the transnational dialectic: The Muhammed cartoons conflict', *Acta Sociologica*, 50: 295–308.

Ong, Aihwa (2005) 'Ecologies of expertise: Assembling flows, managing citizenship', in Ong, Aihwa and Collier, Stephen J. (eds), *Global Assemblages*. Malden, MA, USA: Blackwell, pp. 337–53.

Oreget, Kristin Skare (2010) 'Mediated culture and the well-informed global citizen', *Nordicom Review* 31(2): 47–61.

Pantti, Mervi; Wahl-Jorgensen, Karin; Cottle, Simon (2012) *Disasters and the Media*. New York; Peter Lang.

Papacharissi, Zizi (2007) 'Audiences as media producers: Content analysis of 260 blogs', in Tremayne, Mark (ed.), *Blogging, Citizenship, and the Future of Media*. New York, London: Routledge, pp. 21–38.

Pariser, Eli (2011) *The Filter Bubble: What the Internet is Hiding from You*. New York. Penguin,

Parks, Lisa (2009) 'Signals and oil. Satellite footprints and post-communist territories in Central Asia', *European Journal of Cultural Studies* 12(2): 137–56.

Parks, Lisa (2012) 'Footprints of the global south: Venesat-1 and Rascom QAF/ IR as counter-hegemonic satellites', in Volkmer, Ingrid (ed.), *Handbook of Global Media Research*. Malden, MA: Wiley-Blackwell, pp. 123–42.

Peters, Chris (2012) 'Journalism to go', *Journalism Studies* 13(5–6): 695–705.

Pieterse, Jan Nederveen (1995) 'Globalization as hybridization', in Featherstone, Mike; Lash, Scott; Robertson, Roland (eds) *Global Modernities*. London: Sage, pp. 45–68.

Plyers, Geoffrey (2010) *Alter-Globalization. Becoming Actors in a Global Age*. Cambridge: Polity.

Pretes, Michael and Katherine Gibson (2008) 'Openings in the body of 'capitalism': Capital flows and diverse economic possibilities in Kiribati', *Asia Pacific Viewpoint* 49(3): 381–91.

Price, Monroe (2002) *Media and Sovereignty*. Cambridge, MA: MIT Press.

Price, Monroe (2010) 'Toward a foreign policy of information space', Thussu, Daya (ed.) *International Communication. A Reader*. London, New York: Routledge, pp. 345–69.

Raboy, Marc (2002) 'Media policy in the new communications environment', in Raboy, Marc (ed.) *Global Media Policy in the New Millenium*. Luton: University of Luton Press, pp. 3–15.

Rantanen, Terhi (2005) *The Media and Globalization*. London, Thousand Oaks, New Delhi: Sage.

Rantanen, Tehri (2010) 'Methodological inter-nationalism in comparative media research. Flow studies in international communication', in Rooscall, Anna and Salovaara-Moring, Inka (eds), *Communicating the Nation*. Gothenburg: Nordicom, pp. 25–40.

Rai, Mughda and Cottle, Simon (2010) 'Global news revisited: Mapping the contemporary landscape of satellite television news', in Cushion, Stephen and Lewis, Justin (eds), *The Rise of 24-Hour News Television*. New York: Peter Lang, pp. 51–80.

Ray, Tapas (2011) 'The 'story' of digital excess in revolutions of the Arab Spring', *Journal of Media Practice* 12(2): 189–97.

Rawls, John (1999) *The Law of Peoples*. Cambridge, MA: Harvard University Press.

Read, Donald (1992) *Power of News: The History of Reuters*. Darby, PA: Diane Publications.

Reguilo, Rosana (2009) 'The warrior's code? Youth, communication and social change', in Tufte, Thomas and Enghel, Florenca (eds) *Youth Engaging with the World*. Gothenburg, Sweden: Nordicom, pp. 21–42.

Renan, Ernest (1996) 'What is a nation?', in Eley, Geoff and Ronald Rigor Suny (eds) *Becoming National*. New York, Oxford: Oxford University Press, pp. 42–56.

Requate, Joerg and Schulze-Wessel, Martin (Hg.) *Europaeische Oeffentlichkeit. Transnationale Kommunikation seit dem 18.Jahrhundert*. Frankfurt/New York: Campus.

Riaz, Saqib and Pasha, Saadia Anwar (2011) 'Role of citizen journalism in strengthening societies', *FWU Journal of Social Sciences* 5(1): 88–103.

Risse, Thomas (2002) 'Zur Debatte um die (Nicht) Existenz einer europaeischen Oeffentlichkeit', *Berliner Debatte Initial* 13(5/6): 15–23.

Risse, Thomas (2010) *A Community of Europeans? Transnational Identities and Public Spheres*. Cornell: Ithaca, New York.

Robertson, Roland (1992) *Globalization. Social Theory and Global Culture*. London, Newbury Park, New Delhi: Sage.

Robertson, Roland (2011) 'Global connectivity and global consciousness', *American Behavioral Scientist* 55(10): 1336–45.

Robertson, Roland and Inglis, David (2004) 'The global animus: In the tracks of world consciousness', *Globalizations* 1(1): 38–49.

Robbins, Bruce (ed.) (1993) *The Phantom Public Sphere*. Minneapolis: University of Minnesota.

Robinson, Piers (2002) *The CNN Effect: The Myth of News, Foreign Policy and Intervention*. London: Routledge.

Roderick, Rick (1989) *Habermas and the Foundations of Critical Theory*. London: Macmillan.

Rosenau, James N. and Hylke, Tromp (1989) (eds) *Interdependence and Conflict in World Politics*. Aldershot, Hants, UK; Brookfield, USA: Avebury.

Rosenau, James N. (1989) 'Global changes and theoretical challenges: Towards a postinternational politics for the 1990s', in, Czempiel, Ernst-Otto and

Rosenau, James N. (eds) *Global Changes and Theoretical Challenges: Approaches to World Politics for the 1990s*. Lexington, MA, USA: Lexington Books, pp. 2–3.

Rosenau, James N. (1995) 'Sovereignty in a turbulent world', in Lyons, Gene M, Mastanduno, Michael (eds), *Beyond Wesphalia? State Sovereignty and International Intervention*. Baltimore: Johns Hopkins University Press, pp. 191–227.

Rossfall, Anna and Salovaara-Moring, Inka (2010) 'Introduction', Roosvall, Anna and Salovaara-Moring, Ika (eds), *Communicating the Nation*. Gothenburg: Nordicom, pp. 9–24.

Ruggie, John Gerard (1993) 'Territoriality and beyond: Problematizing modernity in international relations', *International Organization* 47(1): 139–74.

Sakr, Naomi (2001) *Satellite Realms: Transnational Television, Globalization and the Middle East*. London, New York: I. B. Tauris.

Sakr, Naomi (ed.), (2007a) *Arab Media and Political Renewal*. London, UK: I. B. Tauris.

Sakr, Naomi (2007b) *Arab Television Today*. London, New York: I. B. Tauris.

Sarikakis, Katherine (2012) 'Securitization and legitimacy in global media governance', in Volkmer, Ingrid (ed.), *The Handbook of Global Media Research*. Maidenhead, MA: Wiley-Blackwell, pp. 143–55.

Sassen, Saskia (1991) *The Global City; New York, London, Tokyo*. Princeton, NJ; Princeton University Press.

Sassen, Saskia (1996) *Losing Control? Sovereignty in the Age of Globalization*. New York: Columbia University Press.

Sassen, Saskia (2005) 'Electronic markets and activist networks: The weight of social logics in digital formations', in Latham, Robert and Sassen, Saskia (eds) *Digital Formations. IT and New Architectures in the Global Realm*. Princeton: Princeton University Press, pp. 37–53.

Sassen, Saskia (2006) *Territory, Authority, Rights: From Medieval to Global Assemblages*. Princeton: Princeton University Press.

Sassen, Saskia (2007) 'Toward a multiplication of specialized assemblages of territory, authority and rights', *Pallax* 13(1): 87–94.

Sassen, Saskia (2007a) 'The places and spaces of the global: An expanded analytic terrain', in Held, David and McGrew, Anthony (eds), *Globalization Theory*. Cambridge: Polity, pp. 79–105.

Sassen, Saskia (2012) 'Digitization and knowledge systems of the powerful and the powerless', in Volkmer, Ingrid (ed.), *The Handbook of Global Media Research*. Malden, MA, USA: Wiley-Blackwell, pp. 74–91.

Saward, Michael (2002) 'Rawls and deliberative democracy', in D'Entrèves, Maurizio Passerin (ed.), *Democracy as Public Deliberation*. Manchester, New York: Manchester University Press, pp. 112–32.

Scheuerman, William E. (2008) *Frankfurt School Perspectives on Globalization, Democracy, and the Law*. New York, London: Routledge.

Schulz, Markus S. (2011) 'Values and the conditions of global communication', *Current Sociology* 59: 2324–51.

Schiller, Herbert I (1976) *Communication and Cultural Domination*. White Plains, NY: International Arts and Sciences Press.

Semetko, Holly and Schoenbach, Klaus (1994) *Germany's 'Unity Election' – Voters and the Media*. Cresskill, NJ: Hampton Press.

Schaar, Stuart (2011) 'Revolutionary challenges in Tunisia and Egypt: genera-tions in conflict', *New Politics* 12(3): 19–16.

Scholte, Jan Aart (1993) *International Relations of Social Change*. Open University Press: Buckingham, Philadelphia.

Scholte, Jan Aart (2000) *Globalization. A Critical Introduction*. Houndsmills, UK: Macmillan.

Schuetz, Alfred (1971) *Collected Papers*. The Hague, Netherlands: Nijhoff.

Schuetz, Alfred and Luckmann, Thomas (1973, 1989) *The Structures of the Life-world*. Evanstan: NorthWestern University Press.

Schuler, Douglas and Day, Peter (eds) (2004) *Shaping the Network Society*. Cambridge, MA: MIT Press.

Schwartz, Stephanie (2010) *Youth in Post-Conflict Reconstruction*. Washington: United States Institute of Peace Press.

Semmel, A.K. (1976) 'Foreign News in four US elite dailies: some comparisons', *Journalism Quarterly* 53(4): 732–6.

Sheller, Mimi and Urry, John (2003) 'Mobile transformations of 'public' and 'private' life', *Theory, Culture and Society*, 20(3): 107–25.

Shin, Jang-Sup (2009) 'Globalization and challenges to the developmental state: a comparison between south Korea and Singapore', in Shin, Jang-Sup (ed.), *Global Challenges and Local Responses*, London: Routledge, pp. 31–49.

Siedschlag, Alexander (2007) 'Digital democracy and its application to the international arena – From 'deliberation' to 'decision', in Dunn, Myriam et al. (eds), *The Resurgence of the State*. Aldershot, UK: Ashgate, pp. 35–58.

Sifry, Micah (2011) *Wikileaks and the Age of Transparency*. Berkeley, CA, USA: Counterpoint.

Sikkink, Kathryn (2005) 'Patterns of dynamic multilevel governance and the insider–outsider coalition', in Della Porta, Donatella (ed.), *Transnational Protest and Global Activism*. Lanham, Boulder, New York, Toronto, Oxford: Rowman and Littlefield, pp. 151–74.

Silverstone, Roger (1999) *Why Study The Media?* London: Sage.

Silverstone, Roger (2007) *Media and Morality. On the Rise of the Mediapolis.* London: Polity.

Slade, Christina (2010) 'Media and citizenship: Transnational television cul-tures reshaping political identities in the European union', *Journalism: Theory, Practice and Criticism* 11(December): 733–7.

Slade, Christina and Volkmer, Ingrid (2012) 'Media research and satellite cul-tures: Comparative research among Arab communities in Europe', in Volkmer, Ingrid (ed.), *Handbook of Global Media Research*. Malden, MA, USA: Wiley-Blackwell, pp. 397–410.

Slaughter, Anne-Marie (2005) 'Disaggregated sovereignty: Towards public accountability of global government networks', in Held, David and Koenig-Archibugi, Mathias (eds), *Global Governance and Public Accountability*. Malden, USA: Blackwell, pp. 35–66.

Slevin, James (2000) *The Internet and Society*. Cambridge: Polity.

Snow, Nancy (2010) 'What's that I chirping I hear?: From the CNN effect to the Twitter effect', in Kamalipour, Yahya R. (ed.), *Media, Power, and Politics in the Digital Age*. London: Rowman and Littlefield, pp. 97–104.

Sparks, Colin (2000) 'The global, the local and the public sphere', in Wang, Georgette, Servaes, Jan and Goonasekera, Anura (eds), *The New*

Communications Landscape. Demystifying Media Globalization. London and New York: Routledge, pp. 74–95.

Sparks, Colin (2007) *Globalization, Development and the Mass Media*. London, Los Angeles, New Delhi, Singapore: Sage.

Spichal, Slavko (2012) *Transnationalizaton of the Public Sphere and the Fate of the Public*. New York: Hampton Press.

Stern, Robert (2002) *Hegel and the Phenomenology of Spirit*. Routledge: Abingdon, UK.

Strange, Susan (1996) *The Retreat of the State: The Diffusion of Power in the World Economy*. Cambridge: Cambridge University Press.

Stern, Robert (2002) *Hegel and the Phenomenology of Spirit*. Milton Park, USA: Routledge.

Stephens, Mitchell (1988) *History of News. From the Drum to the Satellite*. New York: Viking.

Stevenson, Robert L. and Shaw, Donald Lewis (1984) *Foreign News and the New World Information Order*. Ames: Iowa State University Press.

Stichweh, Rudolf (2007) 'Dimensionen des Weltstaats im System der Weltpolitik', in Albert, Mathias and Rudolf Stichweh (eds), *Weltstaat und Weltstaatlichkeit*. Wiesbaden: VS Verlag, pp. 25–36.

Tarro, Sidney and McAdam, Doug (2005) 'Scale shift in transnational contention', in della Porta and Tarrow *Transnational Protest and Global Activism*. Lanham, MD: Rowman and Littlefield, pp. 121–50.

Taylor, Charles (2004) *Modern Social Imaginaries*. Durham and London: Duke University Press.

Tennant, Evelyn W. (2007) 'Locating transnational activists. The United States anti-apartheid movement and the confines of the national', in Sassen, Saskia (ed.), *Deciphering the Global*. New York, London: Routledge, pp. 119–38.

Toennies, Friedrich (1957) *Community and Society*. New York: Harper and Row.

Thompson, J. B. (1993) 'The theory of the public sphere', *Theory, Culture and Society* 10(3): 173–89.

Thompson, J. B. (1995) *The Media and Modernity. A Social Theory of the Media*. Cambridge: Polity.

Thussu, Daya (2000) *International Communication. Continuity and Change*. London: Arnold.

Thussu, Daya (2007) 'Mapping flow and contra flow', in Thussu, Daya (ed.), *Media on the Move. Global Flow and Contra-Flow*. London: Routledge, pp. 10–29.

Tomlinson, John (1999) *Globalization and Culture*. Cambridge: Polity.

Tomlinson, John (2006) 'Globalization and cultural analysis', Held, David and McGrew, Anthony (eds), *Globalization Theory*. Cambridge: Polity, pp. 148–70.

Tittey, Wisdom (2009) 'Transnationalization, the Africa diaspora, and the deterritorialized politics of the internet', in Mudhai, Okoth Fred; Tettey, Wisdom J; Banda, Fackson (eds), *African Media and the Digital Public Sphere*. Palgrave Macmillan, pp. 143–64.

Tremayne, Mark (2007) 'Examining the blog–media relationship', in Tremayne, Mark (ed.), *Blogging, Citizenship, and the Future of Media*. New York, London: Routledge, pp. ix–xix.

Tufte, Thomas; Corrigan, Aran; Ekstroem, Ylva; Fuglesang, Minou; Rweye-mamu, Datius (2009) 'From voice to participation? Analysing youth agency in letter writing in Tanzania', in Tufte, Thomas and Enghel, Forencia (eds), *Youth Engaging with the World.* Gothenburg: Nordicom, pp. 155–72.

Turkle, Sherry (1995) *Life on the Screen: Identity in the Age of the Internet.* New York: Simon and Schuster.

Turner, Bryan S (2002) 'Cosmopolitan virtue, globalization and patriotism', *Theory, Culture and Society* 19(1–2): 45–63.

Urry, John (2003) *Global Complexity.* Cambridge: Polity.

Vann, Dann and VanArsdel, Rosemary (1996) 'Outposts of the Empire', in Vann, Dann and VanArsdel, Rosemary (eds), *Periodicals of Queen Victoria's Empire.* Toronto, Buffalo: University of Toronto Press, pp. 301–23.

Valtysson, Bjarki (2012) 'Facebook as a digital public sphere: Processes of colonialization and emanicipation', *tripleC* 10(1): 77–91.

Varnelis, Kazys and Friedberg, Anne (2008) 'Place: The networking of public space', in Varnelis, Kazys (ed.), *Networked Publics*, Cambridge, MA; MIT Press, pp. 15–42.

Virilio, Paul (1997) *Open Sky.* New York, London: Verso.

Volkmer, Ingrid (1999) *News in the Global Sphere.* Luton: University of Luton Press.

Volkmer, Ingrid (2002, 2011) 'Journalism and political crises in the global network society', in Zelizer, Barbie and Allan, Stuart (eds), *Journalism after September 11.* London, New York: Routledge, pp. 308–18.

Volkmer, Ingrid (2006) Globalization, generational entelechies and the global public space', in Volkmer, Ingrid (ed.), *News in Public Memory.* New York: Peter Lang, pp. 251–68.

Volkmer, Ingrid (2007) 'Governing the 'spatial reach'? Spheres of influence and challenges to global media policy', *International Journal of Communication* 1: 56–73.

Volkmer, Ingrid (2010) 'Between 'publicness' and 'publicity': Conceptualizing discourse 'assemblages' of public legitimacy in transnational spaces', *Review of Communication, Journal of the American National Communication Association,* Taylor and Francis.

Volkmer, Ingrid and Deffner, Florian (2010) 'Eventspheres as discursive form (re-)negotiating the 'mediated center' in new network cultures', in Couldry, Nick; Hepp, Andreas; Krotz, Friedrich (eds), *Media Events in a Global Age.* London, New York: Routledge, pp. 217–30.

Volkmer, Ingrid (2012) 'Deconstructing the "methodological paradox": Comparative research between national centrality and networked spaces', in Volkmer, Ingrid (ed.), *Handbook of Global Media Research.* Malden, MA: Wiley-Blackwell, pp. 110–22.

Volkmer, Ingrid and Firdaus, Amira (2013) 'Between networks and "hierarchies of credibility": Navigating journalistic practice in a sea of user-generated content', in Broersma, Marcel and Peter, Chris (eds), *Rethinking Journalism.* London: Routledge, pp. 101–13.

Wallerstein, Immanuel (1974) *The Modern World-System.* New York: Academic Press.

Wallerstein, Immanuel (1991) *Unthinking Social Science.* Cambridge: Polity.

Wallerstein, Immanuel (1999) *The End of the World as We Know it*. London, Minneapolis: University of Minnesota Press.

Walzer, (1983) *Spheres of Justice: A Defense of Pluralism and Equality*. New York: Basic books; Oxford: Martin Robertson.

Warner, Michael (1992) 'The mass public and the mass subject', in Calhoun, Craig (ed.) *Habermas and the Public Sphere*. Cambridge, MA: MIT Press, pp. 377–401.

Watzlawick, Paul; Beavin, Janet Helmick; Jackson, Don D. (1967) *Pragmatics of Human Communication: A Study of Interactional Patterns, Pathologies, and Paradoxes*. New York: Norton.

Weaver, David and Willnat, Lars (2012) *The Global Journalist in the 21st Century*. London: Routledge.

Webby, Elizabeth (1996) 'Australia', in Vann, Don J. and VanArsdel, Rosemary (eds), *Periodicals of Queen Victoria's Empire*. Toronto, Buffalo: University of Toronto Press, pp. 19–60.

Westphal, Kenneth R. (1989) *Hegel's Epistemological Realism*. Dordrecht, Boston, London: Kluwer Academic Publishers.

Wiley, Stephen B. Crofts (2004) 'Rethinking nationality in the context of globalization', *Communication Theory* 14(1): 78–96.

Wilkins, Karin Gwinn (2004) 'International development communication', in Mody, Bella (ed.), *International and Development Communication. A 21st century Perspective*. Thousand Oaks, London, New Delhi: Sage, pp. 245–60.

Williams, Howard (1983) *Kant's Political Philosophy*, Oxford: Blackwell.

Wimmer, Andreas and Glick Schiller, Nina (2002)'Methodological nationalism and beyond: Nation-building, migration, and the social sciences', *Global Networks* 2(4): 301–34.

Witteborn, Saskia (2011) 'Constructing the forced migrant and the politics of space and place-making', *Journal of Communication* 61: 1142–60.

Wolfsfeld, G. (1997) *The Media and Political Conflict*. Cambridge: Cambridge University Press.

Wolin, Sheldon (1960) *Politics and Vision: Continuity and Innovation in Western Political Thought*. Boston: Little, Brown and Co.

Wright, Scott (2012) Politics as usual? Revolution, normalization and a new agenda for online deliberation', *New Media Society* 14: 244–61.

Wuthnow, Robert (1989) *Communities of Discourse*. Cambridge, MA; London, England: Harvard University Press.

Young, Iris Marion (1996) 'Communication and the other: Beyond deliberative democracy', Benhabib, Seyla (ed.), *Democracy and Difference: Contesting the Boundaries of the Political*. Princeton, New Jersey: Princeton University Press, pp. 121–35.

Yuan, Elaine (2011) 'News consumption across multiple media platforms', *Information, Communication and Society* 14(7): 998–1016.

Zaret, David (1999) 'Religion, science, and printing in the public spheres in seventeenth-century England' in Calhoun, Craig (ed.), *Habermas and the Public Sphere*. Cambridge, MA: MIT Press, pp. 212–35.

Zimmer, Matthias (2008) *Moderne, Staat und internationale Politik*. Wiesbaden, Germany: VS Verlag fuer Sozialwissenschaften.

Zuern, Michael (2005) 'Globalizing interests and introduction' in Zuern, Michael and Gregor Walter (ed.), *Globalizing Interests. Pressure Groups and Denationalization*. New York: State University of New York Press, pp. 1–29.

Index